Dialectical
Investigations

Dialectical Investigations

By Bertell Ollman

Routledge
New York • London

Published in 1993 by

Routledge
An imprint of Routledge, Chapman and Hall, Inc.
29 West 35th Street
New York, NY 10001

Published in Great Britain by

Routledge
11 New Fetter Lane
London EC4P 4EE

Acknowledgments and thanks are offered to the journals in which earlier versions of several of our chapters have appeared: "Putting Dialectics to Work: the Process of Abstraction in Marx's Method," *Rethinking Marxism* (Spring, 1990); "The Regency of the Proletariat in Crisis: a Job for Perestroika," *P.S.: Political Science and Politics* (Sept., 1991); "How to Study Class Consciousness . . . and Why We Should," *Critical Sociology* (Winter, 1987); "The Meaning of Dialectics," *Monthly Review* (Nov., 1986); "Theses on the Capitalist State," *Monthly Review* (Dec., 1982); "Toward a Marxist Interpretation of the U.S. Constitution," *Monthly Review* (Dec., 1987); and "The Ideal of Academic Freedom as the Ideology of Academic Repression, American Style," *Monthly Review* (Mar., 1984).

Ollman, Bertell.
    Dialectical investigations / Bertell Ollman.
       p.   cm.
    Includes bibliographical references and index.
    ISBN 0-415-90679-2 — ISBN 0-415-90680-6 (pbk.)
    1. Dialectic. 2. Dialectical materialism. 3. Philosophy,
Marxist.   I. Title.
B809.8.0444   1992
335.4'11—dc20   92-24355
                                                 CIP

ISBN 0-415-90679-2 (HB)
ISBN 0-415-90680-6 (PB)

"What is decisive in Marxism . . . [is]
its revolutionary dialectics."
—V.I. Lenin

"Orthodox Marxism . . . does not imply the uncritical
acceptance of the results of Marx's investigations. It
is not the 'belief' in this or that thesis, nor the
exegesis of a 'sacred' book . . . [it] refers exclusively
to method."
—George Lukacs

"Marxism is above all a method of analysis—not
analysis of texts, but analysis of social relations."
—Leon Trotsky

"The dialectic . . . [is] the very marrow of
historiography and the science of politics."
—Antonio Gramsci

"We have to popularize dialectics and dialectics has
to be developed. In a word, I ask that dialectics be
popularized step by step so that we will have 600
million dialecticians."
—Mao Tse-Tung

Contents

Acknowledgments ———————————————————

The honor roll of friends and colleagues who have read one or another version of the present work and offered useful criticisms is a long one. It includes Maximilien Rubel, Wal Suchting, John McMurtry, Frank Cunningham, Ralph Miliband, Paul Sweezy, Randhir Singh, Richard Wolff, G. A. Cohen, David Harvey, Vincente Navarro, Joel Kovel, Gunder Frank, Ira Gollobin, Bill Ash, Tony Smith, Steve Gold, Bob Stone, Joe Walsh, John Ehrenberg, Ariel Salleh, Jose Sanchez, Ray Rakow, Hayward Alker, Peter Heymans, Eli Messinger, Mitchel Cohen, Al Prago, Francis Feeley, Mahdu Sarin, Ted Perlmutter, Jonathan Birnbaum, Edward Vernoff, and Chris Sciabarra. I am deeply grateful for their help. Three people, from whom I received especially provocative criticisms more often than even I would have wished, are Bill Livant, Michael Brown, and Paule Ollman, my wife. To them I owe much of what is best in this book. None of the above, of course, bear any responsibility for my opinions or for the errors and omissions that may have escaped our combined efforts to catch them. I also want to thank my son, Raoul Ollman, for designing the cover for the book.

General Introduction _____

Marxism, understood as the ideas of Karl Marx, has suffered four major onslaughts during the 140 or so years of its history: revisionism, which directed most of its barbs against what were said to be Marx's "overemphasis" on economic processes and his "faulty predictions"; "officialism," or its adoption, beginning in 1917, by a variety of underdeveloped countries as the official doctrine of the regime, with a subsequent shift in Marxism's meaning from an analysis and criticism of capitalism to a rationalization and organizing ideology for a "socialist" state; sectarianism, particularly in the West, where the word and quote often got substituted for Marx's argument and way of thinking; and, most recently, by a kind of eclecticism run wild, a "good times Marxism" denuded of its working class, in which Marx's ideas have been married to a variety of mismatched suitors from the bourgeois academy to produce as many hyphenated offspring. In itself, this last would not be a terrible thing if it were not invariably accompanied by a displacement of Marx's primary focus along with a drastic dilution of his social analysis and political program.

Throughout these attacks on the integrity of Marxism, no element of Marx's thinking has received sorrier treatment—whether through direct criticism, gross distortion, or total neglect—than the dialectic. Yet it is just here, with Marx's dialectical method, that any serious attempt to recover what is of value in Marx's contribution toward remaking our world must begin.

If Marx's theories deal essentially with his understanding of capitalist society, its origins, and probable future, then Marx's dialectical method is how he went about acquiring this understanding, including how he structured it and the order and forms in which he presented it. Marx's method, one might say, is to his theories what grand strategy is to the outcome of a war. It not only plays a decisive role in determining who wins (what works) or loses (fails), but helps define what either means.

Despite its crucial importance for his work, Marx's scattered remarks on dialectics are never more than suggestive, always highly provocative and enticing, but invariably incomplete. In *Capital*, volume I, for example, Marx claimed, "In its mystified [Hegelian] form, dialectics became the fashion in Germany, because it seemed to transfigure and glorify the existing state of things. In its rational form it is a scandal and abomination to bourgeoisdom and its doctrinaire professors, because it includes in its comprehension and affirmation recognition of the existing state of things, at the same time also, the recognition of the negation of that state, of its inevitable breaking up; because it regards every historically developing social form as in fluid movement, and therefore takes into account its transient nature not less than its momentary existence; because it lets nothing impose upon it, and is in its essence critical and revolutionary" (1958, 20). Left as it is, which is how Marx left it, this is little more than a promissory note. It remains for us to cash it in.

Marx himself seemed only partly and intermittently aware of the difficulty most people had in grasping dialectics. In an 1858 letter to Engels, he says that if time permits he would "like to make accessible to the ordinary human intelligence" the rational core of the method Hegel had wrapped in mysticism (Marx and Engels, 1941, 102). Unfortunately, his life as a revolutionary and journalist as well as the need to finish his political economy left Marx with no time to undertake such a work. "Ordinary human intelligence" was left to make sense of his widespread use of dialectics without any direct help from Marx himself. The chapters devoted to dialectics in Engels' *Anti-Dühring* (1878), a work that Marx read and approved before its publication, simplifies some aspects of dialectics but at the cost of overschematizing and rigidifying processes that Marx had used with exemplary flexibility.

As a result of the prevailing uncertainty surrounding dialectics, many of Marx's readers do not see it operating in his works, while others, who do, take it as an unnecessary intrusion, an irksome throwback to his Hegelian past. In both cases, Marx's analysis is made that much poorer, for dialectics—as I hope to show—is not a simple garment that can be ignored or removed at will, something thrown over the shoulder to produce a special effect. It belongs, instead, to the substance as well as to the form of Marx's theories, being part of what holds them up as well as of what binds them together.

Marxism without dialectics, a stew served up by an increasing number of Marx's academic followers, is but another, perhaps more wordy version of standard radical thinking. But it is in just those ways that Marxism is more than radical thinking that its chief value lies, both for understanding the world and for changing it. After all, many thinkers, both before and after Marx, have drawn our attention to the less savory aspects of capitalist life, to its painful inequalities, irrational waste of people and resources, blatant biases on behalf of those who need help least, sickening hypocrisies, and so on. Because capitalist schools and media generally avoid such facts, simply presenting them—as Barrington Moore has pointed out—carries the ring of radical exposure (Wolff, 1965, 61). Likewise, many socialists have accompanied their exposures with visions of a more humane social order with which they would replace the present one. But there is an important difference between radical exposure, with or without an alternative vision of the future, and scientific analysis; between getting the "facts" right and explaining them.

We still want—and need—to know why these injustices occur. Where do they fit and how do they function as part of the present system? How have they come about and what changes are they undergoing at this very moment? Who and what are responsible for them? And, in light of what is learned, what can we do to help bring about a new and better way of life? Marx's analysis provides answers to such questions, but these answers are arrived at as well as structured with the aid of his dialectical method. And we can only fully understand, let alone evaluate, and—where necessary— revise these answers, the theories of Marxism, if we are familiar with this method. Marx really should have found the time to do the promised work on dialectics.

No introduction to a book on dialectics written in the last days of 1991 can ignore the implications of the revolutions in Eastern Europe for the validity of Marx's approach. Many writers, of course, have interpreted these events as the demise not only of particular regimes and forms of social organization but of the Marxist world view to which, at least verbally, their leaders seemed so attached. Leaving aside such obviously important questions as whether and to what extent these regimes were socialist, let alone Marxist, I would just like to point out that the most striking feature of all the social explosions of the past few years—and remarked upon by virtually every observer—is just how unexpected they were. What existed before, however one evaluated it, was taken as given and unchanging; just as most people treat the situation that has emerged as a new given and equally unchanging. It is the same mistake that was made in 1789, again in 1848, and again in 1917. These revolutions, too, surprised almost everyone, and as soon as they happened almost everyone alive at the time thought—wrongly—that they were over.

Surely there is something seriously faulty about a way of thinking that leaves people so unprepared for the political and economic upheavals that occupy such a central place in our history. Is it too much to suggest that dialectical method, which takes change as the given and treats apparent stability as that which needs to be explained, and which provides the specialized concepts and frameworks to explain it, that dialectics so construed, might have a role to play in correcting this imbalance? Though Marx's dialectical method, like the theories constructed with its help, is mainly concerned with capitalism (and only in this context and with this object do all its parts come into play), it contains a good deal, as we shall see, that is applicable to change of other kinds, in other places, and at other times. Hence, rather than serving as an epitaph to Marxism, the rapid transformations occurring in Eastern Europe may have made Marx's dialectical method and a dialectically conceived Marxism more essential than ever.

My own involvement with dialectics began with my first book, *Alienation: Marx's Conception of Man in Capitalist Society* (1971), where I devoted most of six chapters to presenting just enough dialectics to help me explain some troubling features in Marx's theory of alienation. In 1973, this was followed by a long essay, "Marxism and Political Science: Prolegomenon to a Debate on Marx's Method," where I divided this method into its five constituent moments—ontology, epistemology, inquiry, self-clarification, and exposition—and showed how they are related. Though still in general agreement with the analysis found in these works, it soon became clear that my efforts to explain dialectics had failed in at least three major respects: it was not simple enough (it was very difficult for absolute beginners at this subject, which is to say most people, to begin); it was not advanced enough (the problems raised by my interpretation of dialectics, especially in the discussion of "internal relations," were not resolved in a way that enabled people to use this method effectively in their own work); and there were not enough good examples illustrating the use of this method, as I interpret it, from sources other than Marx and Engels. Nor was I able to find other works on dialectics that dealt more satisfactorily with any of these matters. Consequently, my main scholarly activity in recent years has gone into addressing these shortcomings, particularly the gap between dialectics as a world view and dialectics as a workable method for studying the problems of our society. The present book—with sections on Introductions to Dialectics, Advanced Dialectics, and Dialectical Investigations—offers a kind of interim report on my progress.

Throughout this book, readers should bear in mind that my chief purpose has not been to explain the world, or even Marx's theories about the world, but to use these theories to illustrate his methodological practice. Should my account of this practice prove useful in explaining these theories, which in turn help clarify what is happening in the world, that is, of course, a bonus I would be only too pleased to accept.

It may not be amiss to signal, too, that the project of which this volume is the opening salvo will, upon completion, contain three more volumes: a comprehensive account of Marx's dialectical method organized around the five moments sketched in my 1973 article; a popular manual presenting dialectics as a bundle of mental skills closely tied to but not identical with the dialectical structures and movements found in this work; and a reader that will bring together not only what Marx and Engels wrote on this subject but other important contributions to dialectics from outside as well as from inside the Marxist tradition. With this road map of where I have come from as well as where I am headed, readers should also be in a better position to take from the present study no less but also no more than I intend it to convey.

The chapters that have been published previously as articles have all been revised for this book. Chapter two, in particular, is about a third longer than the version of it that appeared in *Rethinking Marxism*. Footnotes will be found at the end of each chapter, and a substantial—though still selective—bibliography of works on Marx's method is provided at the end of the book for readers whose appetite for this subject I hope to have whetted.

A final word for those who consider Marx's dialectics an early Hegelian aberration: I have made a special effort to explain dialectics relying mainly on Marx's later non-philosophical writings. Readers familiar with this debate may be surprised to discover that most of the citations in both of the chapters dealing with dialectics come from Marx's *Theories of Surplus Value,* volumes I–III. My intention, of course, is to show how thoroughly dialectical Marx is, even where one would least expect this to be so.

References

Engels, F. 1934. *Herr Eugen Dühring's Revolution in Science [Anti-Dühring]*. Translated by E. Burns. London: Lawrence and Wishart.

Marx, K. 1958. *Capital.* Vol. 1. Translated by S. Moore and E. Aveling. Moscow: Foreign Languages Publishing House.

———. 1963. *Theories of Surplus Value.* Part 1. Translated by E. Burns. Moscow: Progress Publishers.

———. 1968. *Theories of Surplus Value.* Part 2. Translated by S. Ryazanskaya. Moscow: Progress Publishers.

———. 1971. *Theories of Surplus Value.* Part 3. Translated by J. Cohen and S. W. Ryazanskaya. Moscow: Progress Publishers.

Marx, K., and Engels, F. 1941. *Selected Correspondence.* Translated by D. Torr. London: Lawrence and Wishart.

Ollman, B. 1971. *Alienation: Marx's Conception of Man in Capitalist Society.* Cambridge: Cambridge University Press.

Ollman, B. 1973. "Marxism and Political Science: Prolegomenon to a Debate on Marx's Method", *Politics and Society* (Summer, 1973). Reprinted in Ollman, B. 1978. *Social and Sexual Revolution.* Boston: South End Press.

Wolff, R. P., Moore, B. Jr., and Marcuse, B. 1965. *A Critique of Pure Tolerance.* Boston: Beacon.

Part I

Introduction to Dialectics

1

The Meaning of Dialectics _____

Have you ever tried to hop on a car while it was still moving? How different was it from entering a car that was stationary? Would you have been able to get into the moving car if you were blindfolded? Would you have been able to do it if you were not only blindfolded but didn't know in which direction it was moving or even how fast it was moving?

Why all these silly questions? Obviously, we all agree on the answers, and anyone in his right mind would make sure to know how fast and in which direction a car is moving before trying to climb aboard. Well, what about society? Society is like a vehicle that every one of us tries to climb aboard to find a job, a home, various social relationships, goods to satisfy our needs and fancies—in short, a whole way of life. And who can doubt that society is changing. In fact, no century has experienced as much social change as ours, and no period has experienced faster change than the period since World War II. But just how fast is it changing, and, more important, in what direction?

Will American, or British, or Japanese society as it is coming to be in the next few years be able to give you the things you want from it, that you are expecting, that you are preparing for? Being an optimist, you may answer "yes," but if so, you are looking—and none too closely—at things as they are now. But society, as you admit, is changing, and very fast. Have you studied what our democratic capitalist society is changing into, or are you like the blindfolded person trying to get onto a moving vehicle, not knowing either the speed or direction in which it is traveling?

How, then, does one study the infinitely complex organism that is modern society as it evolves and changes over time? Marxism enters the picture as the most systematic (though, obviously, still incomplete) effort yet undertaken to provide such an analysis. Focusing on how goods get produced, exchanged, and distributed in the capitalist era, it tries to account for the structure as well as the dynamics of the entire social system, including both its origins and likely future. We also learn how the few who benefit most from capitalism use a mixture of force and guile to order the lives and thinking of the great majority who would benefit most from a radical change. Finally, Marxism also lays out a method (dialectics) and a practice (class struggle) for updating this study and helping to bring about the most desirable outcome. No one who is about to climb aboard the moving vehicle that is our rapidly changing society can afford to proceed without it.

What we understand about the world is determined by what the world is, who we are, and how we conduct our study. As regards this last, in our day the problems involved in grasping reality have been compounded by an approach that privileges whatever makes things appear static and independent of one another over their more dynamic and systemic qualities. Copernicus could have been speaking about the modern academy instead of the astronomers of his day when he said, "With them it is as though an artist were to gather the hands, feet, head, and other members for his images from diverse models, each part excellently drawn, but not related to a single body, and since they in no way match each other, the result would be a monster rather than man" (Kuhn, 1962, 83). The existing breakdown of knowledge into mutually indifferent and often hostile academic disciplines, each with its own range of problematics and methods, has replaced the harmonious enlightenment we had been promised with a raucous cacophony of discordant sounds. In the confusion, the age-old link between knowledge and action has been severed, so that scholars can deny all responsibility for their wares while taking pride in knowing more and more about less and less. It is as a way of criticizing this state of affairs and developing an integrated body of knowledge that a growing number of researchers are turning to Marxian dialectics.

With all the misinformation conveyed about dialectics, it may be useful to start by saying what it is *not*. Dialectics is not a rock-ribbed triad of thesis-antithesis-synthesis that serves as an all-purpose explanation; nor does it provide a formula that enables us to prove or predict anything; nor is it the motor force of history. The dialectic, as such, explains nothing, proves nothing, predicts nothing, and causes nothing to happen. Rather, dialectics is a way of thinking that brings into focus the full range of changes and interactions that occur in the world. As part of this, it includes how to organize a reality viewed in this manner for purposes of study and how to present the results of what one finds to others, most of whom do not think dialectically.

The main problem to which dialectics is addressed is set out clearly in Marx's retelling of the Roman myth of Cacus (1971, 536–37). Half man, half demon, Cacus lived in a cave and came out only at night to steal oxen. Wishing to mislead his pursuers, Cacus forced the oxen to walk backward into his den so that their footprints made it appear that they had gone out from there. The next morning, when people came looking for their oxen, all they found were footprints. Based on the evidence of these footprints, they concluded that, starting from the cave, their oxen had gone into the middle of a field and disappeared.

If the owners of the oxen had taken a methodology course at an American university, they might have counted the footprints and measured the depth of each step—but they would have arrived at the same conclusion. The problem here arises from the fact that reality is more than appearances, and that focusing exclusively on appearances, on the evidence that strikes us immediately and directly, can be extremely misleading. How typical is the error found in this example? According to Marx, rather than the exception, this is how most people in our society understand the world. Basing themselves on what they see, hear, and bump into in their immediate surroundings—on footprints of various kinds—they arrive at conclusions that are in many cases the exact opposite of the truth. Most of the distortions associated with bourgeois ideology are of this kind.

To understand the real meaning of the footprints, the owners of the oxen had to find out what happened the night before and what was going on in the cave that lay just over their horizon. In a similar way, understanding anything in our everyday experience requires that we know something about how it arose and developed and how it fits into the larger context or system of which it is a part. Just recognizing this, however, is not enough. For nothing is easier than slipping back into a narrow focus on appearances. After all, few would deny that everything in the world is changing and interacting at some pace and in one way or another, that history and systemic connections belong to the real world. The difficulty has always been how to think adequately about them, how not to distort them and how to give them the attention and weight that they deserve. Dialectics is an attempt to resolve this difficulty by expanding our notion of anything to include, as aspects of what it is, both the process by which it has become that and the broader interactive context in which it is found. Only then does the study of anything involve one immediately with the study of its history and encompassing system.

Dialectics restructures our thinking about reality by replacing the common sense notion of "thing," as something that *has* a history and *has* external connections with other things, with notions of "process," which *contains* its history and possible futures, and "relation," which *contains* as part of what it is its ties with other relations. Nothing that didn't already exist has been added here. Rather, it is a matter of where and how one draws boundaries and establishes units (the dialectical term is "abstracts") in which to think about the world. The assumption is that while the qualities we perceive with our five senses actually exist as parts of nature, the conceptual distinctions that tell us where one thing ends and the next one begins both in space and across time are social and mental constructs. However great the influence of what the world is on how we draw these boundaries, it is ultimately we who draw the boundaries, and people coming from different cultures and from different philosophical traditions can and do draw them differently.

In abstracting capital, for example, as a process, Marx is simply including primitive accumulation, accumulation, and the concentration of capital, in sum its real history, as part of what capital is. While abstracting it as a relation brings its actual ties with labor, commodity, value, capitalists, and workers—or whatever contributes to its appearance and functioning—under the same rubric as its constituting aspects. All the units in which Marx thinks about and studies capitalism are abstracted as both processes and relations. Based on this dialectical conception, Marx's quest—unlike that of his common sense opponents—is never for why something starts to change, but for the various forms this change assumes and why it may *appear* to have stopped. Likewise, it is never for how a relation gets established, but again for the different forms it takes and why aspects of an already existing relation may *appear* to be independent. Marx's critique of the ideology that results from an exclusive focus on appearances, on the footprints of events separated from their real history and the larger system in which they are found, is also of this order.

Besides a way of viewing the world, Marx's dialectical method includes how he studied it, how he organized what he found, and how he presented these findings to his chosen audience. But how does one inquire into a world that has been abstracted into mutually dependent processes? Where does one start and what does one look for? Unlike non-dialectical research, where one starts with some small part and through establishing its connections tries to reconstruct the larger whole, dialectical research begins with the whole, the system, or as much of it as one understands, and then proceeds to an examination of the part to see where it fits and how it functions, leading eventually to a fuller understanding of the whole from which one has begun. Capitalism serves Marx as his jumping-off point for an examination of anything that takes place within it. As a beginning, capitalism is already contained, in principle, within the interacting processes he sets out to investigate as the sum total of their necessary conditions and results. Conversely, to begin with a supposedly independent part or parts is to assume a separation with its corresponding distortion of meaning that no amount of later relating can overcome. Something will be missing, something will be out of place, and, without any standard by which to judge, neither will be recognized. What are called "interdisciplinary studies" simply treat the sum of such defects coming from different fields. As with Humpty Dumpty, who after the fall could never be put together again, a system whose functioning parts have been treated as independent of one another at the start can never be reestablished in its integrity.

The investigation itself seeks to concretize what is going on in capitalism, to trace the means and forms through which it works and has developed, and to project where it seems to be tending. As a general rule, the interactions that constitute any problem in its present state are examined before studying their progress over time. The order of inquiry, in other words, is system before history, so that history is never the development of one or two isolated elements with its suggestion, explicit or implicit, that change results from causes located inside that particular sphere (histories of religion, or of culture, or even of economics alone are decidedly undialectical). In Marx's study of any specific event or institutional form, these two types of inquiry are always interwoven. The fuller understanding of capitalism that is the major result of such a study is now ready to serve as a more effective starting point for the next series of investigations.

Given an approach that proceeds from the whole to the part, from the system inward, dialectical research is primarily directed to finding and tracing four kinds of relations: identity/difference, interpenetration of opposites, quantity/quality, and contradiction. Rooted in his dialectical conception of reality, these relations enable Marx to attain his double aim of discovering how something works or happened while simultaneously developing his understanding of the system in which such things could work or happen in just this way.

In what Marx calls the common sense approach, also found in formal logic, things are either the same/identical or different, not both. On this model, comparisons generally stop after taking note of the way(s) any two entities are either identical or different, but for Marx this is only the first step. Unlike the political economists, for example, who stop after describing the obvious differences between profit, rent, and interest, Marx goes on to bring out their identity as forms of surplus-value (that is, wealth created by workers that is not returned to them in the form of wages). As relations, they all have this quality, this aspect that touches upon their origins, in common. The interest Marx takes in delineating the special features of production and of the working class without neglecting all they have in common with other economic processes and other classes respectively are good examples of his approaching identity and difference from the side of identity. The relations that stand in for things in Marx's dialectical conception of reality are sufficiently large and complex to possess qualities that—when compared to the qualities of other similarly constituted relations—appear to be identical and others that appear to be different. In investigating what these are and, especially, in paying extra attention to whichever half of this pairing is currently most neglected, Marx can arrive at detailed descriptions of specific phenomena without getting lost in one-sidedness.

While the relation of identity/difference treats the various qualities that are examined with its help as given, the interpretation of opposites is based on the recognition that to a very large degree how anything appears and functions is due to its surrounding conditions. These conditioning factors apply to both objects and the persons perceiving them. As regards the former, for example, it is only because a machine is owned by capitalists that it is used to exploit workers. In the hands of a consumer or of a self-employed operator, that is, conditioned by another set of factors, operating under different imperatives, it would not function in this way. As regards the latter, when a capitalist looks at a machine, he sees a commodity he has bought on the market, perhaps even the price he has paid for it, and something that is going to make him a profit. A worker, on the other hand, looking at the same machine sees an instrument that will determine his movements in the production process.

The perspectival element—recognizing that things appear very different depending on who is looking at them—plays a very important role in dialectical thought. This doesn't mean that the truths that emerge from viewing reality from different vantage points are of equal value. Involved as they are in the work of transforming nature, workers enjoy a privileged position from which to view and make sense out of the developmental character of the system, and with his interest in the evolution of capitalism this is the vantage point that Marx most often adopts for himself.

The notion of the interpenetration of opposites helps Marx to understand that nothing—no event, institution, person, or process—is simply and solely what it seems to be at a particular place and time, that is situated within a certain set of conditions. Viewed in another way or by other people, or viewing them under drastically changed conditions may produce not only a different but the exact opposite conclusion or effect. Hence, the interpenetration of opposites. A losing strike in one context may serve as the start of a revolution in another; an election that is a farce because one party, the Republicrats, has all the money and the workers' parties none could, with an equalization of the conditions of struggle, offer a democratic choice; workers who believe that capitalism is an ideal system when they have a good job may begin to question this when they become unemployed. Looking for where and how such changes have already occurred and under what set of still-developing conditions new effects are likely to occur helps Marx gauge both the complexity of the part under examination and its dependence on the evolution of the system overall.

What is called quantity/quality is a relation between two temporally differentiated moments within the same process. Every process contains moments of before and after, encompassing both buildup (and build-down) and what that leads to. Initially, movement within any process takes the form of quantitative change. One or more of its aspects— each process being also a relation composed of aspects—increases or decreases in size or number. Then, at a certain point—which is different for each process studied—a qualitative transformation takes place, indicated by a change in its appearance and/or function. It has become something else while, in terms of its main constituting relationships, remaining essentially the same. This qualitative change is often, though not always, marked by the introduction of a new concept to designate what the process has become.

Only when money reaches a certain amount, Marx says, does it become capital, that is, can it function to buy labor-power and appropriate surplus-value (Engels, 1934, 140). Likewise, the cooperation of many people becomes a new productive power that is not only more but qualitatively different than the sum of individual powers that compose it (Ibid., 142). Looking for quantity/quality change is Marx's way of bringing into single focus the before and after aspects in a development that most non-dialectical approaches treat separately and even causally. It is a way of uniting in thought the past and probable future of any ongoing process at the expense (temporary expense) of its relations in the broader system. And it is a way of sensitizing oneself to the inevitability of change, both quantitative and qualitative, even before research has helped us to discover what it is. While the notion of quantity/quality is in no sense a formula for predicting the future, it does encourage research into patterns and trends of a kind that enables one to project the likely future, and it does offer a framework for integrating such projections into one's understanding of the present and the past.

Of the four major relations Marx investigated in his effort to make dialectical sense out of capitalist reality, contradiction is undoubtedly the most important. According to Marx, "in capitalism everything seems and in fact is contradictory" (1963, 218). He also believes it is the "contradictory socially determined features of its elements" that is "the predominant characteristic of the capitalist mode of production" (1973, 491).

Contradiction is understood here as the incompatible development of different elements within the same relation, which is to say between elements that are also dependent on one another. What is remarked as differences are based, as we saw, on certain conditions, and these conditions are constantly changing. Hence, differences are changing; and given how each difference serves as part of the appearance and/or functioning of others, grasped as relations, how one changes affects all. Consequently, their paths of development do not only intersect in mutually supportive ways, but are constantly blocking, undermining, otherwise interfering with and in due course transforming one another. Contradiction offers the optimal means for bringing such change and interaction as regards both present and future into a single focus. The future finds its way into this focus as the likely and possible outcomes of the interaction of these opposing tendencies in the present, as their real potential. It is contradiction more than any other notion that enables Marx to think accurately about the organic and historical movements of the capitalist mode of production, how they affect each other and develop together from their origins in feudalism to whatever lies just over the horizon.

The common sense notion of contradiction is that it applies to ideas about things and not to things themselves, that it is a logical relation between propositions ("If I claim 'X,' I can't at the same time claim 'not X' "), and not a real relation existing in the world. This common sense view, as we saw, is based on a conception of reality divided into separate and independent parts—a body moves when another body bumps into it. Whereas non-dialectical thinkers in every sphere of scholarship are involved in a nonstop search for the "outside agitator," for something or someone that comes from outside the problem under examination that is the cause for whatever occurs, dialectical thinkers attribute the main responsibility for all change to the inner contradictions of the system or systems in which it occurs. Capitalism's fate, in other words, is sealed by its own problems, problems that are internal manifestations of what it is and how it works and are often parts of the very achievements of capitalism, worsening as these achievements grow and spread. Capitalism's extraordinary success in increasing production, for example, stands in contradiction to the decreasing ability of the workers to consume these goods. Given capitalist relations of distribution, they can buy ever smaller portions of what they themselves produce (it is the proportion of such goods and not the actual amount that determines the character of the contradiction), leading to periodic crises of overproduction/underconsumption. For Marx, contradiction belongs to things in their quality as processes within an organic and developing system. It arises from within, from the very character of these processes (it is "innate in their subject matter"), and is an expression of the state of the system (Ibid., 137).

Without a conception of things as relations, non-dialectical thinkers have great difficulty focusing on the different sides of a contradiction at the same time. The result is that these sides are examined, if at all, in sequence, with one invariably receiving less attention than the other, their mutual interaction often mistaken for causality. A frequent criticism Marx makes of political economists is that they try to "exorcise contradictions" (1968, 519). By viewing capitalist forces of production and capitalist relations of distribution separately they miss the contradiction. A lot of effort of bourgeois ideology goes into denying, hiding, or otherwise distorting contradictions. Bad faith and interest politics, however, account for only a small part of these practices. For non-dialectical thinkers, operating out of a common sense view, real contradictions can be understood only as differences, paradox, opposition, strain, tension, dislocation, imbalance, or, if accompanied by open strife, conflict. But without the dialectical notion of contradiction, they seldom see and can never adequately grasp the underlying forces responsible for these appearances. And, of course, they can never grasp the development or gauge the force of these tendencies before they have made their way to the surface of events. For Marx, on the other hand, the study of capitalist contradictions is also a way of discovering the main causes of *coming* conflict.

On the basis of what he uncovers in his study of identity/difference, the interpenetration of opposites, quantity/quality, and contradiction—a study that starts with the whole and proceeds inward to the part, and which conceives of all parts as processes in relations of mutual dependence— Marx reconstructed the working of capitalist society. Organizing reality in this way, he was able to capture both the organic and historical movements of capitalism in their specific interconnections. The still unfinished results of this reconstruction are the particular laws and theories we know as Marxism.

It is clear that Marx could not have arrived at his understanding of capitalism without dialectics, nor will we be able to develop this understanding further without a firm grasp of this same method. No treatment of dialectics however brief, therefore, can be considered complete without a warning against some of the more common errors and distortions associated with this way of thinking. For example, if non-dialectical thinkers often miss the forest for the trees, dialectical thinkers just as often do the opposite, that is, play down or even ignore the parts, the details, in deference to making generalizations about the whole. But the capitalist system can be grasped only through an investigation of its specific parts in their interconnection. Dialectical thinkers also have a tendency to move too quickly to the bottom line, to push the germ of a development to its finished form. In general, this error results from not giving enough attention to the complex mediations, both in space and over time, that make up the joints of any social problem.

There is also a related tendency to overestimate the speed of change along with a corresponding tendency to underestimate the barriers to change. Relatively minor cracks on the surface of capitalist reality are too easily mistaken for gaping chasms on the verge of becoming earthquakes. If non-dialectical thinking leads people to be surprised whenever a major change occurs, because they aren't looking for it and don't expect it, because it isn't an internal part of how they conceive of the world at this moment, dialectical thinking—for just the opposite reasons—can lead people to be surprised when such change takes so long in coming. In organizing reality for purposes of grasping change, relative stability does not always get the attention that it deserves. These are all weaknesses inherent in the very strengths of dialectical method. Ever present as temptations, they offer an easier way, a quick fix, and have to be carefully guarded against.

Nothing that we have said in our account so far should be taken to deny the empirical character of Marx's method. Marx does not deduce the workings of capitalism from the meanings of words or from the requirements of his theories, but like any good social scientist he does research to discover what is the case. And in his research he made use of the entire range of materials and resources that were available in his time. Nor do we wish to claim that Marx was the only dialectical thinker. As is well known, most of his dialectic was taken over from Hegel, who merely (?) filled in and systematized a way of thinking and an approach to studying reality that goes all the way back to the Greeks. And in our time there are non-Marxist thinkers, such as Alfred North Whitehead and F. H. Bradley, who have developed their own versions of this approach. Despite its heavy ideological content, common sense, too, is not without its dialectical moments, as is evidenced by such maxims as "Every cloud has its silver lining" and "That was the straw that broke the camel's back." Elements of dialectics can also be found in other social science methods, such as structural functionalism, systems theory, and ethnomethodology, where it constitutes most of what is of value in these approaches.

What stands out about Marx's dialectical method is the systematic manner in which he works it out and uses it for the study of capitalist society (including—because the dialectic requires it—its origins and probable future), the united theory of knowledge (set out in the still incomplete theories of Marxism) to which it leads, the sustained critique of non-dialectical approaches (suggested in our remarks on ideology throughout) that it makes possible, and—perhaps most striking of all—its emphasis on the necessary connection posed by dialectics itself between knowledge and action.

As regards this last, Marx claims, the dialectic "is in its essence critical and revolutionary" (1958, 20). It is revolutionary because it helps us to see the present as a moment through which our society is passing, because it forces us to examine where it has come from and where it is heading as part of learning what it is, and because it enables us to grasp that as actors, as well as victims, in this process in which everyone and everything are connected, we have to power to affect it. In keeping in front of us the simple truth that everything is changing, the future is posed as a choice in which the only thing that cannot be chosen is what we already have. Efforts to retain the status quo in any area of life never achieve quite that. Fruit kept in the refrigerator too long goes rotten; so do emotions and people; so do whole societies (where the proper word is *disintegration*). With dialectics we are made to question what kind of changes are already occurring and what kind of changes are possible. The dialectic is revolutionary, as Brecht points out, because it helps us to pose such questions in a manner that makes effective action possible (Lit., Sci., Ideol., 1972, 1).

The dialectic is critical because it helps us to become critical of what our role has been up to now. In Marxist terms, one doesn't advocate class struggle or choose to participate in it (common bourgeois misconceptions). The class struggle, representing the sum of the contradictions between workers broadly defined and capitalists, simply is, and in one way or another we are all already involved. On learning about it and where we fit into it, however, we can decide to stop acting as we have been (the first decision to take) and what more or else we can do to better serve our own interests. What *can* be chosen is what side to take in this struggle and how to conduct it. A dialectical grasp of our society conditioned roles and the equally necessary limits and possibilities that constitute the present provides the opportunity for making a conscious and intelligent choice. In this manner does knowledge of necessity usher in the beginnings of real freedom.

References

Engels, F. 1934. *Herr Eugene Duhring's Revolution in Science* [*Anti-Dühring*]. Translated by Emile Burns. London: Lawrence and Wishart.
Kuhn, T. 1962. *The Structure of Scientific Revolution.* Chicago: Univ. of Chicago Press. 1972. *Literature, Science, Ideologie,* No. 1 (May/June).
Marx, K. 1958. *Capital.* Vol. 1. Translated by S. Moore and E. Aveling. Moscow: Foreign Languages Publishing House.
———. 1963. *Theories of Surplus Value.* Part 1. Translated by E. Burns. Moscow: Progress Publishers.
———. 1968. *Theories of Surplus Value.* Part 2. Translated by S. Ryazanskaya. Moscow: Progress Publishers.
———. 1973. *Theories of Surplus Value.* Part 3. Translated by J. Cohen and S. W. Ryazanskaya. Moscow: Progress Publishers.

Part II

Advanced Dialectics

2

Putting Dialectics to Work:
The Process of Abstraction
in Marx's Method

I. The Problem: How to Think Adequately about Change and Interaction

Is there any part of Marxism that has received more abuse than his dialectical method? And I am not just thinking about enemies of Marxism and socialism, but also about scholars who are friendly to both. It is not Karl Popper, but George Sorel in his Marxist incarnation who refers to dialectics as "the art of reconciling opposites through hocus pocus," and the English socialist economist, Joan Robinson, who on reading *Capital* objects to the constant intrusion of "Hegel's nose" between her and Ricardo (Sorel, 1950, 171; Robinson, 1953, 23). But perhaps the classic complaint is fashioned by the American philosopher, William James, who compares reading about dialectics in Hegel—it could just as well have been Marx—to getting sucked into a whirlpool (1978, 174).

Yet other thinkers have considered Marx's dialectical method among his most important contributions to socialist theory, and Lukacs goes so far as to claim that orthodox Marxism relies solely upon adherence to his method (1971, 1). Though Lukacs may be exaggerating to make his point, it is not—in my view—by very much. The reasons for such widespread disagreement on the meaning and value of dialectics are many, but what stands out is the inadequate attention given to the nature of its subject matter. What, in other words, is dialectics about? What questions does it deal with, and why are they important? Until there is more clarity, if not consensus, on its basic task, treatises on dialectics will succeed only in piling one layer of obscurity upon another. So this is where we must begin.

First and foremost, and stripped of all qualifications added by this or that dialectician, the subject of dialectics is change, all change, and interaction, all kinds and degrees of interaction. This is not to say that dialectical thinkers recognize the existence of change and interaction, while non-dialectical thinkers do not. That would be foolish. Everyone recognizes that everything in the world changes, somehow and to some degree, and that the same holds true for interaction. The problem is how to think adequately about them, how to capture them in thought. How, in other words, can we think about change and interaction so as not to miss or distort the real changes and interactions that we know, in a general way at least, are there (with all the implications this has for how to study them and to communicate what we find to others)? This is the key problem addressed by dialectics, this is what all dialectics is about, and it is in helping to resolve *this* problem that Marx turns to the process of abstraction.

II. The Solution Lies in the Process of Abstraction

In his most explicit statement on the subject, Marx claims that his method starts from the "real concrete" (the world as it presents itself to us) and proceeds through "abstraction" (the intellectual activity of breaking this whole down into the mental units with which we think about it) to the "thought concrete" (the reconstituted and now understood whole present in the mind) (1904, 293–94). The real concrete is simply the world in which we live, in all its complexity. The thought concrete is Marx's reconstruction of that world in the theories of what has come to be called "Marxism." The royal road to understanding is said to pass from the one to the other through the process of abstraction.

In one sense, the role Marx gives to abstraction is simple recognition of the fact that all thinking about reality begins by breaking it down into manageable parts. Reality may be in one piece when lived, but to be thought about and communicated it must be parceled out. Our minds can no more swallow the world whole at one sitting than can our stomachs. Everyone then, and not just Marx and Marxists, begins the task of trying to make sense of his or her surroundings by distinguishing certain features and focusing on and organizing them in ways deemed appropriate. "Abstract" comes from the Latin, *abstrahere*, which means "to pull from." In effect, a piece has been pulled from or taken out of the whole and is temporarily perceived as standing apart.

We "see" only some of what lies in front of us, "hear" only part of the noises in our vicinity, "feel" only a small part of what our body is in contact with, and so on through the rest of our senses. In each case, a focus is established and a kind of boundary set within our perceptions distinguishing what is relevant from what is not. It should be clear that "What did you see?" (What caught your eye?) is a different question from "What did you *actually* see?" (What came into your line of vision?). Likewise, in thinking about any subject, we focus on only some of its qualities and relations. Much that could be included—that may in fact be included in another person's view or thought, and may on another occasion be included in our own—is left out. The mental activity involved in establishing such boundaries, whether conscious or unconscious—though it is usually an amalgam of both—is the process of abstraction.

Responding to a mixture of influences that include the material world and our experiences in it as well as to personal wishes, group interests, and other social constraints, it is the process of abstraction that establishes the specificity of the objects with which we interact. In setting boundaries, in ruling this far and no further, it is what makes something one (or two, or more) of a kind, and lets us know where that kind begins and ends. With this decision as to units, we also become committed to a particular set of relations between them—relations made possible and even necessary by the qualities that we have included in each—a register for classifying them, and a mode for explaining them.

In listening to a concert, for example, we often concentrate on a single instrument or recurring theme and then redirect our attention elsewhere. Each time this occurs, the whole music alters, new patterns emerge, each sound takes on a different value, etc. How we understand the music is largely determined by how we abstract it. The same applies to what we focus on when watching a play, whether on a person, or a combination of persons, or a section of the stage. The meaning of the play and what more is required to explore or test this meaning alters, often dramatically, with each new abstraction. In this way, too, how we abstract literature, where we draw the boundaries, determines what works and what parts of each work will be studied, with what methods, in relation to what other subjects, in what order, and even by whom. Abstracting literature to include its audience, for example, leads to a sociology of literature, while an abstraction of literature that excludes everything but its forms calls forth various structural approaches, and so on.

From what has been said so far, it is clear that "abstraction" is itself an abstraction. I have abstracted it from Marx's dialectical method, which in turn was abstracted from his broad theories, which in turn were abstracted from his life and work. The mental activities that we have collected and brought into focus as "abstraction" are more often associated with the processes of perception, conception, defining, reasoning, and even thinking. It is not surprising, therefore, if the process of abstraction strikes many people as both foreign and familiar at the same time. Each of these more familiar processes operate in part by separating out, focusing, and putting emphasis on only some aspects of that reality with which they come into contact. In "abstraction," we have simply separated out, focused, and put emphasis on certain common features of these other processes. Abstracting "abstraction" in this way is neither easy nor obvious, and therefore few people have done it. Consequently, though everyone abstracts, of necessity, only a few are aware of it as such. This philosophical impoverishment is reinforced by the fact that most people are lazy abstractors, simply and uncritically accepting the mental units with which they think as part of their cultural inheritance.

A further complication in grasping "abstraction" arises from the fact that Marx uses the term in three different, though closely related, senses. First, and most important, it refers to the mental activity of subdividing the world into the mental constructs with which we think about it, which is the process that we have been describing. Second, it refers to the results of this process, the actual parts into which reality has been apportioned. That is to say, for Marx, as for Hegel before him, "abstraction" functions as a noun as well as a verb, the noun referring to what the verb has brought into being. In these senses, everyone can be said to abstract (verb) and to think with abstractions (noun). But Marx also uses "abstraction" in a third sense, where it refers to a suborder of particularly ill fitting mental constructs. Whether because they are too narrow, take in too little, focus too exclusively on appearances, or are otherwise badly composed, these constructs do not allow an adequate grasp of their subject matter.

Taken in this third sense, abstractions are the basic unit of ideology, the inescapable ideational result of living and working in alienated society. "Freedom," for example, is said to be such an abstraction whenever we remove the real individual from "the conditions of existence within which these individuals enter into contact" (1973, 164). Omitting the conditions that make freedom possible (or impossible)—including the real alternatives available, the role of money, the socialization of the person choosing, etc.—from the meaning of "freedom" leaves a notion that can only distort and obfuscate even that part of reality it sets out to convey. A lot of Marx's criticism of ideology makes use of this sense of "abstraction," as when he says that people in capitalist society are "ruled by abstractions" (1973, 164). Such remarks, of which there are a great many in his writings, however, must not keep us from seeing that Marx also abstracts in the first sense given above and, like everyone else, thinks with abstractions in the second sense, and that the particular way in which he does both goes a long way in accounting for the distinctive character of Marxism.

Despite several explicit remarks on the centrality of abstraction in Marx's work, the process of abstraction has received relatively little attention in the literature on Marxism. Serious work on Marx's dialectical method can usually be distinguished on the basis of which of the categories belonging to the vocabulary of dialectics is treated as pivotal. For Lukacs, it was the concept of "totality" that played this role (1971); for Mao, it was "contradiction" (1968); for Raya Dunayevskaya, it was the "negation of negation" (1982); for Scott Meikle, it was "essence" (1985); for the Ollman of *Alienation,* it was "internal relations", and so on (1976). Even when abstraction is discussed—and no serious work dismisses it altogether— the main emphasis is generally on what it is in the world or in history or in Marx's research into one or the other that is responsible for the particular abstractions made, and not on the process of abstraction as such, on what exactly he does and how he does it.[1] Consequently, the implications of Marx's abstracting practice for the theories of Marxism remain clouded, and those wishing to develop these theories and where necessary revise them receive little help in their efforts to abstract in the manner of Marx. In what follows, it is just this process of abstraction, how it works and particularly how Marx works it, that serves as the centerpiece for our discussion of dialectics.

III. How Marx's Abstractions Differ

What then is distinctive about Marx's abstractions? To begin with, it should be clear that Marx's abstractions do not and cannot diverge com- pletely from the abstractions of other thinkers both then and now. There has to be a lot of overlap. Otherwise, he would have constructed what philosophers call a "private language," and any communication between him and the rest of us would be impossible. How close Marx came to fall into such an abyss and what can be done to repair some of the damage already done is discussed in the longer work of which this essay is a part. Second, in depicting Marx's process of abstraction as a predominantly conscious and rational activity, I do not mean to deny the enormous degree to which what results accurately reflects the real world. However, the materialist foundations of Marx's thinking are sufficiently (though by no means "adequately") understood to be taken for granted here while we concentrate on the process of abstraction as such.

---

1. Possible exceptions to this relative neglect of abstractions in discussions of Marx's method include E. V. Ilyenkov (1982), where the emphasis is on the relation of abstract to concrete in *Capital;* A. Sohn-Rethel (1978), which shows how commodity exchange produces abstraction; D. Sayers (1987), which concentrates on the ideological products of the process of abstractions; L. Nowak (1980), which presents a neo-Weberian reconstruction of some aspects of this process, and P. Sweezy (1956) (still the best short introduction to our subject) which stresses the role of abstraction in isolating the essentials of a problem. Insightful, though limited treatments of abstraction can also be found in articles by A. Sayers (1981), J. Allen (1983), and J. Horvath and K. D. Gibson (1984). An early philosophical account of abstraction, which Marx himself had a chance to read and admire, is found in the work of Joseph Dietzgen (1928).

Keeping these two qualifications clearly in mind, we can now say that what is most distinctive about Marx's abstractions, taken as a group, is that they focus on and incorporate both change and interaction (or system) in the particular forms in which these occur in the capitalist era. It is important to underline from the start that Marx's main concern was with capitalism. He sought to discover what it is and how it works, as well as how it emerged and where it is tending. We shall call the organic and historical processes involved here the double movement of the capitalist mode of production. Each movement affects the other, and how one grasps either affects one's understanding of both. But how does one study the history of a system, or the systemic functioning of evolving processes, where the main determinants of change lie within the system itself? For Marx, the first and most important step was to incorporate the general form of what he was looking for, to wit—change and interaction, into all the abstractions he constructed as part of his research. Marx's understanding of capitalism, therefore, is not restricted to the theories of Marxism, which relate the components of the capitalist system, but some large part of it is found within the very abstractions with which these theories have been constructed.

Beginning with historical movement, Marx's preoccupation with change and development is undisputed. What is less known, chiefly because it is less clear, is how he thought about change, how he abstracted it, and how he integrated these abstractions into his study of a changing world. The underlying problem is as old as philosophy itself. The ancient Greek philosopher, Heraclitus, provides us with its classic statement when he asserts that a person cannot step into the same river twice. Enough water has flowed between the two occasions so that the river we step into the second time is not the same river we walked into earlier. Yet our common sense tells us that it is, and our naming practice reflects this view. Heraclitus, of course, was not interested in rivers, but in change. His point is that change goes on everywhere and all the time, but that our manner of thinking about it is sadly inadequate. The flow, the constant alteration of movement away from something and toward something else, is generally missing. Usually, where change takes place very slowly or in very small increments, its impact can be safely neglected. On the other hand, depending on the context and on our purpose in it, even such change—because it occurs outside our attention—may occasionally startle us and have grave consequences for our lives.

Even today few are able to think about the changes they know to be happening in ways that don't distort—usually by underplaying—what is actually going on. From the titles of so many works in the social sciences it would appear that a good deal of effort is being directed to studying change of one kind or another. But what is actually taken as "change" in most of these works? It is not the continuous evolution and alteration that goes on in their subject matter, the social equivalent of the flowing water in Heraclitus' river. Rather, almost invariably, it is a comparison of two or more differentiated states in the development of the object or condition or group under examination. As the sociologist, James Coleman, who defends this approach, admits, "The concept of change in science is a rather special one, for it does not immediately follow from our sense impressions. . . . It is based on a comparison, or difference between two sense impressions, and simultaneously a comparison of the times at which the sense impressions occurred." Why? Because, according to Coleman, "the concept of change must, as any concept, itself reflect a state of an object at a point in time" (1968, 429). Consequently, a study of the changes in the political thinking of the American electorate, for example, gets translated into an account of how people voted (or responded to opinion polls) in 1956, 1960, 1964, etc., and the differences found in a comparison of these static moments is what is called "change." It is not simply, and legitimately, that the one, the difference between the moments, gets taken as an indication of or evidence for the other, the process; rather, it stands in for the process itself.

In contrast to this approach, Marx set out to abstract things, in his words, "as they really are and happen," making how they happen part of what they are (Marx and Engels, 1964, 57). Hence, capital (or labor, money, etc.) is not only how capital appears and functions, but also how it develops; or rather, how it develops, its real history, is also part of what it is. It is also in this sense that Marx could deny that nature and history "are two separate things" (Marx and Engels, 1964, 57). In the view which currently dominates the social sciences, things exist *and* undergo change. The two are logically distinct. History is something that happens to things; it is not part of their nature. Hence, the difficulty of examining change in subjects from which it has been removed at the start. Whereas Marx, as he tells us, abstracts "every historical social form as in fluid movement, and therefore takes into account its transient nature *not less* than its momentary existence" (1958, 20). (My emphasis.)

But history for Marx refers not only to time past but to time future. So that whatever something is becoming—whether we know what that will be or not—is in some important respects part of what it is along with what it once was. For example, capital, for Marx, is not simply the material means of production used to produce wealth, which is how it is abstracted in the work of most economists. Rather, it includes the early stages in the development of these particular means of production, or "primitive accumulation," indeed whatever has made it possible for it to produce the kind of wealth it does in just the way it does (viz. permits wealth to take the form of value, something produced not because it is useful but for purposes of exchange). Furthermore, as part of its becoming, capital incorporates the accumulation of capital that is occurring now together with its tendency toward concentration and centralization, and the effect of this tendency on both the development of a world market and an eventual transition to socialism. According to Marx, the tendency to expand surplus-value and with it production, and therefore to create a world market, is "directly given in the concept of capital itself" (1973, 408).

That capital contains the seeds of a future socialist society is also apparent in its increasingly socialized character and in the growing separation of the material means of production from the direct control of capitalists, making the latter even more superfluous. This "history" of capital is part of capital, contained within the abstraction that Marx makes of capital, and part of what he wants to convey with its covering concept. All of Marx's main abstractions—labor, value, commodity, money, etc.—incorporate process, becoming, history in just this way. Our purpose here is not to explain Marx's economics, but simply to use some of his claims in this area to illustrate how he integrates what most readers would take to be externally related phenomena, in this case its real past and likely future, into his abstraction of its present form.

Marx often uses the qualifying phrase "in itself" to indicate the necessary and internal ties between the future development of anything and how it presents itself at this moment. Money and commodity, for example, are referred to as "in themselves" capital (1963, 396). Given the independent form in which they confront the worker in capitalist society—something separate from him but something he must acquire in order to survive—money and commodity ensure the exchange of labor power and through it their own transformation into means of production used to produce new value. Capital is part of what they are becoming, part of their future, and hence part of them. Just as money and commodity are parts of what capital are, parts of its past, and hence parts of it. Elsewhere, Marx refers to money and commodity as "potential capital," as capital "only in intention, in their essence, in what they were destined to be" (1971, 465; 1963, 399–400). Similarly, all labor is abstracted as wage-labor, and all means of production as capital, because this is the direction in which they are evolving in capitalist society (1963, 409–10).

To consider the past and likely future development of anything as integral to what it is, to grasp this whole as a single process, does not keep Marx from abstracting out some part or instant of this process for a particular purpose and from treating it as relatively autonomous. Aware that the units into which he has subdivided reality are the results of his abstractions, Marx is able to re-abstract this reality, restricting the area brought into focus in line with the requirements of his current study. But when he does this, he often underlines its character as a temporally stable part of a larger and ongoing process by referring to it as a "moment." In this way, commodity is spoken of as a "moment in exchange," money (in its aspect as capital) as a "moment" in the process of production, and circulation in general as a "moment in the system of production" (1973, 145, 217). Marx's naming practice here reflects the epistemological priority he gives to movement over stability, so that stability—whenever it is found—is viewed as temporary and/or only apparent, or, as he says on one occasion, as a "paralysis" of movement (1971, 212). With stability used to qualify change rather than the reverse, Marx—unlike most modern social scientists—did not and could not study why things change (with the implication that change is external to what they are, something that happens to them). Given that change is always a part of what things are, his research problem could only be *how, when,* and *into what* they change and why they sometimes appear not to (ideology).

Before concluding our discussion of the place of change in Marx's abstractions, it is worth noting that thinking in terms of processes is not altogether alien to common sense. It occurs in abstractions of actions, such as eating, walking, fighting, etc., indeed whenever the gerund form of the verb is used. Likewise, event words, such as *war* and *strike,* indicate that to some degree at least the processes involved have been abstracted as such. On the other hand, it is also possible to think of war and strike as a state or condition, more like a photo than a motion picture, or if the latter, then a single scene that gets shown again and again, which removes or seriously underplays whatever changes are taking place. And unfortunately, the same is true of most action verbs. They become action "things." In such cases, the real processes that go on do not get reflected—certainly not to any adequate degree—in our thinking about them. It is my impression that in the absence of any commitment to bring change itself into focus, in the manner of Marx, this is the more typical outcome.

Earlier we said that what distinguishes Marx's abstractions is that they contain not only change or history but also some portion of the system in which it occurs. Since change in anything only takes place in and through a complex interaction between closely related elements, treating change as intrinsic to what anything is requires that we treat the interaction through which it occurs in the same way. With a static notion of anything it is easy to conceive of it as also discrete, logically independent of and easily separable from its surrounding conditions. They do not enter directly into what it is. While viewing the same thing as a process makes it necessary to extend the boundaries of what it is to include at least some part of the surrounding conditions that enter into this process. In sum, as far as abstractions are concerned, change brings mutual dependence in its wake. Instead of a mere sequence of events isolated from their context, a kind of one-note development, Marx's abstractions become phases of an evolving and interactive system.

Hence, capital, which we examined earlier as a process, is also a complex relation encompassing the interaction between the material means of production, capitalists, workers, value, commodity, money, and more—and all this over time. Marx says, "the concept of capital contains the capitalist"; he refers to workers as "variable capital" and says capital is "nothing without wage-labor, value, money, price, etc." (1973, 512; 1958, 209; 1904, 292). Elsewhere, the "processual" character of these aspects of the capital relation is emphasized in referring to them as "value in process" and "money in process" (1971, 137). If capital, like all other important abstractions in Marxism, is both a process and a relation, viewing it as primarily one or the other could only be a way of emphasizing either its historical or systemic character for a particular purpose.

As in his abstractions of capital as a process, so too in his abstractions of it as a relation, Marx can focus on but part of what capital contains. While the temporally isolated part of a process is generally referred to as a "moment," the spatially isolated aspect of a relation is generally referred to as a "form" or "determination." With "form," Marx usually brings into focus the appearance and/or function of any relation, that by which we recognize it, and most often it is its form that is responsible for the concept by which we know and communicate it. Hence, value (a relation) in its exchangeable form is called "money"; while in the form in which it facilitates the production of more value, it is called "capital"; and so on. "Determination," on the other hand, enables Marx to focus on the transformational character of any relational part, on what best brings out its mutual dependence and changeability within the interactive system. Upon analysis, moments, forms, and determinations all turn out to be relations. So that after referring to the commodity as a moment in wealth, Marx immediately proceeds to pick it apart as a relation (1973, 218). Elsewhere, Marx refers to interest, profit, and rent as forms which through analysis lose their "apparent independence," and are seen to be relations (1971, 429).

Earlier, we saw that some abstractions that contain processes could also be found in what we called common sense. The same is true of abstractions that focus on relations. Father, which contains the relation between a man and a child, is one. Buyer, which contains the relations between a person and something sold or available for sale, is another. But compared to the number and scope of relations in the world, such relations are few and meager in their import. Within the common sense of our time and place, most social ties are thought about in abstractions that focus on the parts one at a time, separately as well as statically. Marx, however, believes that in order to adequately grasp the systemic connections that constitute such an important part of reality one has to incorporate them—along with the ways in which they change—into the very abstractions in and with which one thinks about them. All else is make-do patchwork, a one-sided, lopsided way of thinking that invites the neglect of essential connections together with the distortion of whatever influence they exert on the overall system.

Where have we arrived? Marx's abstractions are not things but processes. These processes are also, of necessity, systemic relations in which the main processes with which Marx deals are all implicated. Consequently, each process serves as an aspect, or subordinate part, of other processes, grasped as clusters of relations, just as they do in it. In this way, Marx brings what we have called the double movement of the capitalist mode of production (its history and organic movement) together in the same abstractions, uniting in his thinking what is united in reality. And whenever he needs to focus on but part of this complex, he does so as a moment, a form or a determination.

Marx's abstractions seem to be very different, especially as regards the treatment of change and interaction, from those in which most people think about society. But if Marx's abstractions stand out as much as our evidence suggests they do, it is not enough to display them. We also need to know what gives Marx the philosophical license to abstract as he does. Whence comes his apparent facility in making and changing abstractions? And what is the relation between his abstractions and those of common sense? It is because most readers cannot see how Marx could possibly abstract as he does that they continue to deny—and perhaps not even notice—the widespread evidence of his practice. Therefore, before making a more detailed analysis of Marx's process of abstraction and its place and role in his dialectical method and broader theories, a brief detour through his philosophical presuppositions is in order.

IV. The Philosophy of Internal Relations

According to Marx, "The economists do not conceive of capital as a relation. They cannot do so without at the same time conceiving of it as a historically transitory, i.e., a relative—not an absolute—form of production" (1971, 274). This is not a comment about content of capital, about what it is, but about the *kind* of thing it is—to wit, a relation. To grasp capital, as Marx does, as a complex relation which has at its core internal ties between the material means of production and those who own them, those who work on them, their special product, value, and the conditions in which owning and working go on is to know capital as a historical event, as something that emerged as a result of specific conditions in the lifetime of real people and that will disappear when these conditions do. Viewing such connections as external to what capital is—which, for them, is simply the material means of production or money used to buy such— the economists fall into treating capital as an ahistorical variable. Without saying so explicitly and certainly without ever explicitly defending this position, capital becomes something that has always been and will always be.

The view held by most people, scholars and others, in what we've been calling the common sense view, maintains that there are things and there are relations, and that neither can be subsumed in the other. This position is summed up in Bishop Butler's statement, which G. E. Moore adopts as a motto: "Everything is what it is, and not another thing," taken in conjunction with Hume's claim, "All events seem entirely loose and separate" (1903, title page; 1955, 85). On this view, capital may be found to have relations with labor, value, etc., and it may even be that accounting for such relations plays an important role in explaining what capital is; but capital is one thing and its relations quite another. Marx, on the other hand, following Hegel's lead in this matter, rejects what is, in essence, a logical dichotomy. For him, as we saw, capital is itself a relation, in which the ties of the material means of production to labor, value, commodity, etc., are interiorized as parts of what capital is. Marx refers to "things themselves" as "their interconnections" (Marx and Engels, 1950, 488). Moreover, these relations extend backward and forward in time, so that capital's conditions of existence as they have evolved over the years and its potential for future development are also viewed as parts of what it is.

On the common sense view, any element related to capital can change without capital itself changing. Workers, for example, instead of selling their labor-power to capitalists, as occurs in capitalism, could become slaves or serfs or owners of their own means of production, and in every case their instruments of work would still be capital. The tie between workers and the means of production here is contingent, a matter of chance, and therefore external to what each really is. In Marx's view, a change of this sort would mean a change in the character of capital itself, in its appearance and/or functioning no matter how far extended. The tie is a necessary and essential one; it is an internal relation. Hence, where its specific relationship to workers has changed, the means of production become something else, and something that is best captured by a concept other than "capital." Every element that comes into Marx's analysis of capitalism is a relation of this sort. It is this view that underlies and helps explain his practice of abstraction and the particular abstractions that result, along with all the theories raised on them.

It appears that the problem non-Marxists have in understanding Marx is much more profound than is ordinarily thought. It is not simply that they don't grasp what Marx is saying about capital (or labor, or value, or the state, etc.) because his account is unclear or confused, or that the evidence for his claims is weak or undeveloped. Rather, it is that the basic form, the relation, in which Marx thinks about each of the major elements that come into his analysis is unavailable, and therefore its ideational content is necessarily misrepresented, if only a little (though usually it is much more). As an attempt to reflect the relations in capitalist society by incorporating them into its core abstractions, Marxism suffers the same distorting fate as these relations themselves.

In the history of ideas, the view that we have been developing is known as the philosophy of internal relations. Marx's immediate philosophical influences in this regard were Leibniz, Spinoza, and Hegel, particularly Hegel. What all had in common is the belief that the relations that come together to make up the whole get expressed in what are taken to be its parts. Each part is viewed as incorporating in what it is all its relations with other parts up to and including everything that comes into the whole. To be sure, each of these thinkers had a distinctive view of what the parts are. For Leibniz, it was monads; for Spinoza, modes of nature or God; and for Hegel, ideas. But the logical form in which they construed the relation between parts and the whole was the same.

Some writers on Marx have argued for a restricted form of internal relations that would apply only to society and not to the natural world (Rader, 1979, chapter 2). But reality doesn't allow such absolute distinctions. People have bodies as well as minds and social roles. Alienation, for example, affects all three, and in their alienated forms each is internally related to the others. Likewise, capital, commodities, money, and the forces of production all have material as well as social aspects. To maintain that the philosophy of internal relations does not respect the usual boundaries between nature and society does not mean that Marx cannot for certain purposes abstract units that fall primarily or even wholly on one or the other side of this divide. Whenever he speaks of "thing" or, as is more frequent, of "social relations," this is what occurs, but in every case what has been momentarily put aside is internally related to what has been brought into focus. Consequently, he is unlikely to minimize or dismiss, as many operating with external relations do, the influences of either natural or social phenomena on the other.

What is the place of such notions as "cause" and "determine" within a philosophy of internal relations? Given the mutual interaction Marx assumes between everything in reality, now and forever, there can be no cause that is logically prior to and independent of that to which it is said to give rise and no determining factor that is itself not affected by that which it is said to determine. In short, the common sense notions of "cause" and "determine" that are founded on such logical independence and absolute priority do not and cannot apply. In their stead we find frequent claims of the following kind: the propensity to exchange is the "cause or reciprocal effect" of the division of labor; and interest and rent "determine" market prices and "are determined" by it (1959a, 134; 1971, 512). In any organic system viewed over time, each process can be said to determine and be determined by all others. However, it is also the case that one part often has a greater effect on others than they do on it; and Marx also uses "cause" and especially "determine" to register this asymmetry. Thus, in the interaction between production, distribution, exchange, and consumption—particularly though not exclusively in capitalism—production is held to be more determining (1904, 274ff.). A good deal of Marx's research is devoted to locating and mapping whatever exercises a greater or special impact on other parts of the capitalist system, but, whether made explicit or not, this always takes place on a backdrop of reciprocal effect. (Another complementary sense of "cause" and "determine" will be presented later.)

Returning to the process of abstraction, it is the philosophy of internal relations that gives Marx both license and opportunity to abstract as freely as he does, to decide how far into its internal relations any particular will extend. Making him aware of the need to abstract—since boundaries are never given and when established never absolute—it also allows and even encourages re-abstraction, makes a variety of abstractions possible, and helps to develop his mental skills and flexibility in making abstractions. If "a relation," as Marx maintains, "can obtain a particular embodiment and become individualized only by means of abstraction," then learning how to abstract is the first step in learning how to think (1973, 142).

Operating with a philosophy of external relations doesn't absolve others from the need to abstract. The units in and with which one thinks are still abstractions and products of the process of abstraction as it occurs during socialization and, particularly, in the acquisition of language. Only, in this case, one takes boundaries as given in the nature of reality as such, as if they have the same ontological stature as the qualities perceived. The role played by the process of abstraction is neither known nor appreciated. Consequently, there is no awareness that one can—and often should— re-abstract, and the ability and flexibility for doing so is never acquired.

Whatever re-abstraction goes on, of necessity, as part of learning new languages or new schools of thought, or as a result of important new experiences, takes place in the dark, usually unconsciously, certainly unsystematically, with little understanding of either assumptions or implications. Marx, on the other hand, is fully aware that he abstracts and of its assumptions and implications both for his own thinking and that of others—hence the frequent equation of ideology in those he criticizes with their inadequate abstractions.

In order to forestall possible misunderstandings it may be useful to assert that the philosophy of internal relations is not an attempt to reify "what lies between." It is simply that the particular ways in which things cohere become essential attributes of what they are. The philosophy of internal relations also does not mean—as some of its critics have charged—that investigating any problem can go on forever (to say that boundaries are artificial is not to deny them an existence, and, practically speaking, it is simply not necessary to understand everything in order to understand anything); or that the boundaries which are established are arbitrary (what actually influences the character of Marx's or anyone else's abstractions is another question); or that we cannot mark or work with some of the important objective distinctions found in reality (on the contrary, such distinctions are a major influence on the abstractions we do make); or, finally, that the vocabulary associated with the philosophy of internal relations—particularly "totality," "relation," and "identity"—cannot also be used in subsidiary senses to refer to the world that comes into being after the process of abstraction has done its work.

In the philosophy of internal relations, "totality" is a logical construct that refers to the way the whole is present through internal relations in each of its parts. Totality, in this sense, is always there, and adjectives like "more" and "less" simply don't apply. But Marx's work also contains constructed or emergent totalities, which are of a historical nature, and great care must be taken not to confuse the two. In the latter case, a totality or whole or system is built up gradually as its elements emerge, cohere, and develop over time. "The circumstances under which a relation occurs for the first time," Marx says, "by no means shows us that relation either in its purity or in its totality" (1971, 205). Here, too, unlike logical totalities, some systems can be said to be more or less complete than others, or than itself at an earlier stage. There is nothing in the philosophy of internal relations that interferes with the recognition of such totalities. All that is required is that at every stage in its emergence each part be viewable as a relational microcosm of the whole, including its real history and potential for future development.

The advantages of using any relational part as a starting point for reconstructing the interconnections of the whole, of treating it as a logical totality, will increase, of course, as its social role grows and its ties with other parts become more complex, as it becomes in other words more of an emergent totality. One would not expect the commodity, for example, to serve as a particularly useful starting place from which to reconstruct slave society or feudalism, where it exists but only on the fringes (to the extent that there is some wage-labor and/or some trade between different communities), but it offers an ideal starting place from which to reconstruct the capitalist system in which it plays a central role (1971, 102–3).

A somewhat similar problem exists with the concept of "relation." Perhaps no word appears more frequently in Marx's writings than *Verhaltnis* (*relation*). The crucial role played by *Verhaltnis* in Marx's thinking is somewhat lost to non-German-language readers of his works as a result of translations that often substitute *condition, system,* and *structure* for *relation*. *Verhaltnis* is usually used by Marx in the sense given to it by the philosophy of internal relations, where parts such as capital, labor, etc., are said to be relations containing within themselves the very interactions to which they belong. But Marx also uses *Verhaltnis* as a synonym of *Beziehung* (*connection*), as a way of referring to ties between parts that are momentarily viewed as separate. Taken in this sense, two parts can be more or less closely related, have different relations at different times, and have their relations distorted or even broken. These are, of course, all important distinctions, and it should be obvious that none of them are foreign to Marx's writings. Yet if the parts are themselves relations, in the sense of internal relations, possessing the same logical character no matter what changes they undergo, it would seem that such distinctions could not be made. And, indeed, this belief lays behind a lot of the criticism directed at the philosophy of internal relations.

The two different senses of "relation" found in Marx's writings, however, simply reflect two different orders of relation in his understanding. The first comes out of his philosophy of internal relations and applies to how he views anything. The second is of a practical, empirical sort, and applies to what is actually found between two or more elements (each also relations in the first sense) that are presently viewed as separate. How Marx separates out parts that are conceived of as logically internal to one another is, of course, the work of the process of abstraction. Once abstracted, all manner of relations between these parts can be noted and are in fact noted whenever relevant. Refusing to take the boundaries that organize our world as given and natural, the philosophy of internal relations admits a practice of abstraction that allows for an even greater variety of second-order relations than exists on the common sense view.

V. Three Modes of Abstraction: Extension

Once we recognize the crucial role abstraction plays in Marx's method, how different his own abstractions are, and how often and easily he re-abstracts, it becomes clear that Marx constructs his subject matter as much as he finds it. This is not to belittle the influence of natural and social conditions on Marx's thinking, but rather to stress how, given this influence, the results of Marx's investigations are prescribed to a large degree by the preliminary organization of his subject matter. Nothing is made up of whole cloth, but at the same time Marx only finds what his abstractions have placed in his way. These abstractions do not substitute for the facts, but give them a form, an order, and a relative value; just as frequently changing his abstractions does not take the place of empirical research, but does determine, albeit in a weak sense, what he will look for, even see, and of course emphasize. What counts as an explanation is likewise determined by the framework of possible relationships imposed by Marx's initial abstractions.

So far we have been discussing the process of abstraction in general, our main aim being to distinguish it from other mental activities. Marx's own abstractions were said to stand out in so far as they invariably include elements of change and interaction, while his practice of abstracting was found to include more or less of each as suited his immediate purpose. Taking note of the importance Marx gave to abstractions in his critique of ideology, we proceeded to its underpinnings in the philosophy of internal relations, emphasizing that it is not a matter of this philosophy making such moves possible—since everybody abstracts—but of making them easier, and enabling Marx to acquire greater control over the process. What remains is to analyze in greater detail what actually occurs when Marx abstracts, and to trace its results and implications for some of his major theories.

The process of abstraction, which we have been treating as an undifferentiated mental act, has three main aspects or modes, which are also its functions vis à vis the part abstracted on one hand and the system to which the part belongs and which it in turn helps to shape on the other. That is, the boundary setting and bringing into focus that lies at the core of this process occurs simultaneously in three different, though closely related, senses. These senses have to do with extension, level of generality, and vantage point. First, each abstraction can be said to achieve a certain extension in the part abstracted, and this applies both spatially and temporally. In abstracting boundaries in space, limits are set in the mutual interaction that occurs at a given point of time. While in abstracting boundaries in time, limits are set in the distinctive history and potential development of any part, in what it once was and is yet to become. Most of our examples of abstraction so far have been drawn from what we shall now call "abstraction of extension."

Second, at the same time that every act of abstraction establishes an extension, it also sets a boundary around and brings into focus a particular level of generality for treating not only the part but the whole system to which it belongs. The movement is from the most specific, or that which sets it apart from everything else, to its most general characteristics, or what makes it similar to other entities. Operating rather like a microscope that can be set at different degrees of magnification, this mode of abstraction enables us to see the unique qualities of any part, or the qualities associated with its function in capitalism, or the qualities that belong to it as part of the human condition (to give only the most important of these levels of generality). In abstracting capital, for example, Marx gives it an extension in both space and time as well as a level of generality such that only those qualities associated with its appearance and functioning as a phenomenon of capitalism are highlighted (i.e., its production of value, its ownership by capitalists, its exploitation of workers, etc.). The qualities a given capital may also possess as a Ford Motor Company assembly line for making cars or as a tool in general—that is, qualities that it has as a unique object or as an instance of something human beings have always used—are not brought into the picture. They are abstracted out. This aspect of the process of abstraction has received least attention not only in our own discussion but in other accounts of dialectics. In what follows, we shall refer to it as "abstraction of level of generality."

Third, at the same time that abstraction establishes an extension and a level of generality, it also sets up a vantage point or place within the relationship from which to view, think about, and piece together the other components in the relationship; meanwhile the sum of their ties (as determined by the abstraction of extension) also becomes a vantage point for comprehending the larger system to which it belongs, providing both a beginning for research and analysis and a perspective in which to carry it out. With each new perspective, there are significant differences in what can be perceived, a different ordering of the parts, and a different sense of what is important. Thus, in abstracting capital, Marx not only gives it an extension and a level of generality (that of capitalism), he also views the interrelated elements that compose it from the side of the material means of production and, simultaneously, transforms this configuration itself into a vantage point for viewing the larger system in which it is situated, providing himself with a perspective that influences how all other parts of the system will appear (one that gives to capital the central role).

We shall refer to this aspect of abstraction as "abstraction of vantage point." By manipulating extension, level of generality, and vantage point, Marx puts things into and out of focus, into better focus, and into different kinds of focus, enabling himself to see more clearly, investigate more accurately, and understand more fully and more dynamically his chosen subject.

As regards the abstraction of extension. Marx's general stand in favor of large units is evident from such statements as, "In each historical epoch, property has developed differently and under a set of entirely different social relations. Thus, to define bourgeois property is nothing else than to give an exposition of all these social relations of bourgeois production. . . . To try to give a definition of property an independent relation, a category apart, an abstraction and eternal idea, can be nothing but an illusion of metaphysics and jurisprudence" (n.d., 154). Obviously, large abstractions are needed to think adequately about a complex, internally related world.

The specifics of Marx's position emerge from his frequent criticisms of the political economists for offering too narrow abstractions (narrow in the double sense of including too few connections and too short a time period) of one or another economic form. Ricardo, for example, is reproached for abstracting too short a period in his notions of money and rent, and for omitting social relations in his abstraction of value (1968, 125; 1971, 131). One of the most serious distortions is said to arise from the tendency among political economists to abstract processes solely in terms of their end results. Commodity exchange, for example, gets substituted for the whole of the process by which a product becomes a commodity and eventually available for exchange (1973, 198). As Amiri Baraka so colorfully points out: "Hunting is not those heads on the wall" (1966, 1973). By thinking otherwise for the range of problems with which they are concerned, the political economists avoid seeing the contradictions in the capitalist specific processes that give rise to these results.

The same narrowing of abstractions obtains a similar ideological result in thinking about human beings. In order to maximize individual freedom, Max Stirner sought to abstract an "I" without any messy presuppositions, whether natural or social. Marx's response is that by excluding all that brought it into existence and the full context in which it acts, this "I" is not a particularly helpful abstraction for understanding anything about the individual, least of all his freedom (Marx and Engels, 1964, 477–82). Yet something like Stirner's "I," in the person of the isolated individual, has become the standard way of thinking about human nature in capitalist society. It is the preferred abstraction of extension in which bourgeois ideology treats human beings.

Granted the unusually large extensions Marx gives his abstractions, we now need to know how this practice affects his work. What do such abstractions make possible, perhaps even necessary, and what do they make impossible? Consider all that a wide-angle photograph does in giving value to what is included, to what crowds the edges as well as to what appears at the center. Notice the relations it establishes as important, or at least relevant, and even the explanations that are implicit in what is included and what is left out. Something very similar occurs through the extension given to units of thinking in the process of abstraction. It is by placing so much in his abstractions—and by altering them as often as he does—that Marx greatly facilitates his analysis of what we've called the double motion of the capitalist mode of production. In particular, Marx's practice in abstracting extension serves as the basis for his theory of identity; it underlies his criticism of existing systems of classification and their replacement by the various classificatory schemes that distinguish his theories, i.e., the class division of society, forces/relations of production, appearance/essence, etc.; and it enables him to capture in thinking the real movements that go on in both nature and society.

As regards identity, Marx claims, "It is characteristic of the entire crudeness of 'common sense,' which takes its rise from the 'full life' and does not cripple its natural features by philosophy or other studies, that where it succeeds in seeing a distinction it fails to see a unity, and where it sees a unity it fails to see a distinction. If 'common sense' establishes distinction determinations, they immediately petrify surreptitiously and it is considered the most reprehensible sophistry to rub together these conceptual blocks in such a way that they catch fire" (Marx and Engels, 1961, 339). According to the common sense approach, things are either the same (the sense in which Marx uses "unity" here) or different. A frequent criticism Marx makes of the political economists is that they see only identity or difference in the relations they examine (1971, 168, 497, 527). Marx has it both ways—he is forever rubbing these blocks together to make fire. Most striking are his numerous references to what most people take as different subjects as identical. Such is his claim that "The social reality of nature and human natural science, or natural science about man are identical terms" (1959a, 111). Demand and supply (and in a "wider sense" production and consumption) are also said to be identical (1968, 505). And the list of such claims, both with and without the term *identity*, is very long. An example of the latter is his reference to "Bourgeoisie, i.e., capital" (Marx and Engels, 1945, 21).

In one place, Marx says by "identity" he means a "different expression of the same fact" (1968, 410). This appears straightforward enough, but in Marx's case, this "fact" is relational, composed of a system of mutually dependent parts. Viewing this mutual dependence within each of the interacting parts, viewing the parts as necessary aspects of each other, they become identical in expressing the same extended whole. Consequently, Marx can claim that labor and capital are "expressions of the same relation, only seen from opposite poles" (1971, 491). Underlying all such claims are abstractions of extension that are large enough to contain whatever is held to be identical.

Marx's theory of identity also helps us understand the pivotal role he gives to the notion of form. A form, we will recall, is that aspect of a relation, centering either on appearance or function, from which its covering concept is usually drawn. But "form" is also Marx's chief way of telling us that he has found an identity in difference, as when he says rent, profit, and interest, which are clearly different in many respects, are identical as forms of surplus-value (Marx and Engels, 1941, 106). What is called "Marxism" is largely an investigation of the different forms human productive activity takes in capitalist society, the changes these forms undergo, how such changes are misunderstood, and the power acquired by these changed and misunderstood forms over the very people whose productive activity brought them into existence in the first place. Value, commodity, capital, money, etc., could only be grasped as forms of labor (and, eventually, of each other) and investigated as such because Marx abstracts each of these units large enough to contain all these elements in their distinctive relations. Marx's theories of alienation and of the metamorphosis of value, in particular, offer many examples of this practice. Abstracted more narrowly, as typically occurs in bourgeois ideology, the identity of such elements gives way to similarity and other vague kinds of connection, with the result that some part of the effect and/or influence brought into focus by Marx's encompassing abstractions is lost or seriously distorted.

In adhering to a philosophy of internal relations, the commitment to view parts as identical exists even before they have been abstracted from the whole, so that one can say that, in a sense, identity precedes difference, which only appears with the abstraction of parts based on some appreciation of their distinctiveness. Such differences, when found, do nothing to contradict the initial assumption of identity, that each part through internal relations can express the same whole. Hence, the coexistence of identity and difference.

It was noted earlier that Marx used "totality" and "relation" in two senses, a logical sense having to do with how he viewed all reality and a reconstructed or emergent sense that applied to particular kinds of ties uncovered in his research between parts that had already been abstracted as separate parts. "Identity," as we have been using it so far, belongs to this logical vocabulary and "difference" to the reconstructed one. However, "identity," like "totality" and "relation," is sometimes used in this second, subsidiary sense to highlight closely related aspects of parts whose different appearances or functions have already led to their abstraction as separate parts. In which case, one can also speak of things as being more or less identical.

Besides its effect on the relation of identity, Marx's practice in abstracting extension also has major implications, as I have indicated, for the various classificatory schemes that frame his theories. Every school of thought stands out in large measure by the distinctions it makes and doesn't make, and by those it singles out as being in some respect the most important. Marxism is no exception. Among the better-known classifications found in Marx's work are the juxtapositions of forces and relations of production, base and superstructure, materialism and idealism, nature and society, objective and subjective conditions, essence and appearance, the periodization of history based on different modes of production, and the class division of society (particularly the split between workers and capitalists).

Most accounts of Marxism try very hard to establish where one element in each of these classifications ends and the next one beings, to define neatly and permanently the boundaries that subdivide the structures into which Marx organizes human existence. However, given what has just been said about Marx's practice of abstracting extension and his philosophy of internal relations, it should be clear that this is a fruitless exercise. It is only because they assume that Marx is operating with a philosophy of external relations in which the boundaries between things are taken to be of the same order as their other sense-perceptible qualities (hence determined and discoverable once and for all) that these critics can so consistently dismiss the overwhelming evidence of Marx's practice. Not only does Marx often redraw the boundaries of each of these units, but with every classification there are instances where his abstractions are large enough to contain most or even all of the qualities that seemed to fall into other contrasting units.

Marx's materialist conception of history, for example, is characterized by a set of overlapping contrasts between mode of production and "social, political, and intellectual life processes," base and superstructure, forces and relations of production, economic structures (or foundations) and the rest of society, and material and social existence (1904, 11–12). Since Marx did not take much care to distinguish these different formulations, there is a lot of dispute over which one to stress in giving an account of his views, but on two points there is widespread agreement: (1) that the first term in each pairing is in some sense determinant of the latter, and

(2) that the boundaries between the terms in each case are more or less set and relatively easy to establish. But how clear cut can such boundaries be if Marx can refer to "religion, family, state, law, morality, science, art, etc." as "particular modes of production," community and the "revolutionary class" as forces of production (which also has "the qualities of individuals" as its subjective side), theory "in so far as it gets ahold of people" as a "material force," and can treat laws regarding private property (which would seem to be part of the superstructure) as part of the base and class struggle (which would seem to be part of political life) as part of the economic structure (1959, 103; 1973, 495; n.d., 196; 1970, 137; Acton, 1962, 164)? It is worth noting, too, that Engels could even refer to race as an economic factor (Marx and Engels, 1951, 517).

To be sure, these are not the main uses to which Marx put these categories, but they do indicate something of their elasticity, something about how encompassing he could make his abstractions if he wanted to. And it does show how futile it is to try to interpret the sense in which one part is said to determine the other before coming to grips with the practice that rearranges the boundaries between them.

A similar problem awaits any reader of Marx who insists on looking for a single fixed boundary between essence and appearance. As Marx's investigation into capitalism is largely a study of essential connections, the importance of this distinction is not in doubt. The abstraction of appearance is relatively easy to determine. It is simply what strikes us when we look; it is what's on the surface, what's obvious. Essence is more problematical. It includes appearance, but goes beyond it to take in whatever gives any appearance its special character and importance. As such, essence generally introduces systemic and historical connections (including where something seems to be heading as well as where it has come from) as parts of what it is. It brings into focus an extended set of internal relations. But what gives appearances their special importance on any occasion is tied to the particular problem Marx is working on. Hence, what he calls the essence of anything varies somewhat with his purpose. So it is that the essence of man, for example, is said to be, in turn, his activity, his social relations, and the part of nature that he appropriates (1959a, 75; Marx and Engels, 1964, 198; 1959a, 106). The answer that it is all these in their interconnection, an answer that would secure a fixed, if not necessarily permanent, essence for human beings, misses the point that it is with "essence" that Marx wishes to single out one connection as decisive.

Within the present discussion, what needs to be stressed is that an approach that focuses on appearances and constructs its explanations on this same plane is rooted in abstractions of extension composed only of appearances. Relevance ends at the horizon marked off by our sense perceptions. The rest, if not unreal, is trivialized as unnecessary for under-standing or dismissed as mystical. A major ideological result of the single-minded attention to appearances is an imaginary reversal of real relations, as what strikes us immediately gets taken as responsible for the more or less hidden processes that have given rise to it. Marx refers to mistaking appearance for essence as "fetishism," and sees it operating throughout society, its best-known example being the fetishism of commodities, where the price of things gets substituted for the relations between the people who made them.

Marx, on the other hand, was aided in his investigation of essences by his practice of abstracting units large enough to contain them. For him the absolute division of reality into appearance and essence does not exist, since his main units of analysis include both appearance and essence, or rather they focus on essence in such a way that its apparent aspects are also brought out. Thus, according to Marx, "only when labor is grasped as the essence of private property can the economic process as such be penetrated in its actual concreteness" (1959a, 129). Labor, by which Marx means the particular kind of productive activity that goes on in capitalism, not only brings private property into existence but gives it all its special qualities, and hence is essential to what it is. It is only by going beyond the apparent thing like qualities of private property, only by seizing its essence of labor (which, again, is dependent on constructing an abstrac-tion that is large enough to contain both in their internal relation), that we can truly grasp private property and the capitalist mode of production in which it is the centerpiece.

Perhaps the classification that has suffered the greatest misunder-standing as a result of readers' efforts to arrive at permanent boundaries is Marx's class division of society. Marx's abstraction of extension for class brings together many people but not everything about them. Its main focus is on whatever it is that both enables and requires them to perform a particular function in the prevailing mode of production. As a complex relation, class contains other aspects, such as distinguishing social and economic conditions (ones that generally accompany their position in the mode of production), a group's opposition to other similarly constituted groups, its cultural level, its state of mind (encompassing both ideology and degree of consciousness of themselves as a class), and forms of inner-class communication and of inter-class political struggle. But how many of these aspects Marx actually includes in abstracting the extension of class or of any one of the classes into which he divides society varies with his problem and purpose at the time. Likewise, since all of these aspects in their peculiar configuration have evolved over time, there is also a decision to make regarding temporal extension, over how much of this evolution to abstract in. How widely Marx's decisions on these matters may differ can be seen from such apparently contradictory claims as "All history is the history of class struggle" (where class contains a bare minimum of its aspects) and "Class is the product of the bourgeoisie" (where class is abstracted as a sum of all these aspects) (Marx and Engels, 1945, 11; Marx and Engels, 1964, 93).

What class any person belongs to and even the number of classes in society are also affected by where exactly Marx draws his boundaries. Thus, "working class," for example, can refer to everyone who is employed by capitalists, or to all the people who work for capitalists but also produce value (a smaller group), or to all the people who not only work for capitalists and produce value but are also organized politically as a class (a smaller group still). As regards temporal extension, Marx can also abstract a particular group to include where they seem to be heading, together with the new set of relations that await them but which they have not yet fully acquired. In the case of peasants who are rapidly losing their land and of small businessmen who are being driven into bankruptcy, this translates into becoming wage-laborers (Marx and Engels, 1945, 16). Hence, the class of workers is sometimes abstracted broadly enough to include them as well, that is, people in the process of becoming workers along with those who function as workers at this moment. Marx's well-known reference to capitalism as a two-class society is based on his abstracting all groups into either workers or capitalists depending on where they seem to be heading, the landlords being the major group that is moving toward becoming capitalists. Abstracting such large spatial and temporal extensions for class is considered helpful for analyzing a society that is rapidly developing toward a situation where everyone either buys labor-power or sells it.

At the same time, Marx could abstract much more restricted extensions, which allowed him to refer to a variety of classes (and fragments of classes) based on as many social and economic differences between these groups. In this way, bankers, who are usually treated as a fragment of the capitalist class, are sometimes abstracted as a separate moneyed or financial class (1968, 123). This helps explain why Marx occasionally speaks of "ruling classes" (plural), a designation that also usually includes landlords, narrowly abstracted (Marx and Engels, 1964, 39).

Obviously, for Marx, arriving at a clear-cut, once-and-for-all classification of capitalist society into classes is not the aim, which is not to deny that one such classification (that of capitalists/landlords/workers) enjoys a larger role in his work or that one criterion for determining class (a group's relationship to the prevailing mode of production) is more important. Much to the annoyance of his critics, Marx never defines "class" or provides a full account of the classes in capitalist society. *Capital,* volume III, contains a few pages where Marx appears to have begun such an account, but it was never completed (1959b, 862–3). In my view, had he finished these pages, most of the problems raised by his theory of class would remain, for the evidence of his flexibility in abstracting class is clear and unambiguous. Thus, rather than looking for what class a person or group belongs to or how many classes Marx sees in capitalist society—the obsession of most critics and of not a few of his followers—the relevant question is, do we know on any given occasion when Marx uses "class," or the label associated with any particular class, who he is referring to and why he refers to them in this way. Only then can the discussion of class advance our understanding, not of anything or of everything, but of what it is Marx is trying to explain. It cannot be repeated too often that Marx is chiefly concerned with the double movement of the capitalist mode of production, and arranging people into classes based on different though interrelated criteria is a major means for uncovering this movement. Rather than simply a way of registering social stratification as part of a flat description or as a prelude to rendering a moral judgment, which would require a stable unit, class helps Marx to analyze a changing situation in which it is itself an integral and changing part (Ollman, 1978, chapter 2).

Besides making possible his theory of identity and the various classifications that mark his theories, Marx's practice of abstracting broad extensions for his units also enables him to capture in thought the various movements he sets out to investigate in reality. In order to grasp things "as they really are and happen," Marx's stated aim, in order to trace their happening accurately and give it its due weight in the system(s) to which it belongs, Marx extends his abstractions—as we saw—to include how things happen as part of what they are (1964, 35). Until now, change has been dealt with in a very general way. What I have labeled the double movement (organic and historical) of the capitalist mode of production, however, can only be fully understood by breaking it down into a number of submovements, the most important of which are quantity/quality, metamorphosis and contradiction.[2] These are some of the main ways in which things move or happen; they are forms of change. Organizing becoming and time itself into sequences, they are some of the pathways that bring

---

2. Other important dialectical movements are mediation, interpenetration of polar opposites, negation of the negation, precondition and result, and unity and separation. These are all treated in the longer work of which this essay is a part, and the role that abstraction plays in constructing and helping to make visible the movements of quantity/quality change, metamorphosis, and contradiction applies equally to them.

order to the flow of events. As such, they help structure all of Marx's theories, and are indispensable to his account of how capitalism works, how it developed, and where it is tending.

Quantity/quality change is a historical movement encompassing both buildup and what it leads to. One or more of the aspects that constitute any process-cum-relation gets larger (or smaller), increases (or decreases) in number, etc. Then, with the attainment of a critical mass—which is different for each entity studied—a qualitative transformation occurs, understood as a change in appearance and/or function. In this way, Marx notes, money becomes capital, i.e., acquires the ability to buy labor-power and produce value only when it reaches a certain amount (1958, 307–8). In order for such change to appear as an instance of the transformation of quantity into quality, Marx's abstractions have to contain the main aspects whose quantitative change is destined to trigger off the coming qualitative change as well as the new appearances and/or functions embodied in the latter, and all this for the time it takes for this to occur. Abstracting anything less runs the risk of first dismissing and then missing the coming qualitative change and/or misconstruing it when it happens, three frequent errors associated with bourgeois ideology.

Metamorphosis is an organic movement of interaction within a system in which qualities (occasionally appearances but usually functions) of one part get transferred to other parts so that the latter can be referred to as forms of the former. In what is undoubtedly the key distinguishing movement in Marx's labor theory of value, value—through its production by alienated labor and entry into the market—gets metamorphosed into commodity, money, capital, wages, profit, rent, and interest. The metamorphosis of value takes place in two circuits. What Marx calls the "real metamorphosis" occurs in the production process proper, where commodities are transformed into capital and means of subsistence, both forms of value, which are then used to make more commodities. A second circuit, or "formal metamorphosis," occurs where the commodity is exchanged for money, another form of value, and on one occasion, Marx goes so far as to equate "metamorphosed into" and "exchanged for" (1973, 168). The value over and above what gets returned to the workers as wages, or what Marx calls "surplus-value," undergoes a parallel metamorphosis as it gets transferred to groups with various claims on it, appearing as rent, interest, and profit. In both real and formal metamorphosis, new forms are signaled by a change in who possesses the value and in how it appears and functions for them, i.e., as a means of subsistence, a means of producing more value, a means of buying commodities, etc.

In metamorphosis, a process is abstracted that is large enough to include both what is changing and what it is changing into, making the transformation of one into the other an internal movement. Thus, when value metamorphoses into commodity or money, for example, the latter assume some of the alienated relationships embodied in value as their own, and this is seen as a later stage in the development of value itself. Otherwise, operating with smaller abstractions, commodity or money could never actually become value, and speaking of them as "forms of value" could only be understood metaphorically.

The essentially synchronic character of metamorphosis, no matter the number of steps involved, is also dependent on the size of the abstraction used. To some it may appear that the various phases in the metamorphosis of value occur one after another, serially, but this is to assume a brief duration for each phase. When, however, all the phases of this metamorphosis are abstracted as ongoing, as Marx does in the case of value— usually as aspects of production abstracted as reproduction—then all phases of the cycle are seen as occurring simultaneously (1971, 279–80). Events occur simultaneously or in sequence depending on the temporal extension of the units involved. When Marx refers to all the production that goes on in the same year as simultaneous production, all its causes and effects are viewed as taking place at the same time, as parts of a single interaction (1968, 471). To grasp any organic movement as such, it is simply that one must allow enough time for the interactions involved to work themselves out. Stopping too soon, which means abstracting too short a period for each phase, leaves one with an incompleted piece of the interaction, and inclines one to mistake what is an organic connection for a causal one.

In sum, metamorphosis, as Marx understands it, is only possible on the basis of an abstraction of extension that is sufficiently large to encompass the transfer of qualities from one element in an interaction to others over time, which assumes a particular theory of forms (movement is registered through elements becoming forms of one another), which assumes in turn a particular theory of identity (each form is both identical to and different from the others), that is itself a necessary corollary of the philosophy of internal relations (the basic unit of reality is not a thing but a relation).

If quantity/quality is essentially a historical movement and metamorphosis an organic one, then contradiction has elements of both. As a union of two or more processes that are simultaneously supporting and undermining one another, a contradiction combines five distinct though closely intertwined movements. But before detailing what they are, it is worth stressing once again the crucial role played by Marx's philosophy of internal relations. As regards contradictions, Engels says, "So long as we consider things as static and lifeless, each one by itself, alongside of and after each other, it is true that we do not run up against any contradiction in them. We find certain qualities which are partly common to, partly diverse from, and even contradictory to each other, *but which in this case are distributed among different objects and therefore contain no contradiction.* . . . But the position is quite different as soon as we consider things in their motion, their change, their life, their reciprocal influence on one another. Then we immediately become involved in contradictions" (Engels, 1934, 135). (My emphasis.) Elsewhere, referring to the bourgeois economists' treatment of rent, profit, and wages, Marx asserts where there is "no inner connection," there can be no "hostile connection," no "contradiction" (1971, 503). Only when apparently different elements are grasped as aspects of the same unit can certain of their features be abstracted as a contradiction.

Of the five movements found in contradiction, the two most important ones are the movements of mutual support and mutual undermining. Pulling in opposite directions, each of these movements exercises a constant, if not even or always evident, pressure on events. The uneasy equilibrium that results lasts until one or the other of these movements predominates.

In the contradiction between capital and labor, for example, capital, being what it is, helps bring into existence labor of a very special kind, that is alienated labor, that will best serve its needs as capital. While labor, as the production of goods intended for the market, helps fashion capital in a form that enables it to continue its exploitation of labor. However, capital and labor also possess qualities that exert pressure in the opposite direction. With its unquenchable thirst for surplus-value, capital would drive labor to exhaustion. While labor, with its inherent tendencies toward working less hours, in better conditions, etc., would render capital unprofitable. To avoid the temptation of misrepresenting contradiction as a simple opposition, tension, or dysfunction (common ideological errors), it is essential that the chief movements that reproduce the existing equilibrium as well as those that tend to undermine it be brought into the same overarching abstraction.

A third movement present in contradictions is the immanent unfolding of the processes that make up the "legs" of any contradiction. In this way, a contradiction becomes bigger, sharper, more explosive; both supporting and undermining movements become more intense, though not necessarily to the same degree. According to Marx, the capitalist contradictions "of use-exchange-value, commodity and money, capital and wage-labor, etc., assume ever greater dimensions as productive power develops" (1971, 55). The very growth of the system that contains these contradictions leads to their own growth.

A fourth movement found in contradictions is the change in overall form that many undergo through their interaction with other processes in the larger system of which they are part. Of the contradiction between use and exchange-value, Marx says it "develops further, presents itself and manifests itself in the duplication of the commodity into commodity and money. This duplication appears as a process in the metamorphosis of commodity in which selling and buying are different aspects of a single process and each act of this process simultaneously includes its opposite" (1971, 88). The same contradictions seem to undergo still another meta-morphosis: the contradictions in commodity and money, which develop in circulation, are said "to reproduce themselves" in capital (1968, 512). The contradiction between use and exchange-value with which we began has moved, been transferred, into the relation between commodity and money, and from there into capital. This movement is similar to what occurs in the metamorphosis of value—the systemic interactions are the same. Except here it is an entire contradiction that gets metamorphosed.

The fifth and final movement contained in contradiction occurs in its resolution when one side overwhelms what has hitherto been holding it in check, transforming both itself and all its relationships in the process. The resolution of a contradiction can be of two sorts, either temporary and partial or permanent and total. An economic crisis is an example of the first. Marx refers to crises as "essential outbursts . . . of the immanent contradictions" (1971, 55). The preexisting equilibrium has broken down, and a new one composed of recognizably similar elements, usually with the addition of some new elements, is in the process of replacing it. A partial resolution of a contradiction is more in the order of a readjustment, for it can also be said here that the old contradiction has been raised to a new and higher stage. In the case of simple economic crises, where economic breakdown is followed sooner or later by a renewed burst of accumulation, the initial contradictions are expanded to include more things, a larger area of the globe, more people, and a more highly devel-oped technology. Essentially, the stakes have been raised for the next time around.

A permanent and total resolution occurs when the elements in contra-diction undergo major qualitative change, transforming all their relations to one another as well as the larger system of which they are a part. An economic crisis that gives rise to a political and social revolution is an example of this. Here, the initial contradictions have moved well beyond what they once were, and are often so different that it may be difficult to reconstruct their earlier forms. What determines whether the resolution of a contradiction will be partial or total, of course, is not its dialectical form, the fact that differences get abstracted as contradictions, but its real content. However, such content is unlikely to reveal its secret to anyone who cannot read it as a contradiction. By including the undermining interaction of mutually dependent processes in the same unit, by expanding this unit to take in how such interaction has developed and where it is tending, its metamorphosis through different forms and eventual resolution, it is Marx's broad abstractions of extension that make it possible to grasp such varied movements as internal and necessary elements of a single contradiction.

Finally, Marx's large abstractions of extension also account for how the same factor, as indicated by its proper name, can contain two or more contradictions. Commodity, for example, is said to embody the contradiction between use and exchange-value as well as the contradiction between private and social labor. To contain both contradictions, commodity must be given a large enough extension to include the interaction between the two aspects of value as well as the interaction between the two aspects of labor, and both of them as they develop over time (1971, 130).

VI. Level of Generality

The second main aspect of Marx's process of abstraction, or mode in which it occurs, is the abstraction of level of generality. In his unfinished Introduction to the *Critique of Political Economy,* Marx's only systematic attempt to present his method, great care is taken to distinguish "production" from "production in general" (1904, 268–74). The former takes place in a particular society, capitalism, and includes as part of what it is all the relations of this society that enable it to appear and function as it does. "Production in general," on the other hand, refers to whatever it is that work in all societies have in common—chiefly the purposive activity of human beings in transforming nature to satisfy human needs—leaving out everything that distinguishes different social forms of production from one another.

Marx makes a further distinction within capitalist production between "production as a whole," what applies to all kinds of production within capitalism, and "production as a specific branch of industry," or what applies only to production in that industry (1904, 270). It is clear that more than a change in extension is involved in making these distinctions, especially the first one. The relations of productive activity with those who engage in it as well as with its product are *internal* relations in both cases, but production in capitalism is united with the distinctive capitalist forms of producers and their products, while production in general is united with them in forms that share its own quality as a lowest common denominator.

The abstraction Marx makes in moving from capitalist production to production in general then is not one of extension but one of level of generality. It is a move from a more specific understanding of production that brings into focus the whole network of equally specific qualities in which it functions (and with it the period of capitalism in which all this takes place) to a more general understanding of production that brings into focus the equally general state of those conditions in which it occurs (along with the whole of human history as the period in which these qualities are found).

Something very similar is involved in the distinction Marx makes between "production as a whole" and "production in a particular branch of industry," though the movement here is away from what is more general in the direction of what is more specific. How a particular branch of industry—car manufacturing, for example—appears and functions involves a set of conditions that fall substantially short of applying to the entire capitalist epoch. What appears superficially like a whole-part distinction is—like the earlier distinction between "capitalist production" and "production in general"—one of levels of generality. Both capitalist production (or production as a whole) and production in a particular industry are internally related to the rest of society, but each brings into focus a different period of history, the capitalist epoch in one case and what might be called "modern capitalism," or that period in which this branch of production has functioned in just this way, in the other.

In this Introduction, Marx comes out in favor of concentrating on production in its current historical forms, that is, on capitalist and modern capitalist production, and criticizes the political economists for contenting themselves with production in general when trying to analyze what is happening here and now. Then, falling for the all too common error of mistaking what is more general for what is more profound, the political economists treat the generalizations they have derived from examining various specific forms of production as the most important truths about each historical society in turn, and even as the cause of phenomena that are peculiar to each one. In this way, for example, the general truth that production in any society makes use of material nature, the most general form of property, is offered as an explanation and even a justification for how wealth gets distributed in capitalist society, where people who own property claim a right to part of what gets produced with its help (1904, 271–72).

While Marx's discussion of the political economists in this Introduction oscillates between modern capitalism, capitalism as such, and the human condition, much of what he says elsewhere shows that he can operate on still other levels of generality, and therefore that a more complex breakdown of what are in fact degrees of generality is required. Before offering such a breakdown, I want to make it clear that the boundary lines that follow are all suggested by Marx's own practice in abstracting, a practice that is largely determined by his aim of capturing the double movement of the capitalist mode of production. In other words, there is nothing absolute about the particular divisions I have settled on. Other ways of distinguishing between levels of generality are possible, and for other kinds of problems may be very useful.

Keeping this in mind, there are seven major levels of generality into which Marx subdivides the world, seven plains of comprehension on which he places all the problems he investigates, seven different foci for organizing everything that is. Starting from the most specific, there is the level made up of whatever is unique about a person and situation. It's all that makes Joe Smith different from everyone else, and so too all his activities and products. It's what gets summed up in a proper name and an actual address. With this level—let's call it level one—the here and now, or however long what is unique lasts, is brought into focus.

Level two distinguishes what is general to people, their activities, and products because they exist and function within modern capitalism, understood as the last twenty to fifty years. Here, the unique qualities that justify using proper names, such as Joe Smith, are abstracted out of focus (we no longer see them), and abstracted into focus are the qualities that make us speak of an individual as an engineer or in terms of some other occupation that has emerged in modern capitalism. Bringing these slightly more general qualities into sight, we also end up considering more people—everyone to whom such qualities apply—and a longer period, the entire time during which these qualities have existed. We also bring into focus a larger area, usually one or a few countries, with whatever else has occurred there that has affected or been affected by the qualities in question during this period. Marx's abstraction of a "particular branch of production" belongs to this level.

Capitalism as such constitutes level three. Here, everything that is peculiar to people, their activity, and products due to their appearance and functioning in capitalist society is brought into focus. We encountered this level earlier in our discussion of "production as a whole." The qualities that Joe Smith possesses that mark him as Joe Smith (level one) and as an engineer (level two) are equally irrelevant. Front and center now are all that makes him a typical worker in capitalism, including his relations to his boss, product, etc. His productive activity is reduced to the denominator indicated by calling it "wage-labor," and his product to the denominator indicated by calling it "commodity" and "value." Just as level two widens the area and lengthens the time span brought into focus as compared to level one, so too level three widens the focus so that it now includes everyone who partakes of capitalist relations anywhere that these relations obtain, and the entire 500 or so years of the capitalist era.

After capitalism, still moving from the specific to the general, there is the level of class society, level four. This is the period of human history during which societies have been divided up into classes based on the division of labor. Brought into focus are the qualities people, their activities, and products have in common across the five to ten thousand years of class history, or whatever capitalism, feudalism, and slavery share as versions of class society, and wherever these qualities have existed. Next—level five—is human society. It brings into focus—as we saw in the case of the political economists above—qualities people, their activities, and products have in common as part of the human condition. Here, one is considering all human beings and the entire history of the species.

To make this scheme complete, two more levels will be added, but they are not nearly as important as the first five in Marx's writings. Level six is the level of generality of the animal world, for just as we possess qualities that set us apart as human beings (level five), we have qualities (including various life functions, instincts, and energies) that are shared with other animals. Finally, there is level seven, the most general level of all, which brings into focus our qualities as a material part of nature, including weight, extension, movement, etc.

In acquiring an extension, all Marx's units of thought acquire in the same act of abstraction a level of generality. Thus, all the relations that are constituted as such by Marx's abstractions of extension, including the various classifications and movements they make possible, are located on one or another of these levels of generality. And though each of these levels brings into focus a different time period, they are not to be thought of as "slices of time," since the whole of history is implicated in each level, including the most specific. Rather, they are ways of organizing time, placing the period relevant to the qualities brought into focus in the front and treating everything that comes before as what led up to it, as origins.

It is important, too, to underline that all the human and other qualities discussed above are present simultaneously and are equally real, but that they can only be perceived and therefore studied when the level of generality on which they fall has been brought into focus. This is similar to what occurs in the natural sciences, where phenomena are abstracted on the basis of their biological or chemical or atomic properties. All such properties exist together, but one cannot see or study them at the same time. The significance of this observation is evident when we consider that all the problems from which we suffer and everything that goes into solving them or keeping them from being solved is made up of qualities that can only be brought into focus on one or another of these different levels of generality. Unfolding as they do over time, these qualities can also be viewed as movements and pressures of one sort or another—whether organized into tendencies, metamorphoses, contradictions, etc.—that taken together pretty well determine our existence. Consequently, it is essential, in order to understand any particular problem, to abstract a level of generality that brings the characteristics chiefly responsible for this problem into focus. We have already seen Marx declare that because the classical political economists abstract production at the level of generality of the human condition (level five) they cannot grasp the character of distribution in capitalist society (level three).

A similar situation exists today with the study of power in political science. The dynamics of any power relationship lies in the historically specific conditions in which the people involved live and work. To abstract the bare relation of power from these conditions in order to arrive at conclusions about "power in general" (level five), as many political scientists and an increasing number of social movement theorists have done, ensures that every particular exercise of power will be out of focus and its distinctive features undervalued and/or misunderstood.

Given Marx's special interest in uncovering the double movement of the capitalist mode of production, most of what he writes on man and society falls on level three. Abstractions such as "capital," "value," "commodity," "labor," and "working class," whatever their extensions, bring out the qualities that these people, activities, and products possess as part of capitalism. Pre- and post-capitalist developments come into the analysis done on this level as the origins and likely futures of these capitalist qualities. What Marx refers to in his *Grundrisse* as "pre-capitalist economic formations" (the apt title of an English translation of some historical material taken from this longer work) are just that (1973, 471–513). The social formations that preceded capitalism are mainly viewed and studied here as early moments of capitalism abstracted as a process, as its origins extending back before enough of its distinctive structures had emerged to justify the use of the label "capitalism."

Marx also abstracts his subject matter on levels two (modern capitalism) and four (class society), though this is much less frequent. Where Marx operates on the level of generality of class society, capitalism, feudalism, and slave society are examined with a view to what they have in common. Studies in feudalism on this level of generality emphasize the division of labor and the struggle between the classes that it gives rise to, as compared to the breakdown of the conditions underlying feudal production that gets most of the attention when examining feudalism as part of the origins of capitalism, that is on level three (1958, Part VIII).

An example of Marx operating on level two, modern capitalism, can be found in his discussion of economic crisis. After examining the various ways that the capitalist system, given what it is and how it works, could break down, that is after analyzing it on the level of capitalism as such (level three), he then shows how these possibilities got actualized in the immediate past, in what was for him modern or developed capitalism (1968, 492–535). To explain why the last few crises occurred in just the ways they did, he has to bring into focus the qualities that apply to this particular time period and these particular places, that is recent economic, social, and political history in specific countries. This is also an example of how Marx's analysis can play off two or more different levels of generalization, treating what he finds on the more specific level as the actualization of one among several possibilities present on the more general level(s).

It is instructive to compare Marx's studies of man and society conducted on levels two, three, and four (chiefly three, capitalism) with studies in the social sciences and also with common sense thinking about these subjects, which typically operate on levels one (the unique) and five (the human condition). Where Marx usually abstracts human beings, for example, as classes (as *a* class on level four, as one of the main classes that emerge from capitalist relations of production—workers, capitalists, and sometimes landowners—on level three, and as one of the many classes and fragments of classes that exist in a particular country in the most recent period on level two), most non-Marxists abstract people as unique individuals, where everyone has a proper name (level one), or as a member of the human species (level five). In proceeding in their thinking directly from level one to level five, they may never even perceive, and hence have no difficulty in denying, the very existence of classes.

But the question is not which of these different abstractions is true. They all are in so far as people possess qualities that fall on each of these levels of generality. The relevant question is, which is the appropriate abstraction for dealing with a particular set of problems? More specifically, if social and economic inequality, exploitation, unemployment, social alienation, and imperialist wars are due in large part to conditions associated with capitalist society, then they can only be understood and dealt with through the use of abstractions that bring out their capitalist qualities. And that involves, among other things, abstracting people as capitalists and workers. Not to do so, to insist on sticking to levels one and five, leaves one blaming particular individuals (a bad boss, an evil president) or human nature as such for these problems.

To complete the picture, it must be admitted that Marx occasionally abstracts phenomena, including people, on levels one and five. There are discussions of specific individuals, such as Napoleon III and Palmerston, where he focuses on the qualities that make these people different, and some attention is given, especially in his earliest writings, to qualities that all human beings have in common, to human nature in general. But not only are such digressions an exception, more important for our purposes is that Marx seldom allows the qualities that come from these two levels to enter into his explanation of social phenomena. Thus, when G. D. H. Cole faults Marx for making classes more real than individuals, or Carol Gould says individuals enjoy an ontological priority in Marxism, or, conversely, Althusser denies the individual any theoretical space in Marxism whatsoever, they are all misconstruing the nature of a system that has places—levels of generality—for individuals, classes, and the human species (Cole, 1966, 11; Gould, 1980, 33; Althusser, 1966, 225–58). The very idea of attributing an ontological priority to either individuals, class, or the species assumes an absolute separation between them that is belied by Marx's conception of man as a social relation with qualities that fall on different levels of generality. None of these ways of thinking about human beings is more real or more fundamental than the others. If, despite this, class remains Marx's preferred abstraction for treating human beings, it is only because of its necessary ties to the kind, range, and above all levels of generality of the phenomena he seeks to explain.

It is not only the abstractions in which we think about people but also how we organize our thinking within each of these abstractions that can be set apart on the basis of levels of generality. Beliefs, attitudes, and intentions, for example, are the properties of the unique individuals who inhabit level one. Social relations and interests are the main qualities of the classes and fragments of classes who occupy levels two, three, and four. Powers, needs, and behavior belong to human nature as such, while instincts apply to people as part of human nature but also in their identity as animals. Though there is some movement across level boundaries in the use of these concepts—and some concepts, such as "consciousness," that apply in a somewhat different sense on several levels—their use is usually a good indication of the level of generality on which a particular study falls, and hence, too, of the kind of problems that can be addressed. An integrated conception of human nature that makes full use of all these concepts, which is to say that organically connects up the study of people coming from each of these levels of generality, remains to be done.

By focusing on different qualities of people, each level of generality also contains distinctive ways of dividing up humanity, and with that its own kinds of oppression based on these divisions. Exploitation, for example, refers to the extraction of surplus-value from workers by capitalists that is based on a level three division of society into workers and capitalists. Therefore, as a form of oppression, it is specific to capitalism. The human condition, level five, brings out what all people share as members of our species. The only kind of oppression that can exist here comes from outside the species and is directed against everyone. Material scarcity, a natural condition, is an example of an oppression against people that falls on this level of generality.

Level four, which is marked by a whole series of distinctions between people that are rooted in the division between mental and manual work, enables us to see the beginning of oppressions based on class, nation, race, religion, and sex. Though racial and sexual differences obviously existed before the onset of class society, it is only with the division between those who produce wealth and those who direct its production that these differences become the basis of the distinctive forms of oppression associated with racism and patriarchy. With the appearance of different relationships to the prevailing mode of production and the contradictory interests they generate, with mutual indifference replacing the mutual concern that was characteristic of an earlier time when everything was owned in common, and with the creation of a growing surplus that everyone wishes to possess, all manner of oppressions based on existing divisions of society become possible and for the ruling economic class extremely useful. Racism, patriarchy, nationalism, etc., are chiefly ways of rationalizing these oppressive practices, though, upon frequent repetition, they can sink roots into people's minds and emotions and acquire a relative autonomy from the situation in which they originated.

To be sure, all the oppressions associated with class society also have their capitalist specific forms and intensities having to do with their place and function in capitalism, as a particular form of class society, but the main relations that underlie and give force to these oppressions come from class society as such. Consequently, the abolition of capitalism will not do away with any of these oppressions, only with their capitalist forms. Ending racism, patriarchy, nationalism, etc., in all their forms can only occur when class society itself is abolished, and in particular with the end of the division between mental and manual labor, a world historical change that could only occur, Marx believes, with the arrival of full communism.

If all of Marx's abstractions involve—as I have argued—a level of generality as well as an extension, if each level of generality organizes and even prescribes to some degree the analyses made with its help, that is in its terms, if Marx abstracts this many levels of generality in order to get at different, though related problems (even though his abstraction of capitalism as such, level three, is the decisive one)—then the conclusions of his studies, the theories of Marxism, are all located on one or another of these levels and must be viewed accordingly if they are to be correctly understood, evaluated, and, where necessary, revised.

Marx's labor theory of value, for example, is chiefly an attempt to explain why all the products of human productive activity in capitalist society have a price, not why a particular product costs such and such, but why it costs anything at all. That everything humans produce has a price is an extraordinary phenomenon peculiar to the capitalist era, whose social implications are even more profound because most people view it ahistorically, simply taking it for granted. Marx's entire account of this phenomenon, which includes the history of how a society in which all products have a price has evolved, takes place on the level of generality of capitalism as such, which means that he only deals with the qualities of people, their activities, and products in the forms they assume in capitalism overall. The frequent criticism one hears of this theory that it doesn't take account of competition in real marketplaces and, therefore, cannot explain actual prices is simply off the point—that is the more general point that Marx is trying to make.

To account for the fact that a given pair of shoes costs exactly fifty dollars, for example, one has to abstract in qualities of both modern capitalism (level two) and the here and now (level one) in a way that takes us well beyond Marx's initial project. In *Capital,* volume III, Marx makes some effort to re-abstract the phenomena that enter into his labor theory of value on the level of modern capitalism, and here he does discuss the role of competition among both buyers and sellers in effecting actual prices. Still, the confusion from which innumerable economists have suffered over what has been labeled the "transformation problem" (the transformation of values into prices) disappears once we recognize that it is a matter of relating analyses from two different levels of generality and that Marx gives overriding attention to the first, capitalism, and relatively little attention to the second, which unfortunately is the only level that interests most non-Marxist economists.

The theory of alienation offers another striking example of the need to locate Marx's theories on particular levels of generality if they are not to be distorted. Marx's description of the severed connections between man and his productive activity, products, other people, and the species that lies at the core of this theory falls on two different levels of generality: capitalism (level three) and class society (level four). In his earliest writings, this drama of separation is generally played out in terms of "division of labor" and "private property" (level four). It is clear even from this more general account that alienation reaches its zenith in capitalist society, but the focus is on the class context to which capitalism belongs and not on capitalism as such. Here, capitalism is not so much "it" as the outstanding example of "it."

In later writings, as Marx's concern shifts increasingly to uncovering the double motion of the capitalist mode of production, the theory of alienation gets raised to the level of generality of capitalism (level three). The focus now is on productive activity and its products in their capitalist specific forms, i.e., on labor, commodity, and value; and the mystification that has accompanied private property throughout class history gets upgraded to the fetishism of commodities (and values). The broader theory of alienation remains in force. The context of class society in which capitalism is situated has not changed its spots, but now Marx has developed a version of the theory that can be better integrated into his explanation of capitalist dynamics, especially as found in his labor theory of value. With the introduction of the notion of levels of generality, some of the major disputes regarding Marx's theory of alienation—whether it is mainly concerned with history or with capitalism, and how and to what degree Marx used this theory in his later writings—are easily resolved.

But it is not just Marx's theories whose correct interpretation requires that they be situated on particular levels of generality. The same applies to virtually all of his statements. For example, what is the relation between the claim we have already met in another context that "All history [later qualified to class history] is the history of class struggle" and the claim that "class is the product of the bourgeoisie" (Marx and Engels, 1945, 12; Marx and Engels, 1964, 77)? If "class" in both instances refers to qualities on the same level of generality, then only one of these claims can be true, i.e., either class has existed over the past five to ten thousand years of human history or it only came into existence with capitalism, five to six hundred years ago. However, if we understand Marx as focusing on the qualities common to all classes in the last five to ten thousand years (on level four) in the first claim, and on the distinctive qualities classes have acquired in the capitalist epoch (on level three) in the second (that which makes them more fully classes, involving mainly development in organization, communication, alienation and consciousness), then the two claims are compatible. Because so many of Marx's concepts—"class" and "production" being perhaps the outstanding examples—are used to convey abstractions on more than one level of generality, the kind of confusion generated by such apparent contradictions is all too common.

Marx's remarks on history are particularly vulnerable to being misunderstood unless they are placed on one or another of these levels of generality. The role Marx attributes to production and economics generally, for example, differs somewhat, depending on whether the focus is on capitalism (including its origins), modern capitalism, class societies, or human societies. Starting with human societies, the special importance Marx accords to production is based on the fact that one has to do what is necessary in order to survive before attempting anything else, that production limits the range of material choices available just as, over time, it helps to transform them, and that production is the major activity which gives expression to and helps to develop our peculiarly human powers and needs (1958, 183–84; Marx and Engels, 1964, 117; Ollman, 1976, 98–101). In class society, production plays its decisive role primarily through the division of labor that comes into being in this period and the class divisions and antagonisms that it sets up (1959b, 772; Marx and Engels, 1951, 9–10). It is also on this level that the interaction between the forces and class based relations of production come into focus. In capitalism, the special role of production is shared by everything that goes into the process of capital accumulation (1958, Part VIII). In modern capitalism, it is usually what has happened in a particular phase or sector of capitalist production in a given country in the most recent period (like the development of railroads in India during Marx's time) that is treated as decisive (Marx and Engels, n.d., 79).

Each of these interpretations of the predominant role of production applies only to the level of generality that it brings into focus. No single interpretation comes close to accounting for all that Marx believes needs to be explained, which is probably why, on one occasion, Marx denies that he has any theory of history whatsoever (Marx and Engels, 1952, 278). It might be more accurate, however, to say that he has four complementary theories of history, one for history as abstracted on each of these four levels of generality. The effort by most of Marx's followers and virtually all of his critics to encapsulate the materialist conception of history into a single generalization regarding the role of production (or economics) has never succeeded, therefore, because it could not succeed.

Finally, the various movements Marx investigates, some of which were discussed under abstraction of extension, are also located on particular levels of generality. That is, like everything else, these movements are composed of qualities that are unique, or special to modern capitalism, or to capitalism, etc., so that they only take shape as movements when the relevant level of generality is brought into focus. Until then, whatever force they exercise must remain mysterious, and our ability to use or effect them virtually nil. The movement of the metamorphosis of value, for example, dependent as it is on the workings of the capitalist marketplace, operates chiefly on the levels of generality of capitalism (level three) and modern capitalism (level two). Viewing the products of work on the levels of generality of class society (level four) or the human condition (level five), or concentrating on its unique qualities (level one)—the range of most non-Marxist thinking on this subject—does not keep the metamorphosis of value from taking place, just us from perceiving it. Also, because, "In capitalism," according to Marx, "everything seems and in fact is contradictory", far more so than in any other social formation, it is by abstracting the levels of generality of capitalism and modern capitalism (granted appropriate abstractions of extension) that movements of contradiction become commonplace (1963, 218).

What are called the "laws of the dialectic" are those movements that can be found in one or another recognizable form on every level of generality, that is, in the relations between the qualities that fall on each of these levels, including that of inanimate nature. The transformation of quantity to quality and development through contradiction, which were discussed above, are such dialectical laws. Two other dialectical laws that play important roles in Marx's work are the interpenetration of polar opposites (the process by which a radical change in the conditions surrounding two or more temporarily abstracted elements or in the conditions of the person viewing them produces a striking alteration, even a complete turn about, in their relations), and the negation of the negation (the process by which the most recent phase in a development that has gone through at least three phases will display important similarities with what existed in the phase before last).

Naturally, the particular form taken by a dialectical law will vary considerably, depending on its subject and on the level of generality on which this subject falls. The mutually supporting and undermining movements that lie at the core of contradiction, for example, appear very different when applied to the forces of inanimate nature than they do when applied to specifically capitalist phenomena. Striking differences such as these have led a growing band of critics and some followers of Marx to restrict the laws of dialectic to social phenomena and to reject as "un-Marxist" what they label "Engels' dialectics of nature." Their error, however, is to confuse a particular statement of these laws, usually one appropriate to levels of generality where human consciousness is present, for all possible statements. This error is abetted by the widespread practice—one I also have adopted for purposes of simplification and brevity—of allowing the most general statement of these laws to stand in for the others. Quantity/quality changes, contradictions, etc., that occur among the unique qualities of our existence (level one), or in the qualities we possess as workers and capitalists (levels two and three), or in those we possess as human beings (level five), however, are not simply illustrations for and the working out of still more general natural laws. To be adequately apprehended, the movements of quantity/quality change, contradiction, etc., on each level of generality must be seen as an expression of a law that is specific to that level as well. Most of the work of drafting such multilevel statements of the laws of the dialectic remains to be done.

The importance of the laws of the dialectic for grasping the pressures at work on different levels of generality will also vary. We have just seen Marx claim that capitalism in particular is full of contradictions. Thus, viewing conditions and events in terms of contradictions is far more important for understanding their capitalist character than it is for understanding their qualities as human, or natural, or unique conditions and events. Given Marx's goal to explain the double movement of the capitalist mode of production, no other dialectical law receives the attention given to the law of development through contradiction. Together with the relatively minor role contradiction plays in the changes that occur in nature (level seven), this may also help account for the mistaken belief that dialectical laws are found only in society.

What stands out from the above is that the laws of the dialectic do not in themselves explain, or prove, or predict anything, or cause anything to happen. Rather, they are ways of organizing the most common forms of change and interaction that exist on any level of generality for purposes of study and intervention into the world of which they are part. With their help, Marx was able to uncover many other tendencies and patterns, also often referred to as laws, that are peculiar to the levels of generality with which he was concerned. Such laws have no more force than what comes out of the processes from which they are derived, balanced by whatever countertendencies there are within the system. And like all the other movements Marx investigates, the laws of the dialectic and the level-specific laws they help him uncover are provided with extensions that are large enough to encompass the relevant interactions during the entire period of their unfolding.

Two major questions relating to this mode of abstraction remain to be treated. One is, how do the qualities located on each level of generality effect those on the others? And second, what is the influence of the decision made regarding abstraction of extension on the level of generality that is abstracted, and vice versa? The effect of qualities from each level on those from others, moving from the most general (level seven) to the most specific (level one), is that of a context on what it contains. That is, each level, beginning with seven, establishes a range of possibilities for what can occur on the more specific levels that follow. The actualization of some of these possibilities on each level limits in turn what can come about on the levels next in line, all the way up to level one, that of the unique.

Each more general level, in virtue of what it is and contains, also makes one or a few of the many (though not infinite) alternative developments that it makes possible on less general levels more likely of actualization. Capitalism, in other words, was not only a possible development out of class society, but made likely by the character of the latter, by the very dynamics inherent in the division of labor once it got under way. The same might be said of the relation between capitalism as such and the "modern" English capitalism in which Marx lived, and the relation between the latter and the unique events Marx experienced.

It is within this framework, too, that the relation Marx sees between freedom and determinism can best be understood. Whatever the level of abstraction—whether we are talking about a unique individual, a group in modern capitalism, workers throughout the capitalist era, any class, or human beings as such—there is always a choice to be made and some ability to make it. Hence, there is always some kind and some degree of freedom. On each level of generality, however, the alternatives between which people must choose are severely limited by the nature of their overlapping contexts, which also make one or one set of alternatives more feasible and/or attractive, just as they condition the very personal, class, and human qualities brought into play in making any choice. Hence, there is also a considerable degree of determinism. It is this relationship between freedom and determinism that Marx wishes to bring out when he says that it is people who make history but not in conditions of their own choosing (Marx and Engels, 1951, 225). What seems like a relatively straightforward claim is complicated by the fact that both the people and the conditions referred to exist on various levels of generality, and depending on the level that is brought into focus, the sense of this claim— though true in each instance—will vary.

The view of determinism offered here is different from, but not in contradiction with, the view presented in our discussion of the philosophy of internal relations, where determinism was equated first with the recipro-cal effect found in any organic system and then with the greater or special influence of any one process on the others. To this we can now add a third, complementary sense of determinism that comes from the limiting and prescribing effects of overlapping contexts on all the phenomena that fall within them. Marx's success in displaying how the latter two kinds of determinism operate in the capitalist mode of production accounts for most of the explanatory power that one finds (and feels) in his writings.

Effects of events on their larger contexts, that is, of qualities found on more particular levels on those that fall on more general ones, can also be discerned. Whenever Marx speaks of people reproducing the conditions of their existence, the reference is to how activities whose main qualities fall on one level of generality help to construct the various contexts, including those on other levels of generality, that make the continuation of these same activities both possible and highly likely. Such effects, however, can also be detrimental. In our time, for example, the unregulated growth of harmful features associated with modern capitalist production (level two) have begun to threaten the ecological balance necessary not only for the continuation of capitalism (level three) but for the life of our species (level five).

As for the relation between the choice of extension and that of level of generality, there would seem to be a rough correspondence between narrow abstractions of extension and abstracting very low and very high levels of generality. Once the complex social relations in which a particular phenomenon is situated are put aside through a narrow abstraction of extension, there is little reason to bring these relations into better focus by abstracting the relevant level of generality. Thus, abstracting an extension that sets individuals apart from their social conditions is usually accompanied by an abstraction of level of generality that focuses on what is unique about each (level one). With the social qualities that were abstracted from individuals in extension now attached to the groups to which they belong (viewed as externally related to their members), efforts at generalizing tend to bypass the levels on which these social qualities would be brought into focus (modern capitalism, capitalism, and class society) and move directly to the level of the human condition (level five). So it is that for bourgeois ideology people are either all different (level one) or all the same (level five). While for Marx, whose abstractions of extension usually include a significant number of social relations, privileging the levels of generality of capitalism, modern capitalism, and class society was both easy and obvious; just as giving special attention to these levels led to abstractions of extension that enabled him to take in at one sweep most of the connections that these levels bring into focus.

VII. Vantage Point

The third mode in which Marx's abstractions occur is that of vantage point. Capitalists, as we saw, are referred to as "embodiments of capital"; but capital is also said to function as it does because it is in the hands of people who use it to make profit (1959b, 794, 857–58; 1959a, 79). The state is said to be an instrument of the ruling economic class; but Marx also treats it as a set of objective structures that respond to the requirements of the economy, as an aspect of the mode of production itself (Marx and Engels, 1945, 15; 1959a, 103). There are many similar, apparently contradictory positions taken in Marx's writings. They are the result of different abstractions, but not of extension or level of generality. They are due to different abstractions of vantage point. The same relation is being viewed from different sides, or the same process from its different moments.

In the same mental act that Marx's units of thought obtain an extension and a level of generality, they acquire a vantage point or place from which to view the elements of any particular relation and, given its then extension, from which to reconstruct the larger system to which this relation belongs. A vantage point sets up a perspective that colors everything which falls into it, establishing order, hierarchy, and priorities, distributing values, meanings, and degrees of relevance, and asserting a distinctive coherence between the parts. Within a given perspective, some processes and connections will appear large, some obvious, some important; others will appear small, insignificant, and irrelevant; and some will even be invisible.

In discussing Marx's conception of relation, we saw that it was more than a simple connection. It was always a connection contained in its parts *as seen* from one or another side. So capital and labor, for example, were quoted as being "expressions of the same relation, only seen from the opposite pole" (1971, 491). Or again, Marx says, capital has one "organizational differentiation or composition" (that of fixed and circulating capital) from the point of view of circulation, and another (that of constant and variable capital) from the point of view of production (1968, 579). Both circulation and production are part of the extended capital relation. A criticism of the political economists is that they try to understand capital only from the point of view of circulation, but to grasp the nature of wealth in capitalism, Marx believes, the decisive vantage point is that of production (1968, 578).

It is clear that the decisions Marx makes regarding extension and levels of generality greatly affect the kind of vantage points he abstracts, and vice versa. The amount of mutual dependence and process that is included in an abstraction of extension largely determines what can be seen and studied from this same abstraction taken as a vantage point. Giving production the extension of reproduction, or capital the extension of capital accumulation, for example, enables Marx to bring into view and organize the system of which they are part in ways that would not be possible with narrower (or shorter) abstractions. Likewise, in abstracting a level of generality, Marx brings into focus an entire range of qualities that can now serve individually or collectively (depending on the abstraction of extension) as vantage points, just as other possible vantage points, organized around qualities from other levels of generality, are excluded. Conversely, any commitment as to a particular vantage point predisposes Marx to abstract the extension and level of generality that correspond to

ABSTRACTION IN MARX'S METHOD 69

it and enables him to make the most of it as a vantage point. In practice, these three decisions (really, three aspects of the same decision) as to extension, level of generality, and vantage point are usually made together and their effects are immediate, though on any given occasion one or another of them may appear to dominate.

In the social sciences, the notion of vantage point is most closely associated with the work of Karl Mannheim (1936, Part V). But for Mannheim, a point of view is something that belongs to people, particularly as organized into classes. The conditions in which each class lives and works provides its members with a distinctive range of experiences and a distinctive point of view. Because of their separate points of view, even the few experiences that are shared by people of opposing classes are not only understood but actually perceived in quite different ways. As far as it goes, this view—which Mannheim takes over from Marx—is correct. Marx's conception of point of view goes further, however, by grounding each class' perceptions in the nature of its habitual abstractions, in order to show how starting out to make sense of society from just these mental units, within the perspectives that they establish, leads to different perceptual outcomes. In uncovering the cognitive link between class conditions and class perceptions, Marx helps us understand not only *why* Mannheim is right but *how* what he describes actually works. As part of this, point of view becomes an attribute of the abstraction as such (Marx speaks of the point of view or vantage point of accumulation, relations of production, money, etc.), and only secondarily of the person or class that adopts it (1963, 303; 1971, 156; 1973, 201).

We can now explain why Marx believes workers have a far better chance to understand the workings of capitalism than do capitalists. Their advantage does not come from the quality of their lives and only in small part from their class interests (since the capitalists have an interest in misleading even themselves about how their system works). More important, given what constitutes the lives of workers, the abstractions with which they start out to make sense of their society are likely to include "labor," "factory," "machine," especially "labor," which puts the activity that is chiefly responsible for social change at the front and center of their thinking. Within the perspective set up by this abstraction, most of what occurs in capitalism gets arranged as part of the necessary conditions and results of this activity. There is no more enlightening vantage point for making sense of what is, both as the outcome of what was and as the origins of what is coming into being. This is not to say, of course, that all workers will make these connections (there are plenty of reasons rooted in their alienated lives that militate against it), but the predisposition to do so coming from the initial abstraction of vantage point is there.

For capitalists, just the opposite is the case. Their lives and work incline them to start making sense of their situation with the aid of "price," "competition," "profit," and other abstractions drawn from the market-place. Trying to put together how capitalism functions within perspectives that place labor near the end of the line rather than at the start simply turns capitalist dynamics around. According to Marx, in competition, "everything always appears in inverted form, always standing on its head" (1968, 217). What are predominantly the effects of productive activity appear here as its cause. It is demands coming from the market, itself the product of alienated labor, for example, that seem to determine what gets produced.

As with thinking in terms of processes and relations, common sense is not wholly devoid of perspectival thinking. People occasionally use expressions such as "point of view," "vantage point," and "perspective" to refer to some part of what we have been discussing, but they are generally unaware of how much their points of view affect everything they see and know and of the role played by abstractions in arriving at this result. As with their abstractions of extension and level of generality, most people simply accept as given the abstractions of vantage point that are handed down to them by their culture and particularly by their class. They examine their world again and again from the same one or few angles, while their ability to abstract new vantage points becomes atrophied. The one-sided views that result are treated as not only correct, but as natural, indeed as the only possible view.

Earlier we saw that one major variety of bourgeois ideology arises from using too narrow abstractions of extension (dismissing parts of both processes and relationships that are essential for accurately comprehending even what is included), and that a second comes from abstracting an inappropriate level of generality (inappropriate in that it leaves out of focus the main qualities in which the problem of concern is rooted). There is a third major form of bourgeois ideology that is associated with the abstraction of vantage point. Here, ideology results from abstracting a vantage point that either hides or seriously distorts the relations and movements that one has to perceive in order to adequately comprehend a particular phenomenon. Not everything we need or want to know emerges with equal clarity, or even emerges at all, from every possible vantage point.

A related form of ideology also results from examining a phenomenon from only one side, no matter how crucial, when several are needed—all the while being unaware of the limits on what can be learned from this side alone. This is what Hegel had in mind when he said, to think abstractly (in the ideological sense of the term) is "to cling to one predicate" (1966,

118). Murderers, servants, and soldiers, who serve as Hegel's examples, are all much more than what is conveyed by viewing them from the single vantage point associated with the labels we have given them. Marx is even more explicit when, for example, he berates the economist, Ramsay, for bringing out all the factors but "one-sidedly" and "therefore incorrectly," or equates "wrong" with "one-sided" in a criticism of Ricardo (1971, 351; 1968, 470).

What needs to be stressed is that Marx never criticizes ideology as a simple lie or claims that what it asserts is completely false. Instead, ideology is generally described as overly narrow, partial, misfocused, and/or one-sided, all of which are attributable to limitations in the abstractions of extension, level of generality, and vantage point that are used, where neither these abstractions nor their implications are grasped for what they are. While correctly pointing to the material roots of ideology in capitalist conditions and in the conscious manipulations of capitalists, and bringing out how it functions to serve capitalist interests, most discussions of ideology have completely ignored the misapplication of the process of abstraction that is responsible for its distinctive forms.

Among the major vantage points associated with bourgeois ideology, where the error is not simply one of restricting analysis to a single perspective but where the one or few that are chosen either hide or distort the essential features of capitalism, are the following: the vantage point of the isolated individual, the subjective side of any situation (what is believed, wanted, intended, etc.), the results of almost any process, anything connected with the market, and all of what falls on level five of generality, particularly human nature.

The isolated individual, man separated from both natural and social conditions, is not only the preferred abstraction of extension in which bourgeois ideology treats human beings; it also serves as its preferred vantage point for studying society. Society becomes what social relations look like when viewed from this angle. When one adds that within each person it is such subjective qualities as beliefs, wants, intentions, etc., that are bourgeois ideology's preferred vantage points for viewing the rest of the person, it should be no surprise that the objective features of any situation of which people are a part are so undervalued. In this perspective, an individual is chiefly what he believes himself to be, and society itself what many individuals operating one at a time in the absence of strong social pressures or significant material restraints have made it.

There is also an obvious link between abstracting human beings narrowly in extension, abstracting this extension on levels one and five of generality, and abstracting this extension on these levels of generality as preferred vantage points. By abstracting the isolated individual in extension, one omits the various social and other connections that would incline one to bring levels two, three, and four of generality into focus in order to learn how these connections have acquired the specific characteristics that make them important. And because the contexts associated with modern capitalism, capitalism, and class society are never properly brought into focus, the qualities that fall on these levels can hardly serve as useful vantage points. To the limited extent that anything from these contexts does get examined from vantage points associated with bourgeois ideology, the result is usually a hodgepodge of mismatched qualities from different levels of generality, with some more and some less in focus, all loosely held together by the language of external relations. Whatever integration is achieved by such studies only succeeds in breaking up and dissembling the organic unity that exists on each of these levels, making a systematic understanding of any kind that much more difficult.

Other than the isolated individual and his subjective qualities, another family of vantage points that is well represented in bourgeois ideology are the results of various social processes, especially those found in the market. Already narrowly abstracted in extension as finished products, the processes by which these results have emerged are no longer visible. Thus, capital is simply the means of production; a commodity—any good that is bought and sold; profit—something earned by capitalists; and the market itself—an over-the-counter exchange of goods and services that follows its own extra social laws. When used as vantage points for viewing the capitalist system, these dead building blocks can only construct a dead building, an unchanging system whose emergence at a certain point in history is as much a mystery as its eventual demise. The ultimate distortion occurs in what Marx calls the fetishism of commodities (or capital, or value, etc.), when such results take on a life of their own and are viewed as responsible for their own birth process. Whenever any static and narrowly conceived-of set of results are used as a vantage point for examining origins, there is a danger of turning around cause and effect in this way.

Still other vantage points put to heavy use in bourgeois ideology are whatever is taken to be part of the human condition, the whole of level five and especially human nature as such, or rather what is taken to be human nature. Starting out from these vantage points, phenomena whose most important qualities fall on levels one to four lose their historical specificity and are made to appear as obvious and inevitable as the flat abstractions that introduce them. In this way, approaching capitalist distribution, as the political economists are accused of doing, from the vantage point of a level five notion of production—that is, production in so far as it partakes of the human condition—makes it appear that the existing capitalist division of wealth together with the social mechanisms that are responsible for it are equally part of the human condition.

Marx, who on occasion made use of all these vantage points, favored vantage points connected with production, the objective side of any situation, historical processes generally, and social class, particularly at the level of generality of capitalist society. The reason Marx privileges such vantage points varies, as does the extension he gives them, with the level of generality on which he is operating. Beyond this, Marx's abstraction of vantage point—as indeed of extension and level of generality—can usually be traced to his theories and what they indicate is necessary to uncover some part of the organic or historical movement of the capitalist mode of production. One must be careful, here as elsewhere, not to place within Marx's method many of the judgments and decisions regarding priorities that could only come from the theories he developed with its help.

Equally characteristic of Marx's practice in abstracting vantage points is the easy facility he shows in moving from one to the other. Aware of the limitations inherent in any single vantage point, even that of production, Marx frequently alters the angle from which he examines his chosen subject matter. While whole works and sections of works can be distinguished on the basis of the vantage point that predominates, changes of vantage point can also be found on virtually every page of Marx's writings. Within the same sentence, Marx can move from viewing wages from the vantage point of the worker to viewing it from the vantage point of society as a whole (1963, 108). Marx's analysis of the complex relations between production, distribution, exchange, and consumption, which has already come into this essay on several occasions, also provides what is perhaps the best example of how often he changes his abstractions of both extension and vantage point, and how crucial this practice and his facility in it was for obtaining his results (1904, 274–92).

As with his abstractions of extension and level of generality, Marx's abstractions of vantage point play a crucial role in the construction of all his theories. It is Marx's abstractions of vantage point that enable him to find identity in difference (and vice versa), to actually catch sight of the organic and historical movements made possible by his abstractions of extension, and to classify and reclassify the world of his perceptions into the explanatory structures bound up in what we call Marxism.

Earlier, in discussing Marx's theory of identity, we saw that abstracting an extension that is large enough to contain both identical and different qualities of two or more phenomena is what makes the coexistence of identity and difference possible, but one's ability to actually see and therefore to examine either set of qualities depends on the vantage point adopted for viewing them. Sticking with one vantage point will restrict understanding any relation to its identical or different aspects when, in fact, it contains both. Marx, on the other hand, can approach the relation of profit, rent, and interest from the vantage point of surplus-value, or what they have in common as the portion of value that is not returned to the workers who produced it, their identity, as well as from any of the vantage points located in differences arising from who holds these forms of surplus-value and how each functions in the economic system.

Abstracting vantage points that bring out the differences between two or more aspects of an interactive system also highlights the asymmetry in their reciprocal effect. Granted such reciprocal effect, production was said to play the dominant role on all five levels of generality on which Marx operates. But it is only by abstracting production as a vantage point that its special influence on other economic processes and on society as a whole on each level can be seen for what it is. As Marx says, with the level of class societies in mind, the existence of the ruling class and their functions "can only be understood *from* the specific historical structure of their production relations" (1963, 285). (My emphasis.)

Along with his abstractions of extension, Marx's abstractions of vantage point play an equally important role in establishing the flexible boundaries that characterize all his theories. In Marx's division of reality into objective and subjective conditions, it is by abstracting a vantage point first in one then in the other that he uncovers the more objective aspects of what is ordinarily taken to be subjective (extending the territory of the objective accordingly), and vice versa. Together with the aforementioned theory of identity, it is the abstraction of the vantage point that enables Marx to actually see objective and subjective conditions as "two distinct forms of the same conditions" (1973, 832). Likewise, it is by abstracting a particular vantage point that Marx can see aspects of nature in society, or the forces of production in the relations of production, or economic in non-economic structures, or the base in the superstructure, and vice versa, adjusting the abstraction of extension for each pairing accordingly. Looking at the relations of production from the vantage point of the forces of production, for example, even the cooperative power of workers can appear as a productive force (Marx and Engels, 1964, 46).

Marx's various class divisions of society, based as we saw on different abstractions of extension for class, are also discernible only from the vantage point of the qualities (functions, opposition to other classes, consciousness, etc.) that serve as the criteria for constructing a given classification. That is, if class is a complex relation made up of a number of different aspects, and if the composition of any particular class depends on which ones Marx includes in his abstraction of extension and brings into focus through his abstraction of level of generality, then his ability to actually distinguish people as members of this class depends on his having abstracted just these aspects as his vantage points for viewing them. It also follows that as Marx's vantage point changes, so does his operative division of society into classes. In this way, too, the same people, viewed from the vantage points of qualities associated with different classes, may actually fall in different classes. The landowner, for example, is said to be a capitalist in so far as he confronts labor as the owner of commodities, i.e., functions as a capitalist vis à vis labor (rather than as a landowner vis à vis capitalists), and is viewed from this vantage point (1963, 51).

Viewed from the vantage point of any one of his qualities, the individual's identity is limited to what can be seen from this angle. The qualities that emerge from the use of other vantage points are ignored because for all practical purposes, at *this* moment in the analysis, and for treating *this* particular problem, they simply don't exist. Hence, people abstracted as workers, for example—that is, viewed from one or more of the qualities associated with membership in this class—where the object of study is capitalist political economy, are presented as not having any gender or nation or race. People, of course, possess all these characteristics and more, and Marx—when dealing with other problems—can abstract vantage points (usually as part of non-capitalist levels of generality) that bring out these other identities.

Given Marx's flexibility in abstracting extension, he can also consider people from vantage points that play down their human qualities altogether in order to highlight some special relation. Such is the case when Marx refers to the buyer as a "representative of money confronting commodities"—that is, views him from the vantage point of money inside an abstraction of extension that includes money, commodities, and people (1963, 404). The outstanding example of this practice is Marx's frequent reference to capitalists as "embodiments" or "personifications" of capital, where living human beings are considered from the vantage point of their economic function (1958, 10, 85, 592). The school of structuralist Marxism has performed an important service in recovering such claims from the memory hole in which an older, more class struggle–oriented Marxism had placed them. However useful decentering human nature in this manner is for grasping some of the role-determined behavior that Marx uncovered, there is as much that is volunteerist in his theories that requires the adoption of distinctively human vantage points, and only a dialectical Marxism that possesses sufficient flexibility in changing abstractions—of vantage point as of extension and level of generality—can make the necessary adjustments.

If Marx's abstractions of extension are large enough to encompass how things happen as part of what they are, if such abstractions of extension also allow him to grasp the various organic and historical movements uncovered by his research as essential movements, then it is his abstractions of vantage point that make what is there—what his abstractions of extension have "placed" there—visible. The movement of the transformation of quantity into quality, for example, is made possible as an essential movement by an abstraction of extension that includes both quantitative changes and the qualitative change that eventually occurs. But this transformative process is not equally clear or even visible from each of its moments. In this case, the preferred vantage point is one that bridges the end of quantitative changes and the start of the qualitative one. Viewing the cooperation among workers, for example, from the vantage point of where its transformation into a qualitatively new productive power begins provides the clearest indication of where this change has come from as well as where the process that brought it about was heading.

The movement of metamorphosis, we will recall, is an organic movement in which qualities associated with one part of a system get transferred to its other parts. In the case of the metamorphosis of value, the main instance of this movement in Marx's writings, some of the central relationships that constitute value get taken up by commodity, capital, wage-labor, etc. Only an abstraction of extension that is large enough to include its different phases as internally related aspects of a single system allows us to conceive of metamorphosis as an internal movement and of its subsequent stages as forms of what it starts out as. But to observe this metamorphosis and, therefore too, to study it in any detail, we must accompany this abstraction of extension with an abstraction of vantage point in the part whose qualities are being transferred. Thus, the metamorphosis of value into and through its various forms is only observable as a metamorphosis from the vantage point of value.

As regards contradiction, Marx says, "In capitalism everything seems and in fact is contradictory" (1963, 218). It *is* so—in reality, and with the help of Marx's broad abstractions of extension, which organize the parts as mutually dependent processes. But it *seems* so only from certain vantage points. From others, the incompatible development of the parts would be missed, or misconstrued, or, at a minimum, seriously underestimated. The vantage point from which Marx usually observes contradictions is the intersection between the two or more processes said to be in contradiction. It is a composite vantage point made up of elements from all these processes. Of course, if one has not abstracted differences as processes and such processes as mutually dependent, there is no point of intersection to focus on.

What we've called the double movement of the capitalist mode of production can be approached—that is, viewed and studied—from any of the major contradictions that compose it, and in each case—given internal relations—the elements that are not directly involved enter into the contradiction as part of its extended conditions and results. In this way, the vantage point that is adopted organizes not only the immediate contradiction, but establishes a perspective in which other parts of the system acquire their order and importance. In the contradiction between exchange and use-value, for example, the relations between capitalists and workers are part of the necessary conditions for this contradiction to take its present form and develop as it does, just as one result of this contradiction is the reproduction of the ties between capitalists and workers. Given the internal relations Marx posits between all elements in the system, this makes capitalists and workers subordinate aspects of the contradiction between exchange and use-value. The whole process can be turned around: adopting the vantage point of the contradiction between capitalists and workers transforms the relations between exchange and use-value into its subordinate aspects, again as both necessary preconditions and results. The actual links in each case, of course, need to be carefully worked out. Hence, contradictions can be said to overlap; they cover much the same ground, but this ground is broken up in various ways, along a variety of axes, based on as many different foci.

Even when the shift in vantage points appears to be slight, the difference in the perspective opened up can be considerable. For example, take the contradiction between capital and wage-labor on one hand and that between capitalists and workers on the other. The vantage point for viewing the former is the intersection of two objective functions, while the preferred vantage point for viewing the latter is where the activities and interests of the two classes who perform these functions intersect. Each of these contradictions contains the other as major dependent aspects (neither capital nor capitalists could appear and function as they do without the other, and the same holds for wage-labor and workers). Yet, though both contradictions can be said to cover more or less the same ground, the different perspectives established by these contrasting vantage points allows Marx to distinguish how people create their conditions from how they are created by them, and to trace out the implications of each position without dismissing or undervaluing the other—all the while presenting both contradictions as undergoing similar pressures and in the process of a similar transformation.

Marx's laws offer still another illustration of the crucial role played by the abstraction of vantage point. As was pointed out earlier, all of Marx's laws are tendencies arising from the very nature of whatever it is that is said to have them. In every case, it is Marx's abstraction of extension that brings the various organic and historical movements together under the same rubric, making how things happen a part of what they are, but it is his abstraction of vantage point that enables him (and us) to actually catch sight of them as a single tendency.

The law of the falling rate of profit, for example, is a tendency inherent in the relation of profit to the organic composition of capital, which is the ratio of constant to variable capital, or the amount of surplus labor that can be realized with a given capital (1959b, Part III). Like all tendencies in Marx's work, it is subject to countertendencies (state subsidies, inflation, devaluation of existing capital, etc.), which are often strong enough to keep the falling rate of profit from finding expression in the balance sheet of businessmen at the end of the year. To observe this tendency, therefore, and be in a position to study the constant pressure it exerts on the concentration of capital (another law) and through it on the entire capitalist system, one must follow Marx in abstracting an extension for profit that includes its relation over time to the organic composition of capital, and view this relation from the vantage point of this composition. Without such abstractions of extension *and* vantage point, one simply cannot see, let alone grasp, what Marx is talking about. With them, one can see the law despite all the evidence thrown up by countertendencies. Hence, the irrelevance of various attempts by Marx's critics and followers alike to evaluate the law of the falling rate of profit based on analyses made from the vantage point of one of its possible results (the actual profits of real businessmen) or from capitalist competition or some other vantage point located in the marketplace. All the laws in Marxism can be described, studied, and evaluated only inside the perspectives associated with the particular vantage points from which Marx both discovered and constructed them.

VIII. The Role of Abstractions in the Debates over Marxism _____

It will have become evident by now that it is largely differences of vantage point that lay behind many of the great debates in the history of Marxist scholarship. In the *New Left Review* debate between Ralph Miliband and Nicos Poulantzas on the character of the capitalist state, for example, the former viewed the state chiefly from the vantage point of the ruling economic class, while the latter viewed what are essentially the same set of relations from the vantage point of the socio-economic structures that establish both the limits and the requirements for a community's political functions (Poulantzas, 1969; Miliband 1970).[3] As a result, Miliband is better able to account for the traditional role of the state in serving ruling class interests, while Poulantzas has an easier time explaining the relative autonomy of the state, and why the capitalist state continues to serve the ruling class when the latter is not directly in control of state institutions.

The debate over whether capitalist economic crisis is caused by the tendency of the rate of profit to fall or arises from difficulties in the realization of value, where one side views the capitalist economy from the vantage point of the accumulation process and the other from the vantage point of market contradictions, is of the same sort (Mattick, 1969; Baran and Sweezy, 1966).[4] A somewhat related dispute over the centrality of the capitalist mode of production as compared to the international division of labor (the position of "world system theory") for charting the history and future of capitalism is likewise rooted in a difference of preferred vantage points (Brenner, 1977; Wallerstein, 1974). So, too, is the debate over whether bourgeois ideology is mainly a reflection of alienated life and reified structures or the product of the capitalist consciousness industry, where one side views the construction of ideology from the vantage point of the material and social conditions out of which it arises and the other from that of the role played by the capitalist class in promoting it (Mepham, 1979; Marcuse, 1965).

Earlier, in what is perhaps the most divisive dispute of all, we saw that those who argue for a strict determinism emanating from one or another version of the economic factor (whether simple or structured) and those who emphasize the role of human agency (whether individual or class) can also be distinguished on the basis of the vantage points they have chosen for investigating the necessary interaction between the two (Althusser, 1965; Sartre, 1963). To be sure, each of these positions, here as in the other debates, is also marked by somewhat different abstractions of extension for shared phenomena based in part on what is known and considered worth knowing, but even these distinguishing features come into being mainly as a result of the vantage point that is treated as privileged.

The different levels of generality on which Marx operates is also respon-

---

3. Both thinkers seriously modified the views expressed in these articles in later works (Miliband, 1977; Poulantzas, 1978), and these revisions too can be explained in large part through changes in their abstractions of vantage point.

4. There are still other Marxist interpretations of capitalist crises (as, indeed, of the state) that are also largely dependent on the vantage point adopted. Here, as in the other debates mentioned, it was enough to refer to a single major cleavage to illustrate the general point regarding abstractions.

sible for its share of debates among interpreters of his ideas, the main one being over the subject of the materialist conception of history: is it all history, or all of class history, or the period of capitalism (in which earlier times are conceived of as pre-capitalist) (Kautsky, 1988; Korsch, 1970)? Depending on the answer, the sense in which production is held to be primary will vary as will the abstractions of extension and vantage point used to bring this out.

Finally, the various abstractions of extension of such central notions as mode or production, class, state, etc., have also led to serious disagreements among Marx's followers and critics alike, with most schools seeking to treat the boundaries they consider decisive as permanent. However, as evidenced by the quotations that practically every side in these disputes can draw upon, Marx is capable of pursuing his analysis not only on all social levels of generality and from various vantage points but with units of differing extension, only giving greater weight to the abstractions that his theories indicate are most useful in revealing the particular dynamic he was investigating. The many apparently contradictory claims that emerge from his study are in fact complementary, and all are required to "reflect" the complex double movement (historical—including probable future—and organic) of the capitalist mode of production. Without an adequate grasp of the role of abstraction in dialectical method, and without sufficient flexibility in making the needed abstractions of extension, level of generality, and vantage point, most interpreters of Marx have simply constructed versions of his theories that suffer in their very form from the same rigidity, inappropriate focus, and one-sidedness that Marx saw in bourgeois ideology.

In an often quoted though little analyzed remark in the Introduction to *Capital,* Marx says that value, as compared to larger, more complex notions, has proved so difficult to grasp because "the body, as an organic whole, is more easy to study than are the cells of that body." To make such a study, he adds, one must use the "force of abstraction" (1958, 8). Using the force of abstraction, as I have tried to show, is Marx's way of putting dialectics to work. It is the living dialectic, its process of becoming, the engine that sets other parts of his method into motion. In relation to this emphasis on the force of abstraction, every other approach to studying dialectics stands on the outside looking in, treating the change and interaction that abstractions help to shape in one or another already completed form. The relations of contradiction, identity, law, etc., that they study have all been constructed, ordered, brought into focus, and made visible through prior abstractions. Consequently, while other approaches may help us to understand what dialectics is and to recognize it when we see it, only an account that puts the process of abstraction at the center enables us to think adequately about change and interaction, which is to say—to think dialectically, and to do research and engage in political struggle in a thoroughly dialectical manner.[5]

References

Acton, H. B. 1962. *The Illusion of the Epoch.* London: Cohen and West.

Allen, J. 1983. "In Search of Method: Hegel, Marx and Realism." *Radical Philosophy* (no. 35).

Althusser, L. 1965. *Pour Marx.* Paris: Maspero.

Baraka, A. [Jones, L.]. 1966. *Home Social Essays.* New York: William Morrow and Co.

Baran, P., and P. Sweezy. 1966. *Monopoly Capital.* New York: Monthly Review Press.

Brenner, R. 1977. "The Origins of Capitalist Development: A Critique of Neo-Smithian Marxism." *New Left Review* (no. 104).

Cole, G. D. H. 1966. *The Meaning of Marxism.* Ann Arbor: Michigan University Press.

Coleman, J. 1968. "The Methodological Study of Change." *Methods in Sociological Research.* Edited by H. and A. Blalock. New York: McGraw HIll.

Dietzgen, J. 1928. *The Positive Outcome of Philosophy.* Translated by W. W. Craik. Chicago: Charles H. Kerr.

Dunayevskaya, R. 1982. *Philosophy and Revolution.* Atlantic Highlands, N.J.: Humanities Press.

Engels, F. 1934. *Herr Eugen Dühring's Revolution in Science* [*Anti-Dühring*]. Translated by Emile Burns. London: Lawrence and Wishart.

Gould, C. 1980. *Marx's Social Ontology.* Cambridge, Mass.: M.I.T. Press.

Hegel, G. W. F. 1966. *Hegel: Texts and Commentary.* Edited and translated by W. Kaufman. Garden City, N.Y.: Anchor Press.

Horvath, R. J., and K. D. Gibson. 1984. "Abstraction in Marx's Method." *Antipode* 16.

Hume, D. 1955. *Enquiry Concerning Human Understanding.* Indianapolis: Bobbs-Merrill.

Ilyenkov, E. V. 1982. *The Dialectics of the Abstract and the Concrete in Marx's Capital.* Translated by S. Syrovatkin. Moscow: Progress Publishers.

James, W. 1978. *The Works of William James.* Cambridge, Mass.: Harvard University Press.

Kautsky, K. 1988. *The Materialist Conception of History.* Translated by R. Meyer. New Haven: Yale University Press.

---

5. Not all of the important questions associated with dialectics have been dealt with in this essay. Missing or barely touched on are the place and/or role within dialectical method of reflection, perception, emotion, memory, conceptualization (language), appropriation, moral evaluation, verification, and activity, particularly in production. I am painfully aware of their absence, but my purpose here was not to provide a complete overview of dialectics but to make it possible for people to put it to work by deconstructing the much-neglected process of abstraction, which, along with the philosophy of internal relations, I take to be at the core of this method. My next volume on dialectics, which focuses on the process of appropriation as Marx's preferred abstraction for knowing, being, and doing in their interaction with one another, will try to make up for these lapses. It will also contain a more systematic treatment of the moments of inquiry and exposition, as forms of activity under appropriation, as well as a critical survey of some important contributions to dialectical method that have been passed over in the present introductory work.

Korsch, K. 1970. *Marxism and Philosophy.* Translated by F. Halliday. New York: Monthly Review Press.

Lukacs, G. 1971. *History and Class Consciousness.* Translated by R. Livingstone. Cambridge: M.I.T. Press.

Mannheim, K. 1936. *Ideology and Utopia.* Translated by L. Wirth and E. Shils. New York: Harcourt, Brace and Co.

Mao Tse Tung. 1968. *Four Essays on Philosophy.* Peking: Foreign Languages Press.

Marcuse, H. 1965. "Repressive Tolerance." *A Critique of Pure Tolerance.* Edited by R. W. Wolff, B. Moore, and H. Marcuse. Boston: Beacon Press.

Marx, K. 1904. *A Contribution to the Critique of Political Economy.* Translated by N. I. Stone. Chicago: Charles H. Kerr.

———. 1958. *Capital.* Vol. 1. Translated by S. Moore and E. Aveling. Moscow: Foreign Languages Publishing House.

———. 1959a. *Economic and Philosophical Manuscripts of 1844.* Translated by M. Milligan. Moscow: Foreign Languages Publishing House.

———. 1959b. *Capital.* Vol. 3. Moscow: Foreign Languages Publishing House.

———. 1963. *Theories of Surplus Value.* Part 1. Translated by E. Burns. Moscow: Progress Publishers.

———. 1968. *Theories of Surplus Value.* Part 2. Translated by S. Ryazanskaya. Moscow: Progress Publishers.

———. 1970. *Critique of Hegel's Philosophy of Right.* Edited by J. O'Malley. Translated by A. Jolin and J. O'Malley. Cambridge, Eng.: Cambridge University Press.

———. 1971. *Theories of Surplus Value,* Part 3. Translated by J. Cohen and S. W. Ryazanskaya. Moscow: Progress Publishers.

———. 1973. *Grundrisse.* Translated by M. Nicolaus. Harmondsworth, England: Penguin.

———. n.d. *The Poverty of Philosophy.* Moscow: Foreign Languages Publishing House.

Marx, K., and F. Engels. 1941. *Selected Correspondence.* Translated by D. Torr. London: Lawrence and Wishart.

———. 1945. *The Communist Manifesto.* Chicago: Charles H. Kerr.

———. 1950. *Briefwechsel.* Vol. 3. Berlin: Dietz.

———. 1951. *Selected Works in Two Volumes,* Vol. 1. Moscow: Foreign Languages Publishing House.

———. 1952. *The Russian Menace to Europe.* Edited by P. W. Blackstock and B. F. Hoselitz. Glencoe, Ill.: The Free Press.

———. 1961. *Werke.* Vol. 4. Berlin: Dietz.

———. 1964. *The German Ideology.* Translated by S. Ryazanskaya. Moscow: Progress Publishers.

———. n.d. *On Colonialism.* Moscow: Foreign Languages Publishing House.

Mattick, P. 1969. *Marx and Keynes.* Boston: Porter Sargent Publishers.

Meikle, S. 1985. *Essentialism in the Thought of Karl Marx.* London: Open Court.

Mepham, J. 1979. "The Theory of Ideology in *Capital,*" *Issues in Marxist Philosophy.* Vol. 3. Edited by J. Mepham and D. H. Ruben. Atlantic Highlands, N.J.: Humanities Press.

Miliband, R. 1970. "The Capitalist State: Reply to Nicos Poulantzas." *New Left Review* (no. 59).

———. 1977. *Marxism and Politics.* Oxford: Oxford University Press.

Moore, G. E. 1903. *Principia Ethica.* Cambridge, Eng.: Cambridge University Press.

Novak, L. 1980. *The Structure of Idealization: Toward a Systemic Interpretation of the Marxian Idea of Science.* Dordrecht, Holland: D. Reidel Publishers.

Ollman, B. 1976. *Alienation: Marx's Conception of Man in Capitalist Society.* Cambridge, Eng.: Cambridge University Press.

————. 1978. *Social and Sexual Revolution: Essays on Marx and Reich.* Boston: South End Press.
Poulantzas, N. 1969. "The Problem of the Capitalist State." *New Left Review* (no. 58).
————. 1978. *State, Power, Socialism.* Translated by P. Camiller. London: Verso.
Rader, M. 1979. *Marx's Interpretations of History.* Oxford: Oxford University Press.
Robinson, J. 1953. *On Re-reading Marx.* Cambridge, Eng.: Students Bookshop Ltd.
Sartre, J.-P. 1963. *The Problem of Method.* Translated by H. E. Barnes. London: Methuen.
Sayers, A. 1981. "Abstraction: a Realist Interpretation." *Radical Philosophy* (no. 28).
Sayer, D. 1987. *The Violence of Abstraction.* Oxford: Blackwell.
Sohn-Rethel, A. 1978. *Intellectual and Manual Labor.* London: Macmillan.
Sorel, G. 1956. *Reflexions sur la Violence.* Paris: Marcel Riviere.
Sweezy, P. 1956. *The Theory of Capitalist Development.* New York: Monthly Review Press.
Wallerstein, I. 1974. *The Modern World System.* London: Academic Press.

Part III

Dialectical Investigations _____

The essays in Section III are offered as examples in the use of dialectical method. Too brief to provide an adequate analysis of any of the problems treated, their main purpose is to show how aspects of Marx's method—and, in particular, the abstractions of extension, level of generality, and vantage point that I have stressed—work in investigating a variety of social and historical phenomena. While Marx's theories are only fully applicable to capitalism, including its origins and likely future, his dialectical method can be used more broadly, and I have also tried to suggest something of this extended range by including essays on Soviet politics and the study of history.

The analyses of the state in chapters 3 and 4 are built around different aspects of dialectical method, abstraction of vantage point in "Theses on the Capitalist State," and abstractions of extension and of level of generality in "Why Do We Need a Theory of the State?". Examining freedom and necessity in their relation to the capitalist state (chapter 3) required that abstraction of vantage point occupy the central place in our analysis. While accounting for the flexible boundaries of the state and especially for the patterns found in the practices of state institutions (chapter 4) required that priority be given to abstraction of extension and abstraction of level of generality. A fully adequate theory of the state, which would answer all the important questions people raise about it, could only be constructed by integrating these and still other aspects of dialectical method in ways that we did not consider necessary for our present illustrative purposes.

The chapters in this section also vary a lot in their complexity. Those on the state, Constitution, *Perestroika,* and academic freedom, for example, are written in a relatively popular style, and should be accessible to the average reader. By contrast, the essays on history and class consciousness are more difficult and more weighted with scholarly references. This is mainly due to the fact that, besides being examples of the use of dialectics, the latter two essays carry the theoretical discussion of method beyond what is found in sections I and II. "Studying History Backward" (chapter 8) introduces the dialectical movement of "precondition and result" as a way of integrating past, present, and future forms into the same interaction, while "How to Study Class Consciousness" (chapter 9) develops a framework for conducting dialectical inquiry of various forms of consciousness without distorting or trivializing the objective conditions in which they are found.

In an effort to make the methodological scaffolding with whose help all these essays were constructed more visible, I have also marked the main dialectical steps taken with footnotes and indicated the pages in sections I and II where the relevant theoretical discussions occur. In this way, too, the interested reader can refresh his or her understanding of the dialectical forms used without interfering with the flow of the argument for those whose main concern is with content. Students of method would probably benefit from reading these essays twice, once straight through and the second time looking up the theoretical discussion of each dialectical move as it comes into the text.

Finally, dialectical method also has something to say about how best to present a reality composed of mutually dependent processes whose relations are not only changing but appear differently, depending on the level of generality and vantage point that one adopts for investigating them. There is a story about a Zen monk who was asked why he never spoke to his students. He answered that if they understood him there was no need to speak to them. And, if they didn't understand him, he didn't believe that speaking to them would do any good. Unfortunately, too many of those who write on dialectics appear to have acquired their pedagogy from this venerable monk. Though problems of exposition are not addressed directly in this work, I hope that what follows will make it abundantly clear that I am not among them.[1]

---

1.   For a discussion of the moment of exposition in Marx's dialectical method, see my book, *Alienation*, pp. 65–9.

3

Theses on the Capitalist State _____

(1) One major aim of Marx's analysis of capitalism is to explain how people can make their own history and be made by it at the same time, how we are both free and conditioned, and how the future is both open and necessary.

(2) In Marx's theory of politics, the capitalist state is conceived of as a complex social relation of many different aspects, the main ones being political processes and institutions, the ruling class, an objective structure of political/economic functions, and an arena for class struggle.[1]

(3) These aspects also offer ways into the study of the state as a whole (perspectives from which to view and piece together its constituent elements).

(4) Viewed from one aspect, or one side, the state appears as a one-sided relation—not partial (because in most cases the various parts are all represented), but one-sided (because the parts are structured in function of where one begins, which also affects the attention given to each one).[2]

(5) The main interpretations of Marx's theory of the state—that it is an instrument of the capitalist class (Lenin and Ralph Miliband), an objective structure of political functions interlocked with capitalist economic functions (early Poulantzas), an arena of class struggle (late Poulantzas), the illusory community arising out of alienated social relations (early Ollman), and the hegemonic political ideology (Gramsci)—are such one-sided relations.

(6) None of these interpretations denies the possibility that the institutions of the state at a particular time and place are in the hands of a faction or fragment of the capitalist class (or a coalition of such), who use them to promote their own special interests. Indeed, this is usually the case. Such inner-class political conflict constitutes the subject matter of most political science. The ways in which the state simultaneously represents the interests of the whole capitalist class in opposition to the working class, the former ruling class, other dominated classes, and fragments of

---

1. For abstracting things as relations, see pp. 11–12, and 31–5.
2. For abstraction of vantage point, see pp. 67–78.

the capitalist class itself (including the one that has temporarily come out on top in the inner-class conflict), on the other hand, constitutes the subject matter of a Marxist theory of politics.[3]

(7) Each of these one-sided interpretations of the state (see no. 5) brings out something important about the capitalist state—about its appearance, structure, functioning (including contradictory functioning), ties to the rest of capitalism, and potential for change—just as it hides and distorts much else. And insofar as each of these interpretations integrates politics with economic and social processes, they all carry us outside the boundaries of relevance drawn by orthodox political science.[4]

(8) Some problems are better studied inside one rather than another of these interpretations. How the state protects the *status quo,* for example, is most usefully approached within the framework supplied by the view of the state as the instrument of the capitalist class. But it is the view of the state as a set of objective structures interlocked with capitalist economic processes that provides the most relevant framework in which to examine how the state contributes to the reproduction of capitalist conditions of existence. The requirements of tomorrow's capitalism and how they exert influence today emerge most clearly within this framework. The same political developments, when viewed inside these two different interpretations, will often exhibit a dual role: they defend existing capitalist relations while simultaneously laying down a necessary condition for what they are becoming.

(9) These different Marxist interpretations of the state are dependent to some degree (in when they are formulated, which ones get stressed, etc.) on the conditions and events in the lives of the people who hold them. Allowing for many exceptions, we can say in general that the structural view of the state (the state as a set of objective structures) is most popular in "quiet" periods; the Gramscian view of the state as the hegemonic political ideology, which stresses the capitalists' near perfect control over the workers' thinking, emerges in periods of political reaction; while the views of the state as the instrument of the ruling class and as an arena of class struggle come to the fore in periods of rapid social change.

(10) Some of the interpretations of the state mentioned seem to contradict one another. For example, the view of the state as an instrument of the capitalist class (which suggests that the capitalists are in direct control of the state and consciously use its institutions to promote their interests) appears to contradict the view of the state as a set of objective structures tied to capitalist economic processes whose requirements it must satisfy

---

3. For abstraction of level of generality, see pp. 53–67.
4. For abstraction of extension, see pp. 39–53.

(which suggests that the actions of whichever group controls the state are determined by forces outside its control, given that it does not want to overturn the entire capitalist system).

(11) These apparently contradictory views of the state are equally true—if not equally important (this is determined by research)—representing as they do different tendencies inside the state relation.[5] Dialectical truth does not fit together like the pieces of a puzzle, but allows for the kind of multiple one-sidedness and apparent contradictoriness that results from studying any subject from perspectives associated with its different aspects. (Perhaps the best-known example of this phenomenon in Marxism is the claim that capitalists are an "embodiment of capital," which stands in apparent contradiction to the claim that capital functions as it does because it is in the control of capitalists who use it to further their profit-maximizing interests.)

(12) Particular political developments may also have apparently contradictory meanings when viewed within different Marxist interpretations of the state. For example, a political reform that favors the working class, when viewed within the framework of the capitalist state as an arena of class struggle, appears as a victory for the workers, perhaps one which helps set limits to the exercise of capitalist power. On the other hand, viewing the same reform within the framework of the state as the instrument of the capitalist class leads to the conclusion that the capitalists have adopted a more sophisticated way of controlling or cooling out the workers, that it is a higher-order victory for the capitalists. These different conclusions do not balance out, and a compromise makes no sense. Rather, both conclusions are true, depending as they do on the interpretation of the state in which the event in question is placed.

(13) As regards the future, the apparently contradictory versions of the present that emerge from analyzing the same event within different interpretations of the state indicate the variety of real possibilities that make up the future. In the case of a political reform that seems to favor the workers, it could strengthen their hand in the class struggle; it could also—in quite different ways—weaken them. These alternative futures are part of the present; they don't begin tomorrow. It is only by studying present political developments within different interpretations of the state that we can capture the full potential for change, and change in different directions, which constitutes an essential part of the present moment—and maximize our chances for influencing them.[6]

(14) The widespread debate among Marxists over the relative autonomy

---

5. For contradiction, see pp. 15–17, 50–3, 63–5, and 76–7.
6. For abstractions of extension, see pp. 39–53; for vantage point, see pp. 67–78.

of the state usually goes on at cross purposes because the people involved do not sufficiently distinguish between these different Marxist interpretations of the state, and hence whether (under certain circumstances) the state is relatively autonomous from the ruling capitalist class, or from the economic requirements of capitalism, or from other alienated social relations, etc. As a matter of fact, there is a case to be made for relative autonomy within each of these perspectives on the state. What is important is to avoid the confusion that results from thinking there is only one debate when there are really several.

(15) Note for further research. The model for constructing the relations between the different views of the state arising out of approaches rooted in its different aspects is the complex set of "identities" Marx uncovers between production, distribution, exchange, and consumption in his unfinished Introduction to the *Critique of Political Economy.*[7]

(16) These complementary yet quite distinct Marxist views of the state have somewhat different consequences for the development of political consciousness and revolutionary will. For most people, their eyes are first opened politically when they grasp the state as an instrument of the ruling class; the society-wide dimensions of the problem only come into view when the state is also grasped as an objective structure tied in with capitalist economic structures. Their understanding is deepened—and the problems of organizing against capitalism better appreciated—when they also see the state as the illusory community and the hegemonic political ideology. But only when/if the state is also grasped as an arena of class struggle does Marxism become not only a way of understanding the world but a means for changing it through political activity.

(17) The narrow focus that political science imposes on the study of politics (whether in American Government, Comparative Government, International Relations, or Public Administration), especially when combined with its ahistorical approach, radically falsifies both the degree of freedom and the degree of necessity that characterizes our political lives.[8] In the absence of any inquiry into the state as an instrument of the capitalist class, political science seriously exaggerates the citizen's freedom to use the state to achieve his/her ends. Ignoring the state's character as an objective set of political structures tied in with capitalist economic processes, political science also underestimates the objective constraints under which any party in power acts, given a desire to retain even some capitalist relations (the classic dilemma of social democracy). However,

---

7. For identity/difference, see pp. 13–14, 42–4, and 73–5.
8. For abstraction of extension, see pp. 39–53. For the relation between freedom and determinism, see pp. 65–7.

should such a party decide to do away with capitalism entirely, the same view of the state accords to people greater freedom of action than most political scientists think they have (or could have). Likewise, on the level of individual effectiveness, viewing the state as an arena of class struggle means that people actually have more freedom to determine their lives (because it is only through class struggle that major change occurs) than they do in more traditional political science views of the state, which exalt the role of personal freedom while denying or ignoring class struggle.

(18) The interpretations of the state that contribute most to the development of revolutionary will are those that give a prominent place to the capitalist class, which is to say the view of the state as an instrument or ruling committee of this class and the view of the state as an arena of class struggle. To build up a full head of steam in and for the struggle, to maximize rational hostility as a politically motivating factor, most people require opponents in human form, other people who embody the oppressive functions of the system. It is as hard to hate abstract enemies as it is to love abstract friends. It is true that an analysis of the state as a set of objective structures (and, to a lesser extent, as the illusory community) is necessary to fully grasp the origins of existing oppression, how it works and for whom, the weak points in the armor of oppression, who are one's potential allies, and even how the oppressors themselves may be suffering from the system that carries their name. But it is also true that only by directing the struggle against actual, living capitalists can people be sufficiently motivated to engage in revolutionary struggle. To ignore the structural dimension of the analysis is to increase the danger that revolutionary politics will degenerate into reformism, directed toward removing the worst politicians. Without the class dimension, the danger is that revolutionary politics—lacking "fire in the belly"—will degenerate into scholasticism.

(19) By studying the state from the perspectives associated with its different aspects, Marxism is able to show how in politics people make their own history and are made by it at the same time, how we are both free and conditioned, and how the future is both open and necessary.

4

Why Do We Need a Theory of the State? _____

　　　　　　To his credit, in his article, "The Limits of the State: Beyond Statist Approaches," Tim Mitchell does indeed go "beyond" the boundaries that have been drawn in most debates among political scientists on this subject, but he leaves us with the question of whether he has gone far enough. After effectively criticizing various writers's attempts to establish a clear division between state and society, Mitchell offers a version of their union that emphasizes the numerous everyday activities that constitute the forms and hierarchies of order and control, which are our political institutions, while simultaneously making these institutions appear separate from and independent of the larger social context.[1] The same practices that give rise to the state are held to be primarily responsible for the widespread misunderstanding of its nature, and in particular of its limits.

　　But why do we want to understand what the state is, in the first place? Primarily, I would have thought, it is because we want to understand better what the state does.[2] As this suggests, most people already have a rough idea of what the state does—it makes laws, administers and enforces them, adjudicates disputes on the basis of such laws, and represents people who live under the rule of one state in their dealings with other states. Until greater clarity is attained regarding who and/or what does all this, it is difficult to distinguish the state from such kindred phenomena as the government and the nation, or to understand why setting the boundaries of the state should be such a problem. More important, it is impossible to explain the patterns observed in how the state conducts its work and in the effects that result from it. That is, some groups in the country consistently play a greater role in the higher reaches of the state and benefit to an inordinate degree from most of what the state does. Well, who are they, and why should this be so? And does it have anything

---

Response to Tim Mitchell's "The Limits of the State: Beyond Statist Approaches," *American Political Science Review*, 85 (March 1991).

　1.　For abstraction of extension, see pp. 39–53.
　2.　For abstraction of vantage point, see pp. 67–78.

to do with the nature of the state as such? These would seem to be reasonable and even obvious questions.

While all the writers Mitchell criticizes are indeed guilty of setting up the state as an independent entity, they do at least provide us with answers to these questions—if it is only to deny the accumulated evidence, though it is usually more, such as attributing the observed bias to the decisions of politicians. Mitchell, on the other hand, offers no answers whatsoever. The Foucault-inspired micro-practices of "organization and articulation" (92) that constitute the state in his account are disembodied, depoliticized, declassed, and, despite a couple of vague references to history, ahistorical.[3] Emptied of all social content, they can tell us nothing about why the state acts as it does.

Yet there is much in Mitchell's essay that suggests that he really knows what the answers are. He says, for example, that the spillover of society into what is ordinarily taken to be the state, their internal relation, has to do with how a "social and political order is maintained" (90). But we never learn who benefits most from maintaining the present social order or how exactly the state helps them. The social order itself is never named. Capitalism is nowhere mentioned in his article.

Further, Mitchell is aware that a major effect of the attempt to remove the state from society is that it reinforces the view that the state and/ or officials acting on its behalf are free and independent agents, only occasionally influenced—and then only to a minor degree—by larger social forces.[4] From this, it is but a short step to recognize, as I believe Mitchell must but nowhere makes explicit, that there are few beliefs more important to the health of the status quo than the one which treats state institutions as neutral in the political and economic clashes between different groups, such that each of them has a more or less equal chance of winning the support of these institutions. To believe that the state has special ties to one group, insuring that its major interests always come on top, would cost the state a great deal of its legitimacy and make it far more difficult for it to do whatever it does on behalf of the favored group.

Finally, Mitchell's own examples suggest to us that he knows more than he says. Do the Aramco Oil Company (89) and American banks (90), two of Mitchell's main examples, engage in politics to establish a clear separation between the state and society, or to promote their own money-making interests? The question should answer itself. If in the process of promoting their interests, they make use of means that disguise their

---

3. For abstraction of extension, see pp. 39–53.
4. For the role of irrational abstractions in the construction of ideology, see pp. 26, 41, 45–6, 57–8, and 70–3.

integration into the state—chiefly as a way of avoiding democratic ac-countability—this certainly deserves to be mentioned, but it should not require that we exchange one disguise for another. For while Mitchell isolates a major ideological distortion that emerges from the particular ways in which a favored group helps constitute the state in the very process of using it, he does so in a manner that further mystifies who exactly is acting and why they are acting in just these ways.

Why such hesitancy? After criticizing various thinkers for setting the state out from society, Mitchell seems unwilling to investigate the system-atic bias that he clearly suspects is present in state practices because he fears falling into the same trap as those he criticizes. To present the state consistently acting as it does due to pressures (whatever their form) located in society is to reestablish, he seems to believe, the very separation between state and society that he took such pains to demolish. In short, Mitchell's explanatory framework and commitments keep him from recog-nizing what, at some other level, he knows to be there.

Is there another way of treating this matter that would avoid being caught up in this dilemma? Mitchell's own approach suggests that there is. The key to this approach involves extending the notion of the state back in time to include the wide variety of practices by which the institutions of the state came into being. Having stretched the boundaries of the state so far, there can be no objection in principle to stretching them a little further in order to include who and/or what are primarily responsible for the aforesaid practices. Mitchell's conception of the state, in other words, could—and, in my view, should—include the group(s) whose special ties to the state give its forms and practices their distinctive character.[5] This would enable us to explain the patterns we observe in the latter's effects without introducing a split between state and society. If the everyday activities of citizens helps explain how the state is constituted, it is only the connection between these activities and the requirements of the favored group(s) that can account for why it is constituted in just these ways at just this time.[6] An adequate conception of the state must contain answers to the questions, "why" and "when," as well as to the question, "how."

There is no single answer to where the state ends and where society begins, because these are not neighborhoods separated by broad avenues. Rather, the one performs a range of essential functions within the other. The ways and even the forms through which these functions are per-formed, however, vary considerably depending on both the nature and stage of development of the society in question. They also vary depending

5. For abstraction of extension, see pp. 39–53.
6. For abstraction of vantage point, see pp. 67–78.

on which group has enough power based on its structural position in society to ensure that its interests generally emerge on top, that the requirements rooted in these special interests get taken as society's requirements. Such a group is more accurately referred to as the "ruling class." With changes in society, in its ruling class and in what this class requires to best serve its interests, the functions of the state will also vary and with them the boundaries that establish state limits as well as the very meaning of "state" in our discourse.

Functions imply a system, however, and our quest is complicated by the fact that the functions performed by the state belong to three different, though overlapping, systems. These systems are class society, capitalism, and modern American democratic capitalism.[7] They differ from each other in the degree of generality (or specificity) that mark all their qualities. Which is to say, our society is a class divided society and as such possesses a host of interacting qualities that are similar to those found in other class divided societies during the whole period that they have existed on earth (roughly five to ten thousand years). Ours is also a capitalist society and has many systemic qualities that distinguish it as such, which it shares with all the capitalist societies in the five to six hundred years that this social formation has existed. And, finally, our society is a stage in capitalism that has come to the fore under the special conditions that have developed in America in recent years (say the last twenty to fifty years). What we call "American society," then, is a layered construction composed of sets of internally related qualities that fall on three different levels of generality, indicative of three different time frameworks.

While the qualities that constitute these three systems are often treated together, we can also distinguish among them, and for certain purposes it is essential that we do so. As regards the state, it is clear that what is meant by the ruling class as well as by its requirements varies somewhat as we move from viewing the United States as a class society to viewing it as a capitalist society, to viewing it as modern American democratic capitalism.

At the level of class society, the dominant economic class requires political help in reproducing the conditions that underlie its position of dominance. Such help involves various means of socializing the population, and especially its most oppressed sections, into an acceptance of the status quo and a repressive apparatus—chiefly police, soldiers, and courts—that can be called upon when the former doesn't wholly work. Socialization is aimed primarily at gaining popular acceptance for the institution of private property, for the basis—whether in divine will, birth,

---

7. For abstraction of level of generality, see pp. 53–67.

or money—of the prevailing division of labor, and for the idea that the special interests of the dominant class are the same as the interests of the nation. The mystification involved in the latter leads Marx to refer to the state during the entire period of class history as an "illusory community" (1942, 74). It is a "community" because it tries to reproduce the conditions underlying the mutual dependence of all people living in a given geographical area. It is "illusory" because it privileges the interests of one class under the guise of serving the interests of everyone. So much is true of the state in all class societies.

But, as we said, ours is also a capitalist class society, and as such it requires political help tailored to the peculiar character and interests of the ruling capitalist class. Perhaps the most distinctive feature of the capitalists as a ruling class is their constant drive to accumulate, to treat wealth primarily as a means to produce still more wealth. While socialization and repression remain essential state functions for capitalism, the nature of accumulation in this period requires certain modifications in the forms through which these functions are carried out. To cite just one example, workers perform their roles in accumulation more effectively if they feel they have had some freedom in choosing a job and at least the possibility of influencing state policy in so far as it affects their job. All of which gives to the production of capitalist ideology, and the institutions devoted to this activity, a much more important place in capitalism—and therefore in the capitalist state—than it has in other class societies and their states.

The centrality of accumulation in capitalism also forces the state to undertake a function that does not exist in other class societies, and that is helping the capitalists realize the value of their products. Given how capitalism works, capitalists simply require more direct political help in their efforts to enrich themselves than did feudal aristocrats or the slave owners of antiquity. They require what amounts to state planning on their behalf—and they get it. While rendered mostly invisible by their ideology, such planning covers everything from investing, to financing, to doing research, to training workers, to buying, to selling the finished products. Most of our tax, trade, labor, and monetary policies (including both laws and their administration) come under the rubric of capitalist planning. The political institutions and practices that serve capitalist interests in these ways are essential parts of the capitalist state.[8]

While Mitchell's examples show corporations and banks only interested in making money—an interest aided by "appearing" private, outside the

---

8. For abstraction of extension, see pp. 39–53.

state—he never examines the system in which this occurs. Consequently, there is no mention of capital accumulation and the kind of help this requires from the state. Had he placed his analysis squarely within a capitalist framework, he would have noticed that the state's appearing separate from society is but one of the ways—though, perhaps, ideologically the most important—in which the state serves the interests of the capitalist ruling class.

Just as ours is a class society and a capitalist society, it is also, as we have said, the modern American democratic capitalist society, and some of what our state is and does pertains to the special interests of the American capitalist class, given its place and role in world capitalism at this stage of its development. If the first set of qualities we examined are shared with all societies within the period of class history, and the second with other capitalist societies for the entire period that they have existed, these qualities apply only to the American democratic capitalist society of recent times. Among the new developments that have had a major impact on the character and practices of the state on this level of generality, three seem to stand out. The enormous increase in the gross national product, together with the intensification of competition between capitalist societies in the last few decades, has led to the state taking on a larger and more direct role in the realization of value, while for good ideological reasons insisting ever more loudly that nothing of the kind is happening. Also, the Cold War has given us the National Security State, including the "Military-Industrial Complex," which has greatly facilitated the capitalists' effort to repress internal opposition and bolster their profits by draping both with the mantle of national security. Finally, the development of communications technology has made it possible for the American ruling class to extend the political work of socialization in capitalist ideas and values to the entire globe, transforming the media into an indispensable arm of the state, which is to say into an aspect of the state itself (or what Louis Althusser dubbed an "ideological state apparatus") (1976, 67–126).[9]

As our American capitalist class becomes increasingly international, with more foreign capitalists investing in the United States and more U.S. capitalists investing abroad, the political help required to realize value has led to the development of world institutions such as the IMF, the World Bank, and GATT, whose economic labels disguise their important political functions. They are the beginnings of a world capitalist state, whose origins and development—as with the rise of the national states that occurred earlier—are best understood as political responses to the

---

9. For abstraction of extension, see pp. 39–53.

changing requirements of the ruling capitalist class on the level of generality of modern capitalist society.[10]

The national state in the United States is also losing some of its power to regional political forms, such as the New York Port Authority and the Appalachian Regional Commission, and for similar reasons: the interests of the capitalist class in this period are better served by having certain political functions performed in this way and on this scale. That both world and regional forms of the state are completely unaccountable to their respective constituencies has also contributed to their popularity among the ruling class. Barring a socialist transformation, what we have here is a preview of the next stage of the "American" capitalist state, with the national forms of the state being reduced to performing mainly repressive and socializing functions while most of the help rendered capitalists in their drive to accumulate and maximize profits is provided at the world and regional state levels. How this will affect the national state's ability to perform its repressive and socializing functions remains to be seen.

Viewing political institutions and practices as internally related to the ruling economic class, as equal and necessary aspects of a more broadly conceived notion of the state, viewing such ties as falling on three different levels of generality, does not keep us from recognizing occasions when a set of unusual circumstances allows some government officials, political parties, and even whole institutions to operate in relative autonomy from ruling class imperatives. The point is that this is the exception, and a relative exception at that—meaning short term and for limited purposes—and not the rule, as is the case in most non-Marxist interpretations of the state. Such exceptions are also largely explainable in terms of the special circumstances that apply. These exceptions also become increasingly rare as we move from the more specific level of modern American capitalism to the more general one of capitalism overall to the still more general one of class society, which is to say that it was easier to have a New Deal (the part of it that favored the interests of workers) than it is to interfere with the structures that underlie capitalist and, more generally, ruling class domination.[11]

Nor do I mean to wholly dismiss the struggle by subaltern classes to use some part of the state—taking advantage of the problems and contradictions that come with the territory—to promote their interests. While the cards are carefully stacked against such efforts, it is sometimes possible to win small, or temporarily, or to keep a capitalist initiative from

---

10. For abstraction of extension, see pp. 39–53; for vantage point, see pp. 67–78.
11. For abstraction of level of generality, see pp. 53–67.

succeeding to the extent that it otherwise would. And by reordering power relations even slightly, every victory resets the odds for the major confrontations up ahead, when the problems inherent in the ordinary functioning of the system have reached the explosion point. The larger goal of these confrontations can only be to socialize the means of production and deprive the capitalist ruling class of the basis of its power. Should this succeed, a new ruling class, representing in this case the great majority, would organize the state in a way that would best serve its special interests, once again altering the boundaries of the state in the process. The internal relations between state and society—a very changed society and hence a very different state—would remain the same.

If many political scientists treat the state as a kind of "ghost in the machine" (David Easton's not altogether friendly observation, quoted by Mitchell) (91), it is only because the machine acts in ways that belie all attempts at explanation which are restricted to the decisions of the people who sit at the controls. Something more and different has to be introduced to help account for the persistent patterns found in how the machine works. Until this is done, all attempts to kick the state out the door—in the manner of the political systems' theorists, for example—will only result in having it climb back in through the window. Recognizing this, Mitchell sought to highlight the numerous everyday practices that constitute the state in its present form and enable it to function as it does. In so far as these practices are themselves left unaccounted for, however, he has just substituted one ghost for another. It is only by extending the connections that Mitchell started to trace back further in order to take account of the political requirements of our ruling class—grasped as a ruling class in general, as a capitalist ruling class, and as the modern American capitalist ruling class—that the otherwise inexplicable movements of Easton's ghost (and Mitchell's, too) become comprehensible.

References

Althusser, L. 1976. *Positions*. Paris: Editions Sociales.
Marx, K. and F. Engels. *German Ideology*. Translated by R. Pascal. London: International.
Mitchell, T. 1991. "The Limits of the State: Beyond Statist Approaches." *American Political Science Review*, 85 (March).

5

Toward a Marxist Interpretation of the U.S. Constitution _____

When Moses invented ten fundamental laws for the Jewish people, he had God write them down on stone tablets. Lycurgus, too, represented the constitution he drew up for ancient Sparta as a divine gift. According to Plato, whose book, *The Republic,* offers another version of the same practice, attributing the origins of a constitution to godly intervention is the most effective way of securing the kind of support needed for it to work. Otherwise, some people are likely to remain skeptical, others passive, and still others critical of whatever biases they perceive in these basic laws, and hence less inclined to follow their mandates.

As learned men, the framers of the American Constitution were well aware of the advantages to be gained by enveloping their achievement in religious mystery, but most of the people for whom they labored were religious dissenters who favored a sharp separation between church and state; and since most of the framers were deists and atheists themselves, this particular tactic could not be used. So they did the next best thing, which was to keep the whole process of their work on the Constitution a closely guarded secret. Most Americans know that the framers met for three months in closed session, but this is generally forgiven on the grounds that the then Congress of the United States had not commissioned them to write a new Constitution, and neither revolutionaries nor counter-revolutionaries can do all their work in the open. What few modern-day Americans realize, however, is that the framers did their best to ensure that we would never know the details of their deliberations. All the participants in the convention were sworn to life-long secrecy, and when the debates were over, those who had taken notes were asked to hand them in to George Washington, whose final task as chairman of the convention was to get rid of the evidence. America's first president, it appears, was also its first shredder.

Fortunately, not all the participants kept their vows of silence or handed in all their notes. But it wasn't until 1840, a half century after the Constitution was put into effect, with the posthumous surfacing of James Madison's extensive notes, that the American people could finally read what had happened in those three crucial months in Philadelphia. What was re-vealed was neither divine nor diabolical, but simply human, an all-too-human exercise in politics. Merchants, bankers, shipowners, planters, slave traders and slave owners, land speculators, and lawyers, who made their money working for these groups, voiced their interests and fears in clear, uncluttered language; and, after settling a few, relatively minor disagreements, they drew up plans for a form of government they believed would serve these interests most effectively. But the fifty years of silence had the desired myth-building effect. The human actors were transformed into "Founding Fathers," their political savvy and common sense were now seen as all-surpassing wisdom, and their concern for their own class of property owners (and, to a lesser extent, sections of the country and occupational groups) had been elevated to universal altruism (in the liberal version) or self-sacrificing patriotism (in the preferred conservative view). Nor have we been completely spared the aura of religious mystery so favored by Plato. With the passage of years and the growing religiosity of our citizenry, it has become almost commonplace to hear that the framers were also divinely inspired.

The year 1987 was the bicentennial of the writing of the Constitution, and wherever one turned in the media, in schools and professional associ-ations, in talks by politicians and other public figures, the same myths appeared. The Commission on the Bicentennial of the U.S. Constitution, which was set up under Chief Justice Burger to coordinate most of these efforts, demonstrated its own commitment to historical truth by initially taking as its slogan "200 Years of Peace, Prosperity, and Liberty."

What is in danger of being lost among all the patriotic non sequiturs is the underside of criticism and protest that has accompanied the Constitu-tion from its very inception. Not everyone has been satisfied to treat this product of men as if it came from God. Even before the Constitution was officially adopted, many people, known to history as Anti-Federalists, questioned whether what was good for the property-owning factions that were so well represented in Philadelphia would be as good for those who owned little or nothing. Then as subsequently, the main questions raised dealt with the limitations on suffrage, the inadequate defense of individual rights and freedoms, the acceptance and even strengthening of the institu-tion of slavery, and the many other benefits given to men of property.

Taken at face value, the Constitution is an attempt to fix the relations between state and federal governments, and between the three branches—legislative, executive, and judiciary—of the latter. And most accounts of this document have concentrated on the mechanical arrangements that make this balancing act possible. In the process, the Constitution's basic assumptions and particularly its social and economic purposes have been grossly neglected. It is a little like learning in some detail how a car works before even knowing what kind of machine it is, what it is supposed to do, and why it was constructed in just this way. Learning the functioning of any system, whether mechanical or institutional, is not without value in determining its meaning and use, but we would do better to approach their symbiosis from the other side, to examine who needed what and how the specific structures created responded to these needs.[1] What is really at stake in any political dispute, the real-life questions involved, and why different people take the positions they do, can never be adequately understood by focusing solely or even mainly on the legalistic forms in which the issues are presented and fought out.[2]

In examining any political phenomena, it is always wise to ask, "Who benefits?" As regards the American constitutional system, the answer was given clearly, if somewhat crudely, by Senator Boies Penrose, a late nineteenth-century Republican from Pennsylvania, who told a business audience: "I believe in a division of labor. You send us to Congress; we pass the laws under which you make money . . . and out of your profits you further contribute to our campaign funds to send us back again to pass more laws to enable you to make more money" (Green, 35). When, a few years later, Charles Beard suggested that the same kind of considerations may have played a role in the writing of the Constitution, he un-leashed a political storm against his book that has few if any parallels in our history. Then-president Taft publicly denounced this unseemly muckraking as besmirching the reputations of our Founding Fathers. Not particularly noted for his indifference to economic gain when he became president, Warren Harding, at that time a newspaper publisher, attacked Beard's "filthy lies and rotten perversions" in an article entitled, "Scavengers, Hyena-Like, Desecrate the Graves of the Dead Patriots We Revere" (McDonald, xix). And even as a growing number of professional historians came to accept Beard's interpretation, the city of Seattle banned his book.

Obviously, Beard had touched a tender nerve, but it is also obvious that economic motivations—as Beard himself recognized—are only part of the explanation for political phenomena. Other factors influence people's behavior, and some people act often and even primarily out of other kinds of motives. The problem is how to credit these necessary qualifications without unduly compromising the original insight (not really that original, since political theory has known about the importance of economic motivation from Plato on).

In an attempt to redirect attention away from the mechanical and socially

---

1. For abstraction of vantage point, see pp. 67–78.
2. For appearance/essence, see pp. 10–11, and 45–6.

uninformative details of checks and balances, criticisms of the Constitution have proceeded on three distinct though closely related levels. The first concentrates on the people who wrote the document, on who they were and what they thought, feared, and wanted. The second deals with the classes and subclasses to which they belonged and which they more or less consciously represented, with the objective interests of these classes and what was required to satisfy them. Here what is decisive are the assumptions and ways of thinking that correspond to membership in a particular class, or the part of human understanding that comes from what we take for granted, not so much because of who we are as because of where we fit in society. Hence, for example, one might favor strong laws to protect private property not because one wants to remain wealthy (though I suspect most wealthy people do), but because one has been socialized as a member of a property-owning class to take this requirement and its connection to life, liberty, and the pursuit of happiness for granted. The third level introduces the nature of the capitalist mode of production, and tries to bring out how the Constitution, together with other political institutions, function as both cause and effect within the life process of a developing capitalist society.[3]

From the start, most criticisms have been situated on the first and second of these levels. However, given the necessary relations between levels, a fully adequate analysis of what our Constitution means would have to devote more attention to the larger context, capitalism, in which it was produced and which it helps in no small measure to reproduce. To be sure, capitalism doesn't exist apart from the social and economic classes whose struggle over opposing interests constitutes its central drama. Nor can these classes be completely understood apart from the lives of the real individuals who compose them. But the reverse is equally true: the actions of the individual framers makes little sense—opening the way for various superficial interpretations—if viewed apart from the class interests which they sought to further; just as the nature of these classes, their specific interests, and the conditions and means available to satisfy them require a contextualization that could only come from an account of the enveloping capitalist system. It was early commercial capitalism in its free worker and slave variants that gave rise to the main property owning classes represented at Philadelphia; that established the conditions for their alliance and made this alliance politically dominant; that led to the most pressing problems from which these classes suffered; and finally that provided both the possibilities and limits for the resolution of these problems. Unfortunately, the book that treats the Constitution as a political extension of the capitalist mode of production, as an organic

---

3. For cause and effect, see p. 36.

function of this historically developing whole, while not losing sight of how it is also a product of a particular class alliance *and* of the real individuals who gathered in Philadelphia remains to be written.[4]

What still needs to be stressed—chiefly because even most critics ignore it—is that on all three levels of analysis and throughout the entire two hundred years of its history, the Constitution has been a way of understanding reality as much as it has served to shape it.[5] And it has succeeded in ordering society in part through how it has made people think about it, just as these practical achievements have secured widespread acceptance for the intellectual modes that they embody. In sum, an important part of the Constitution's work is ideological. As ideology, the Constitution provides us with a kind of bourgeois fairy tale in which claims to equal rights and responsibilities are substituted for the harsh realities of class domination. Through the Constitution, the struggle over the legitimacy of any social act or relationship is removed from the plane of morality to that of law. Justice is no longer what is fair but what is legal, and politics itself is transformed into the technical wrangling of lawyers and judges. The Constitution organizes consent not least by its manner of organizing dissent. The fact that two-thirds of the world's lawyers practice in the United States is not, as they say, a coincidence. The main ideologists in the American system are not teachers, preachers, or media people, but lawyers and judges.

Unlike political theory, the Constitution not only offers us a picture of reality but through the state's monopoly on violence it forces citizens to act, or at least to speak, "as if." Acting as if the rule of Law, equality of opportunity, freedom of the individual, and the neutrality of the state, all of which are inscribed in the Constitution, are more than formally true inhibits people's ability to recognize that they are all practically false, that the society set up with the help of the Constitution simply does not operate in these ways. It is not a matter of reality failing to live up to a set of commendable ideals but of these ideals serving to help mask this reality through misrepresenting what is legal for what is actual, what is permissible in law for what is possible in society. When does an ideal become a barrier to the realization of what it supposedly promotes? When people are encouraged to treat the ideal as a description, however imperfect, of the real, as in the claim that ours is a society ruled by law, where whatever actually exists that goes counter to this claim is relegated to the role of a passing qualification. Viewed in this way, the dynamics of who is doing what to whom and why, together with the structural reforms needed to change things, can never be understood.[6]

---

4. For abstraction of level of generality, see pp. 56–67; for vantage point, see pp. 67–78.
5. For abstraction of extension, see pp. 39–53.
6. For critique of ideology, see pp. 10–11, 26, 41, 45–6, 57–8, and 70–3.

Finally, all such criticisms should not blind us to the many positive and progressive qualities of the Constitution, both for the time in which it was written and for the present day. By 1787 the revolutionary war had been over for four years, but it was still not clear that the English ruling class had accepted its result. What could be done to ensure the country's political independence? And how best to deal with the economic problems resulting from the disruption of trade and investment patterns that accompanied this independence? These problems were not very different from those confronting ex-colonial countries that have gained their independence in our century; and in every case setting up a strong central government has been vital for their solution. Beyond this, and especially for the late eighteenth century, the Constitution deserves high marks for its attempt to limit the arbitrary power of government (providing some protection for its own critics) and for such measures as the elimination of all religious qualifications for voting and holding office.[7]

With the passing years the Constitution has also proved to be admirably suited for a society in transition from early to late capitalism, that is, from one dominated by merchant and financial capitalists and slave owners tied to capital through their production for a world market, to one dominated by industrial and financial capitalists, both domestic and multinational. By facilitating the accumulation of wealth on a scale never before dreamed of in world history, the Constitution can also be viewed as helping to make possible a transition to socialism at a very high level of economic development. Few of these positive qualities come without their regressive aspects or side effects, but that should not keep us from recognizing their existence or importance, or making use of them when we can. Though not the same virtues that are trumpeted in most bicentennial celebrations, they should be enough to show that our criticisms do not lead us to regret that the Constitution was ever written. One studies the past neither to annul it nor to improve it, but to build upon it where that is possible. In learning how the Constitution works, for whom it works better and for whom it works worse, and how and why it acquired its character, we discover not only what the Constitution has meant but what it may yet mean in our future.[8]

Can the Constitution serve a people bent on a democratic socialist transformation of capitalist society? It has done everything a document could possibly do to forestall such an eventuality; and as the central institutional prop of our capitalist society, it continues to act in this way. And yet, despite its lopsided and deceptive form and the worst elitist intentions of its framers, the changes it has undergone in the past two hundred years suggest that

7. For abstraction of vantage point, see pp. 67–78; for the interpenetration of polar opposites, see pp. 14, 48, and 64–5.
8. For abstracting the future aspects of a process, see pp. 29–31, and 76.

this possibility cannot be ruled out. Nothing, of course, came easy. Every amendment to the Constitution, just like most new interpretations by the Supreme Court (in some ways more important than new amendments), and each change of emphasis in its administration and enforcement have come about as a result of popular struggle. Neither blacks, nor women, nor un-propertied males, for example, were simply handed the right to vote. It might be said that the expansion of democracy only occurred after it became clear that the influence of party machines, public education, newspapers, churches, mass spectator sports, patriotism and especially the growth of the economic pie through capitalist development and American imperialistic adventures "abroad" (including Indian and Mexican lands west of the Mississippi) would suffice to ensure that the newly enfranchised publics would not use their power for subversive ends.[9]

But the most fundamental contradiction in the entire Constitution cannot be dismissed so easily. This is the contradiction between political democracy and economic servitude.[10] The framers did everything they could—consistent with winning acceptance for the document—to avoid placing the loaded gun of popular sovereignty in the hands of the people. They had no doubt as to what would happen to the grossly unequal distribution of property in our country (at present, 1 percent of the population own 50 percent of all wealth) should this ever occur (Carter, 35). Well, it has occurred, and the mass of America's citizens have made little use of political democracy to obtain economic democracy. For some, therefore, the trial is over, and the verdict is in. For us, the jury is still out. Capitalism in *extremis* has many catastrophes in store for all of us. And with the stakes so high, history can afford to take its time. Meanwhile, more informed criticism of the one-sided, deceptive, and biased rules of the game by which we are all forced to play can hurry history along just that little bit, and in the process encourage thinking on the role—if any— of the Constitution in the transition to a socialist society.

References

Carter, A. "How About a Capital Accumulation Tax?" *New York Times,* Sept. 23, 1986.
Green, M. "Stamping Out Corruption." *New York Times,* Oct. 28, 1986.
McDonald, F. 1986. New Introduction to Charles Beard's *An Economic Interpretation of the Constitution.* New York: Free Press.

---

9. For identity/difference, see pp. 13–14, 42–4, and 73–5.
10. For contradiction, see pp. 15–17, 50–3, 63–5, and 76–7.

6

The Regency of the Proletariat in Crisis: A Job for Perestroika

The discussion of *Perestroika* has suffered on the whole from inadequate attention paid to the nature of Soviet society. Yet, it is only upon knowing the kind of society we have before us that we can grasp the specificity of its problems and the possibilities within the system for resolving them. Hence any serious inquiry into *Perestroika* and *Glasnost* must begin by determining the best way to characterize the Soviet Union.

There has probably never been a society anywhere that has been burdened with so many different names: "socialism," "communism," "actually existing socialism," "state socialism," "bureaucratically deformed socialism," "dictatorship of the proletariat," "workers' state," "people's democracy," "state capitalism," "totalitarianism," "red fascism," and there are others. The problem of finding the right label, of course, is a reflection of the difficulty people have had in deciding which one or few of its attributes have been decisive in giving the Soviet Union its distinctive character, including too its real history and potential for future change.

Most of the debate has revolved around whether to treat the working class, or the Communist Party, or some combination of bureaucrats and managers as the leading actor in the Soviet drama. Those who opt for the workers, and there are still some who do, have to explain why such groups as the Communist Party, bureaucrats, and managers exercise so much real power. Those who single out the Party have to account for where the Party gets its goals and why there are any social and political limits to its power. Why, for example, should it ever change its policies? The totalitarian model, which this is, assumed that the Soviet Union would remain forever the same. People who give priority to bureaucrats and managers,

This chapter is from a talk given at a conference on *Perestroika* at the Academy of Social Science of the Central Committee of the CPSU in Moscow (the highest Higher Party School), October 17, 1990.

whether taken as a new class or not, have to explain how the Communist Party could exist *before* the rise of this group, whose political instrument, according to this view, the Party is. These are the main reasons I reject these three interpretations of Soviet society and the various labels with which they come. What then to emphasize to get at the distinctive character and dynamics of Soviet society, and what name best captures it?

I choose to emphasize not one group but a relation—until recently an essential, organic relation—between two groups: the workers and the Communist Party. Within this relation, the third group mentioned above, bureaucrats and managers, function as mediators invariably serving the interests of the Communist Party which appoints them and sets their agendas. Those who have caught a glimpse of the importance of this relation have generally cast it as one of "vanguardism," where the Communist Party is viewed as the vanguard of the working class, with the working class viewed as the dominant class in society. But this assumes that the Soviet Union is a dictatorship of the proletariat, which Marx understood as a society in which the workers hold real power. The Soviet Union is not and has never been a dictatorship of the proletariat, because the workers have never held power. Its self-proclaimed vanguard did, and still does. But this vanguard derives its legitimacy from its presumed connection to the working class, whose right to rule is taken as given, and more often than not it was the interests of the workers (as interpreted by the Party, of course) that determined government policy. Given the prevailing ideology, the Party had no other acceptable rationale for acting as it did; nor did the rest of society for going along.

On this interpretation, the Soviet Union is neither socialist nor capitalist, neither a dictatorship, nor a democracy, neither a workers' state nor a bureaucratic state as these characterizations are ordinarily understood, but contains elements of all of these. In my view, the unusual combination suggested by these apparently incompatible qualities is best grasped as a kind of regency. The Soviet Union is a Regency of the Proletariat.[1] The model here is the regency of an earlier time when an established politician, often the uncle of a still-too-young monarch, wielded power in his name, and claimed to act in his interest. Though all effective power was in the hands of the Regent, his legitimacy rested on his relation to the king, whom everyone, including the Regent, considered to be the rightful ruler. As the young king grew up and became capable of governing on his own, the Regent had two choices: either hand over power to the king or eliminate him and assume power in his own name.

As a model of the relation between the Communist Party and the working

1. For abstraction of extension, see pp. 39–53.

class, the idea of regency has several advantages. It makes clear that the only rightful possessor of power, according to the prevailing ideology, is the proletariat; that this power has been exercised for them, and presumable in their interests, by the Communist Party; that the entire basis of the Party's legitimacy lies in its special relationship to the workers; that this relationship has evolved into something quite different than it was at the start; and that with these changes, the Soviet Regent, the Communist Party, had to decide whether to hand over power to the workers or to eliminate them, not physically, of course, but politically and ideologically.

These changes are to be understood not only in terms of a growth in the size, education, and political sophistication of the working class but also in the number of ways their lack of cooperation and generally indifferent work could interfere with the efficient functioning of the Party's economic plan. While the growing complexity of the plan and of the productive tasks it entailed required more care, more commitment, and more cooperation on the part of workers, the latter delivered less and less.[2] With the exception of the war years and the period of recovery immediately afterward, when survival and patriotic sentiments supplemented the Party's traditional appeals, most workers were never able to identify with the planners or accept the plan as their own. Moreover, none of the Party's attempts to entice or force cooperation seemed to make a difference.

There are many factors that play a role in the economic slowdown in the Soviet Union that began as early as 1960. Cold War competition with the West, of course, must not be neglected, but I give primacy of place to this contradictory relation between the evolving requirements of the plan and the decrease in worker effort and cooperation that it elicited.[3] Particularly instructive is the precipitous decline that took place in capital productivity. It is estimated that between 1960 and 1985 the ratio of capital to industrial output in the Soviet Union went down almost 40 percent (Sweezy, 1990, 7). With work quality and intensity dropping, the increase in the number of factories and machines of all sorts did not have the expected impact on the quantity of goods produced.

Poor planning? Probably. Inefficient, self-interested management? Without a doubt. But the key to this unraveling of an economic arrangement that had worked moderately well until then lay in the refusal of most of its participants, deprived of other means of showing their discontent, to accommodate themselves to the changing nature of their tasks. This is not to be viewed as a matter of the workers failing the system, but of the

---

2. For abstraction of process, see pp. 28–31.
3. For contradiction, see pp. 15–17, 50–3, 63–5, and 76–7.

system itself, based on the evolving relation of Party to class, reaching the limits of its adaptability. While the main effect of such resistance was economic, it can also be seen as a kind of half-conscious political protest, guerilla warfare conducted chiefly by working to rule, by workers against a Regency whose *raison d'être* had run its course.[4]

Whatever the initial justification, it would appear that Soviet workers no longer needed, or, in the case of a growing number, wanted, some other group to act on their behalf. What was the response of the Soviet Regent to be? It is this situation that I've described as "The Regency of the Proletariat in Crisis."[5]

This crisis can also be cast within the Marxist framework of the relations between the forces and relations of production. In line with what was said about the Regency, the groups whose interactions earn them pride of place in the relations of production in Soviet society are the workers and the Communist Party. It is through their interaction that Soviet forces of production have developed as far as they have, making the Soviet Union until recently the second largest industrial power on earth. But these same relations in their evolved state have come to impede the further progress of the forces of production. Now something must give.[6]

II ───

In light of this characterization of the Soviet Union as a Regency of the Proletariat, what sense can we make out of *Perestroika* and *Glasnost?* Within this perspective, the policies collectively referred to by these names represent a revolt by the Regents, a counterrevolution, a preemptive strike to forestall the coming to power of the working class.[7] Viewing the Soviet Union as a Regency of the Proletariat, the main aims of *Perestroika* and *Glasnost* appear to be as follows: (1) discipline the workers through the introduction of market mechanisms with their ever-present threat of unemployment; (2) hide the hand, that is, the Party's hand, that disciplines them by giving economic powers that once belonged to central planners, a group easily identified with the Party, to managers and owners on the enterprise level; (3) have the workers participate in their own mystification; and (4) shift the basis of the Party's legitimacy from the working class,

---

4. For identity/difference, see pp. 13–14, 42–4, and 73–5.
5. For quantity/quality change, see pp. 15, 48–9, and 76.
6. For contradiction, see pp. 15–7, 50–3, 63–5, and 76–7.
7. For abstraction of vantage point, see pp. 67–78.

and the Party's supposed position of vanguard to this class, to the public at large by setting up Western-style democratic elections to the government.

(1) *Discipline the workers through the introduction of market mechanisms.* Here is a stick with which to coerce cooperation that was not available before. To the Regents, it must have seemed that everything had been tried to make Soviet workers work more efficiently except the discipline of the capitalist marketplace. Repeated attempts to inspire, entice, and cajole greater cooperation had brought meager results. The guarantee of full employment, persistent labor shortages, and the ideology that this was a workers' state rendered whatever coercion that did occur short-term and generally ineffective. Now, the workers were being asked to work harder, longer, with less job security, and if not for less wages at least for wages that buy less, and all for a promise of more consumer goods at some later time, a promise the majority of workers no longer believe. As always in market economies, the talk from on top is about satisfying pent-up demand and liberating people's desire to get rich, but where the carrot will not or cannot work, the system has at its disposal the biggest stick of all, which is the threat of unemployment with its accompanying social misery.

(2) *Hide the hand,* that is, the Party's hand, that disciplines them by giving economic powers that once belonged to central planners, a group easily identified with the Party, to managers and owners on the enterprise level. The latter, in turn, can blame the impersonal forces of the market for whatever hardships they inflict upon the workers. From the vantage point of the Regents, a major problem of the old system was that it was too transparent. For all the complexity of Soviet bureaucracy, no one ever had any doubts about who made major economic decisions and, consequently, about who to blame when things went wrong. In a market economy, fundamental truths are never so plain. What stands out in the market are the prices of things and the apparent freedom of people to buy and sell whatever they wish without any outside interference. What is carefully hidden from view are the underlying social relations among the workers that get expressed in the prices of their products, as well as the role of monopoly and monetary power in determining both what is available to buy and what people may have to sell.[8] This applies equally to labor power, capital, and finished commodities. In this way, the responsibility of the particular social system and those who rule over it for employment levels and conditions, as well as for what gets made and who benefits most and least from how it gets distributed, is transferred to the decisions of individual buyers and sellers in the market. The market as such, ab-

---

8. For appearance/essence, see pp. 10–11, and 45–6.

stracted from its historically specific context and functions, acquires the aura of a natural phenomenon, and who but a madman would set out to correct nature?[9]

(3) *Have the workers participate in their own mystification.* This is where *Glasnost* comes in: having altered appearances through the above-mentioned reforms, workers can now be allowed to speak freely about what they see, since what they see only confirms their new powerlessness. If people are to believe that they have no one to blame for their worsened economic situation but themselves, because they didn't work hard enough or they suffer from bad luck, they must come to this conclusion on their own. They can't simply be informed, without a chance to question and criticize. The Soviet people had become so skeptical about official pronouncements that they have ceased to believe even the most elemental truths. Witness the widespread disbelief in the inequalities and other injustices in the United States, just because their own government was the messenger. Hence the need for *Glasnost*, for openness.

Rousseau (1969, 277) had pointed out long ago that "there is no subjugation so perfect as that which keeps the appearance of freedom, for in that way one captures volition itself." This lesson has been confirmed time and again throughout the capitalist West, and now Gorbachev has sought to apply it to the Soviet Union. The essential first step was to organize the structure of everyday life so that what emerges on the surface of events, what people see and experience, directs their attention to the economic decisions of individuals as consumers and workers. It is in this manner that *Perestroika* and *Glasnost* are each necessary to the success of the other.

(4) *Shift the basis of the Party's legitimacy as ruler from the working class to the public at large* by setting up Western-style democratic elections to the government. The Communist Party hopes, of course, to retain political power but as the representative of a new coalition, the majority of voters, in which the workers will be one faction among others. In the process, the organic tie which bound the Party, even as Regent, to the working class has been sundered once and for all. There is no longer any reason for the Party to take special account of the interests of workers, and government decisions no longer have to be rationalized in these terms. Deprived of their privileged status, the workers have lost whatever basis they once possessed for demanding special consideration or for complaining when they didn't receive it. There is no longer any reason for them to be treated better than any other group in society, which also means other groups may be treated better than the workers, or rather,

---

9. For abstraction of extension, see pp. 39–53.

since theory lagged behind practice on this matter, for this to occur more openly than before. The political as well as the economic structures for a more thoroughgoing exploitation of the working class are now in place.

Given that the workers never really had much influence over the decisions of the Party, this shift in what the effective rulers of society take to be the basis of their legitimacy may seem to be of little importance. On the contrary, it is of crucial importance, because it occurs at a time when the workers are finally in a position to decide on their interests for themselves, and at a point in Soviet society when these interests have become increasingly opposed to those of managers, bureaucrats, members of the repressive apparat, and so-called entrepreneurs, all of whom have significant representation in the Party. Viewing their class as the only legitimate rulers in society and being confirmed in this view by the official ideology could have proved of inestimable value in any major confrontation between the workers and the Party. The rise of Solidarity in Poland provided the leaders of the CPSU with a frightening example of how this advantage might play itself out. The Regency, as we saw, had reached its limit, and before the workers could take control of the state power that had been functioning in its name, the Party took the initiative and, in effect, changed the rules of the political game.

While most of the discussions of Soviet reforms have centered on the dismantling of an authoritarian state, on expanded freedoms and the development if democratic institutions, it is essential to see that workers have no more control over key economic decisions than before, that profit maximization is replacing serving social needs as the main criterion for determining production choices, and that the workers no longer enjoy a privileged status in society. And for the Party, under its current leadership, it is the latter set of achievements and not the former that are the main objectives of *Perestroika* and *Glasnost*.

Some will object that the interpretation offered here seriously underplays the divisions within the Communist Party as well as the divisions between the Party leadership and its non-Party liberal opposition. However, I consider it more revealing that all the speeches at the 28th Party Congress (July 1990) were in favor of *Perestroika* and *Glasnost* than that some criticisms were raised over what to emphasize and how fast to proceed.[10] It was also at this Congress that Gorbachev, a lifelong apparatchik chosen by other lifelong apparatchiks, declaimed that *Perestroika* was the only way that the Communist Party could stay at the center of Soviet life. "Otherwise, other forces," he warned, "will push us onto the sidelines and we will lose our positions" (*Herald Tribune*, July 1990, 6).

10. For identity/difference, see pp. 13–14, 42–4, 73–5.

I see no reason not to take this remarkably candid admission at face value. The "forces" that have Gorbachev so worried are not, as most foreign observers believe, economic liberals who stand to the right of the Party ("left" for the *New York Times*), but a conscious and aroused working class.

As for the non-Party (chiefly ex-Party and equally non–working class) opposition, who would move even faster toward a full market economy, here too the similarities with Gorbachev's program far outweigh the differences.[11] In virtually all these disputes between different factions of what Daniel Singer has called the Soviet "privilegensia," the main albeit unspoken point at issue is how best to save their collective skins from the threat of a real dictatorship of the proletariat. Whether the parties involved are fully conscious of this or are partly victims of their own rhetoric is, of course, another question. No doubt some are conscious and some are not. It is even possible that Gorbachev and his advisers did not lay out their initial plans in the crude and unqualified manner in which they are formulated above. No matter, for this is what their plans come down to. This is what they really mean. And if the Communist Party leaders once thought that introducing some market mechanisms and retaining a significant degree of central planning would be enough to achieve their goals, the logic of events both in the Soviet Union and in the world capitalist system soon taught them otherwise. Gorbachev had to learn, as he says, that when it comes to the market one cannot be partly pregnant (*Herald Tribune*, June 1990,1).[12]

III

Well, will it work? This is really two questions. First, will it work for the Communist Party? Will they, or at least their leaders, retain power? And, second, will it work for society? Will it resolve the Soviet Union's economic problems? As for whether the Regent will retain power, my answer is "no." Given democratic elections, why should people vote for Communists, even ex-Communists, to put "liberal" economic policies into effect when there are real liberals available to do it? Recent elections in Eastern Europe are a clear sign of what is in store for the CPSU in the very near future. Here the leaders of the Communist Party badly miscalculated.

What about the country? Will *Perestroika* and *Glasnost* resolve the economic crisis? Here, too, unfortunately, my answer has to be "no." If

---

11. Ibid.
12. For abstraction of extension, see pp. 39–53.

Marxist materialism has one basic lesson, it is this: "You can't make something out of nothing." Seventy years ago, the CPSU ignored this lesson and tried to build socialism with "nothing," that is, with none of the necessary material conditions of industry, wealth, skill levels, and democratic traditions. It should be no surprise, therefore, that they failed. Today, they are making the same kind of idealist mistake in trying to construct a version of capitalism without any of the main building blocks of capitalism present.[13] And I am talking not only about Gorbachev's plan but also about all the variations on it offered by his liberal opposition.

Let me just mention three preconditions for capitalism that are missing: first, there is no capitalist class with sufficient accumulated wealth to buy up existing industries, let alone invest in their much-needed modernization. Mafia and managers with some savings, even with the addition of a few foreign companies, don't amount to a capitalist class. Second, there is no working class of the kind an emerging capitalist society requires, that is a desperately poor, beaten down, malleable people ready to do anything to survive. The embers of pride, self-confidence and egalitarianism still found among today's workers will not be put out so quickly. Third, there are no foreign markets for most of what a Soviet capitalism would produce since these are already glutted with better quality and probably cheaper goods from Japan, Korea, Brazil, etc. As if this weren't enough, the timing for acquiring foreign investments and loans, and new markets for anything but raw materials, could not be worse as a result of the economic decline now occurring throughout the capitalist world.[14] There is an old Chinese proverb that says, "Don't tie your boat to tail of capitalist dog just as it is about to go over the waterfalls." But, then, lately even the Chinese haven't been paying much attention to this one.

To conclude: how best to characterize the Soviet Union? It is a Regency of the Proletariat. What then is *Perestroika* and *Glasnost*? It is a counterrevolution, a preemptive strike against the working class. Will it work for the Communist Party? No. For Soviet society as a whole? No. It is unlikely to take seventy years for this idealist attempt to build capitalism in the Soviet Union to fail, but fail it will, and fail decisively.

Paradoxically enough, the objective conditions for socialism in the USSR are now largely present, but because of the unhappy experience with a regime that called itself "socialist" the subjective conditions are absent. It will probably take an experience with a poorly functioning market economy operating in harness with political dictatorship—the most likely next stage—for these subjective conditions to reappear and

---

13.   For identity/difference, see. pp. 13–14, 42–4, and 73–5.
14.   For abstraction of extension, see pp. 39–53.

for a socialist revolution to become a possibility. (This assumes, of course, that in the process the objective conditions embodied in the highly developed economy are not destroyed.) On the other hand, somewhere in the midst of all this, the Soviet Union might be saved by a socialist revolution in the West as our capitalist economy goes into a tailspin. But as an American might say, "Don't count on it." Finally, there is a slight possibility, a very slight one, that Soviet workers, sensing what is about to happen, will make the long-deferred socialist revolution and abort the market dictatorship before it becomes fully operative. Socialism, real, democratic, Marxist socialism is a possible outcome of the current crisis in the Regency of the Proletariat. It is a small possibility, but given the stakes and the horrendous alternative, for the working class at least, there is really no other game in town.[15]

References

International Herald Tribune. June 23, 1990.
International Herald Tribune. July 11, 1990.
Rousseau, Jean-Jacques. 1969. *Emile, Oeuvres Complètes IV.* Paris: Ed. Gallimard.
Sweezy, P., and H. Magdoff, 1990. "Perestroika and the Future of Socialism, Part 2." *Monthly Review*, April.

---

15.   One year after this essay was written, the Regency of the Proletariat appears to have collapsed. In reality it has only entered into a new phase, under new flags and slogans, in which most of the Party elite remain in power as part of an alliance with what had been its ex-Party, liberal opposition. Its free market reforms have no more chance of succeeding now than before, and the threat to its rule from the working class, despite its current low level of consciousness, is greater than ever (May, 1992).

7

The Ideal of Academic Freedom as the Ideology of Academic Repression, American Style

Mark Twain said that we Americans enjoy "three unspeakably precious things: freedom of speech, freedom of conscience, and the prudence never to practice either of them." (1899, 198) Fortunately, some in the universities as elsewhere in our society have lacked this prudence, but they have generally paid a price for it.

Three brief studies: in 1915, Scott Nearing, a socialist professor of economics, was fired from the University of Pennsylvania for publicly opposing the use of child labor in coal mines. With an influential mine owner on the board of trustees, the president of the university decided he had to let Nearing go. As far as I can discover, he is the first professor fired from an American university for his radical beliefs and activities (Frumkin, 1981).

Some have argued that this honor belongs to Edward Bemis, who was dismissed from the University of Chicago in 1894. A major charge in this case was that Bemis had the poor judgment to hold discussions with union leaders during the famous Pullman railroad strike of that year. In a letter to the president of the University of Chicago, Bemis admitted that he had talked to the union officials, but—he insisted—only with the purpose of urging them to give up the strike. It didn't help. The strike went on—and the dismissal stuck (Metzger, 152 ff.). However, in light of Bemis' admission, I find it difficult to view him as the first radical to lose his job because of his political beliefs. That honor belongs to Nearing. This doesn't mean that the universities were tolerant earlier. Before Nearing, there simply were no radical professors, not ones who spoke out, anyway.

Second, in 1940 the Rapp-Coudert Committee of the New York State legislature began its infamous investigation of subversives in the Municipal College System (now City University of New York-CUNY). By 1942, over forty professors were fired or did not get their contracts renewed either because they were communists or because they refused to divulge their political beliefs and connections (Schappes, 1982). [1]

---

1. On October 1981, the board of trustees of the City University of New York voted an apology to Morris Schappes and other victims of the Rapp-Coudert Committee's investigation that took place some forty years before. Similar apologies for "excesses" committed during

Third, in 1978 Joel Samoff was denied tenure by the political science department of the University of Michigan. Though he had published widely and was about to receive the university's Distinguished Service Award for outstanding contributions to the scholarly life of the university, he was faulted for not publishing enough in orthodox political science journals and for using an unscientific Marxist approach to his subject matter.

In each case, a professor's right to pursue truth in his own way was abrogated. In the Nearing case, the ax was wielded by the university's higher administration. For the CUNY forty, it was the government that was primarily responsible for the blow that befell them, while Samoff's academic demise resulted from a decision taken by a majority of his own colleagues.

Where does academic freedom lie in all this? While there is general agreement that academic freedom involves the right of teachers and students to investigate any topic they wish and to freely discuss, teach, and publish their conclusions, there is an anguished debate over where to draw the line (nowhere is everything allowed) and, more particularly, over who should be allowed to do it. Where does the threat to academic freedom come from?

The case against government interference in academic decision making is most easily made and probably most widely supported: academic freedom is assured when the government adopts a hands-off policy toward the university. Many dissatisfied professors and students, however, maintain that a greater danger to academic freedom today comes from university presidents and boards of trustees who try to impose their values and judgments on the entire university community. Still others, including such victims of peer evaluation as Joel Samoff, would argue it is faculty bias that does the most damage, that without a sincere toleration of unorthodox approaches on the part of the professorate there can be no thoroughgoing academic freedom.

The situation is more complicated still, for even the people who advocate government interference in university affairs often do so—in their words—"to protect academic freedom," in this case against the deceivers and manipulators of youth. In short, everyone is in favor of academic freedom; only the emphasis and enemies are different. In 1978, when I was denied a job as chairman of the Government Department at the University of Maryland because of my Marxist political views, I called this denial an attack on my academic freedom. The faculty, who had chosen me for the job, also said their academic freedom had been infringed upon.

---

the McCarthy period were offered recently by the boards of trustees of Reed College (in the case of Stanley Moore) and Temple University (in the case of Barrows Dunham).

Students, who wanted to study with me, made the same claim. President John Toll, who rejected me, insisted he was acting on behalf of academic freedom, his academic freedom to do what he thought best in disregard of all outside pressures. And many state politicians, whose threats of financial retribution against the university constituted the most powerful of these outside pressures, likewise spoke of defending academic freedom against the likes of me.

The problem of sorting out the various uses of "academic freedom" is both very easy and terribly complex: easy, if it is simply a matter of taking a stand, of choosing the notion of "academic freedom" that is most compatible with one's own values and declaring other uses illegitimate. It becomes complex if we try to explore the relations between these different uses to discover what as a group they reveal about the conditions they are intended to describe. It is by taking this latter path that I also hope to cast some light on the state of academic freedom in America today.

The time-honored way of breaking out of the confusion that surrounds the discussion of academic freedom is to label what has hitherto passed for a definition as the ideal, and to add the words, "Unfortunately, it doesn't always apply." The implication, of course, is that this is what most people want, and that actual practice is close and closing in on the ideal. Focusing on the ideal in this way, practice can be short-changed. What actually happens is viewed teleologically, in terms of what one thinks it is going to become eventually, in time, with patience and more propagandizing of the ideal. The possibility that the gap between the actual and the ideal is more or less fixed and *that the ideal may even play a role in keeping it so* is hardly entertained, and can't be so long as what occurs is not examined on its own terms and within its real social and political context.[2] In any case, the confusion over the different uses of "academic freedom" can never be sorted out so long as the discussion remains on the abstract level of ideas. For this, we must keep our feet on solid ground, and find out who is doing what to whom and why.[3]

The locus of our study, of course, will be the university. And not just any university, but the university in capitalist society. Can't we just examine the nature of universities in general? I think not. Why not should be evident if we look no further than the big business dominated boards of trustees of all our major universities. If we were studying institutions of higher learning in a foreign country and discovered that a majority of the members of all their boards of trustees were generals, we would not hesitate to

---

2. For abstraction of extension, see pp. 39–53.
3. For abstraction of vantage point, see pp. 67–78.

make certain conclusions about the character and aim of education there. Yet even people who know that our boards of trustees are run by a business elite seldom question why this is so or try to think through what follows from this fact. Are businesspeople really more clever than the rest of us, or more public spirited, or more concerned with the development of rational and critical thought? If not, we must try to understand what capitalists want from the university and what they do there, and how all this relates to academic freedom.[4]

Capitalism is a form of society where the means of production are privately owned, and all production decisions are made on the basis of what will earn the largest profits for owners. So much holds true for the entire history of our republic. But the American capitalist system has also undergone a number of major changes. Marxist economist Sam Bowles points out that the capitalist economy and riding a bicycle have one important thing in common: in both, forward motion is necessary for stability (1976, 237). As capitalism grows and changes so does the nature of its requirements from education, as, indeed, from other sectors of capitalist life.

Among the major developments in American capitalism over the last one hundred years are the following: with the growth of technology, the amount of capital investment going to workers in the form of wages has decreased as a percentage of total investment, leading to a general and long-term squeeze on profits (surplus-value, of which profit is a portion, is produced by labor; hence, a relatively smaller percentage of investment going to labor means a constricted base for profits); the percentage of the work force that is self-employed (entrepreneurs and professionals) has gone down from 40 percent to 10 percent; in the same period, the number of managers and professionals on salaries (chiefly employed by big business) has increased sevenfold; in big business, complex hierarchies have developed that determine power, status, and salary; more jobs require minimal skills; an intensification of the division of labor has led to an increased fragmentation of tasks for both white- and blue-collar workers, decreasing the degree of control that each individual has over his or her job; mainly in order to maintain profits, the government has come to play a more direct role in running the economy on behalf of the capitalist class; and ideology—that is, one-sided, partial, essentially mystifying interpretations of reality—has spread from the factory to the media, market, courts, and schools, chiefly as a means of disguising the increasingly obvious pro-capitalist bias of the state.

The major changes that have occurred in American higher education

---

4. For abstraction of level of generality, see pp. 53–67.

during the last one hundred years reflect these developments in the capitalist mode of production, and have operated in general to facilitate the efficient functioning of the new capitalist order. For example, whereas in 1870 only 2 percent of the eighteen to twenty one age group went to college, today it is about 50 percent. The liberal arts and classics that formed the core of the old university curriculum have been replaced by science, math, public administration, business, and other vocational training. In both the natural and social sciences, universities have assumed more and more research and development tasks for private industry, upping their profits by reducing their necessary costs.[5]

Increasingly, university life has been organized on the basis of a complex system of tests, grades, and degrees, so that people know exactly where they fit, what they deserve, what has to be done to rise another notch on the scale, and so on. Discounting—as most educators do—their negative effects on scholarship, critical thinking, and collegiality, these practices have succeeded in instilling a new discipline and respect for hierarchy, lowering students' expectations, and generally in creating a sense that you get what you work for and have talent for—and, therefore, that failure is due to some personal fault (laziness, stupidity, or bad will).

Overseeing this reorganization of the academy, codifying its ends and rationalizing its means, dispensing incentives, cost accounting, building bridges to the "community" (chiefly business leaders and politicians) is the work of a vastly expanded cast of professional managers. At Columbia University, for example, in the period 1948–68, the faculty grew by 50 percent, the student body by 100 percent, and the administration by 900 percent (Brown, 46).[6]

Of all the ideas that help keep democratic capitalism in the United States functioning as smoothly as it does, none is more important than the idea of "equality of opportunity." Here, too, the university has a special role to play. It seems that people are willing to live with great social and economic inequalities if they believe they had, or have, or will have the chance to make it up, or even that their children will have such a chance. In the nineteenth century, the belief in equality of opportunity was fed chiefly by the existence of "free" land in the West. When the frontier closed, this dream was kept alive by the possibility of starting a small

---

5. For abstracting past aspects of a process, see pp. 28–31.

6. For more extended discussions of the developments in higher education and their relationship to the changing requirements of capitalism, see Bowles and Gintis, *Schooling*; Ira Shor, *Critical Teaching and Everyday Life* (Boston: South End Press, 1980); Martin Carnoy, ed., *Schooling in Corporate Society: The Political Economy of Education in America* (New York: David McKay, 1972); and Henry A. Giroux, *Ideology, Culture and the Process of Schooling* (Philadelphia: Temple University Press, 1981).

business that, with a little luck and hard work, might one day make you rich. Now that nine out of every ten small businesses end in failure (according to U.S. Commerce Department statistics), it is our relatively open system of higher education that serves as living evidence for the existence of equality of opportunity.

For universities to play their appointed role in this capitalist drama, it is not enough that everyone who wants to get an education be able to get into a university. In both its structure and content, higher education must appear to give everyone a more or less equal chance to prepare for the best jobs. Should the universities be perceived as vocational schools, providing low-level skills and indoctrinating students with the values and attitudes deemed important by their future capitalist employers, as a simple continuation of the tracking system already begun in high schools, the crucial ideological work of the university in promoting belief in the existence of a real equality of opportunity would suffer irreparable damage.

The university's role in helping to justify democratic capitalism carries over, as we might expect, to the content of its courses. Particularly today, with the government's more direct involvement in the economy on the side of the capitalists and so many young members of the working class in college with time to read and think about it, there is a great need for ever more sophisticated rationalizations for the status quo. In this effort, the university must maintain the appearance of allowing all points of view, including some critical of capitalism, to freely contest. Otherwise, the ideas that emerge from universities would be tainted, viewed as propaganda rather than "knowledge" and "science," and have less hold on people. Not only students would be affected, but also the general public, many of whose beliefs and prejudices receive their legitimation as value-free social science by academic decree.[7]

Finally, to complete our list of the main ways in which higher education serves capitalism in the modern period, we should mention that the universities provide local capitalists with a reserve army of low paid, nonunionized, part-time workers, while at the same time offering a kind of custodial care for young people who cannot find jobs, becoming in Ira Shor's apt phrase "warehouses for unneeded workers" (1980, 6). Here, too, students will only willingly accept these degrading roles and conditions if they believe they are receiving a real education and being prepared for something better.

Does all this mean that the university is not a place where knowledge

---

7. For appearance/essence, see pp. 10–11, and 45–6.

and skills get passed on from one generation to the next, and where some people teach and others actually learn how to think more critically? Not al all. Like universities in all periods and virtually all societies, American universities embody, to one degree or another, all the fine qualities that are paraded in Commencement Day speeches.[8] Unfortunately, these speeches neglect to mention other functions which clearly stamp our universities as products of capitalist society, and any attempt to grasp the dynamics of the present situation must begin by focusing on these historically specific qualities.[9]

The time has come to reintroduce the idea of academic freedom and to see how it works. The first thing that strikes us from the above account is that American universities require a little critical thought, which means a few critical teachers, which means too, a little academic freedom for them to work, in order for universities to function as they are meant to and have to in capitalist society. The presence of some radical professors helps to legitimate the bourgeois ideology that comes out of universities as "social science" and the universities themselves as something more than training centers. So a few radical professors are necessary to make the point that real freedom of thought, discussion, and so on exist and that people in the university have the opportunity to hear all sides in the major debates of the day.

But a key question is: at what point do a few radical professors become too many?[10] For the presence of radicals in universities at a time of burgeoning working class enrollment and a declining economy constitutes a real and growing threat to the capitalist system. In the story of the Emperor's New Clothes, it didn't take many voices to convince the crowd that the emperor was naked. At a time of deepening economic crisis, the promises of capitalism are no less vulnerable.

Given the need for some radical professors and the dangers of too many, the debate over where to draw the line, who should draw it, and on the basis of what criteria goes on continually. It goes on in government, in university administrations, and among the faculty in almost every university department. Because the language in which these questions are posed is different on each level, even participants are not always aware that they are involved in the same debate. Without explicit coordination, using apparently different criteria and procedures, and while lost in their own internecine disputes over turf and power, the government, university ad-

---

8.   For interpenetration of polar opposites, see pp. 14, 48, and 64–5.
9.   For abstraction of level of generality, see pp. 53–67.
10.   For quantity/quality change, see pp. 15, 48–9, and 76.

ministrations, and departmental facilities are all taking part in the same balancing act.[11]

Viewed from the perspective of their victims (of those who suffer because they fall on the other side of the line), however, the practice of academic freedom in our universities appears as a kind of policing mechanism that operates on three levels.[12] On the level of government, its means (repressive laws, administrative harassment, threats to reduce funding, etc.) and ends are pretty evident, though even here there is some attempt to disguise the ends in terms of preserving students' academic freedom from the predations of deceptive radical professors. For the administration, the disguise takes the forms of preserving university autonomy from direct government interference on one hand, and making universities run smoothly (radicals tend to make waves) on the other. At the faculty level, this "internal policing," in the words of Marxist scholar Milton Fisk, takes the form of making so-called objective, value-neutral decisions on what constitutes political science or economics or philosophy, and which journals in each discipline warrant the academic Good Housekeeping Seal of Approval—so that publishing elsewhere, which usually means in radical journals, doesn't count for promotion, tenure, and the like (1972, 16).[13]

Only on the first level, that of government, is academic repression expressed in political terms, as an effort to keep radicals or Marxists out of the university because of their political beliefs. Hence, whenever governments are forced to act against radicals, the ideological work of the university, which relies so heavily on the assumption of tolerance, is seriously jeopardized. Better by far if university administrators, using institutional arguments, refuse to hire radical professors or turn them down for tenure. Best of all, of course, is when departmental faculties, using what appear to be purely professional criteria, take the initiative themselves. Consequently, and as a general rule, politicians get involved in academic repression, or threaten to do so, only when university administrators fail to act "responsibly," or give signs that they are about to; while administrators overrule their faculty on this matter only when it is the latter who have failed to act "responsibly."[14]

In distinguishing among the forms of academic repression peculiar to the government, university administrators, and departmental faculties, I do not mean to suggest that these three levels are autonomous. Quite the contrary. The influence of the government on university administrations—

---

11.   For identity/difference, see pp. 13–14, 42–4, and 73–5.

12.   For abstraction of vantage point, see pp. 67–78.

13.   Along with the Brown article cited above, Fisk's essay represents the best of what little work Marxists have done on the subject of academic freedom.

14.   For identity/difference, see pp. 13–14, 42–4, and 73–5.

for example, through appointing presidents and boards of trustees, determining budgets, setting research priorities, licensing programs, etc.— is so overwhelming that one scholar, Michael Brown, would have us view administrations in public universities as part of the state apparatus (1979, 37–39).[15] The situation in what are still called "private" universities differs only in degree. Nor do I wish to play down the ties of interests and values that bind government, university administrations, and most departmental faculties to the capitalist class, a connection Milton Fisk tries to highlight by designating university professors a "class of functionaries" with a special servitor relationship to capitalists.[16] I have been chiefly concerned, however, to examine how the contradictory functions of the capitalist university (in particular, educating, socializing, and legitimating capitalist social relations) result in different kinds of academic repression, which turn out, upon analysis, to be different aspects of the same thing; and this *just because* of the intimate ties (sketched by Brown, Fisk, and others) among the capitalist class, the government, university administrations, and most faculty.[17]

As regards academic freedom, what I have been arguing is that a kind of academic freedom already exists. It takes the form of a three-tiered mechanism of academic repression. It is the way this repression functions, for whom and against what.[18] The underside of who is allowed to teach is who cannot; just as what cannot be studied is organically related to what can be studied. Setting this ever-changing boundary is the act of freedom of some, which determines the kind (muted) and degree (very little) of freedom available to all. Unfortunately, academic freedom, interpreted as the actual practice of freedom in the academy, its expression as repression, is not quite what we always thought it was. What, then, can be said about what we always thought it was, or what is often referred to as the ideal of academic freedom?

First, it is clear that as long as the capitalist class controls the universities, which is to say as long as capitalism exists, the gap between the ideal of academic freedom and its practice (described above) is more or less fixed. But I have also suggested that this ideal itself may play a role in keeping this gap fixed, that rather than part of the solution the ideal of academic freedom may be part of the problem. How can this be so? Partly, it is so because the ideal of academic freedom helps to disguise and distort an essentially repressive practice by presenting it as an imperfect

---

15. For abstraction of vantage point, see pp. 67–78.
16. Ibid.
17. For contradiction, see pp. 15–17, 50–3, 63–5, and 76–7. For identity/difference, see pp. 13–14, 42–4, and 73–5.
18. For abstraction of extension, see pp. 39–53; for vantage point, see pp. 67–78.

version of what should be. Putting what everyone is said to favor in the front (and at the start) relegates what actually exists to the role of a passing qualification. Viewed in this way (and in this order), the dynamics of who is doing what to whom and why, together with the structural reforms needed to change things, can never be understood.[19]

Second, beginning as the admittedly inadequate description of real events, the ideal of academic freedom gradually substitutes itself as an explanation of what is happening that is so feeble that, with minor qualifications, all the worst villains can embrace it. Though everyone may favor academic freedom, it is in the nature of ideals—it is said—that they can never be fully realized. Something similar occurs with the ideal of consumer sovereignty in which the assumed goal of the exercise replaces and then helps to explain what people actually do in supermarkets, where they generally choose products that they have been socialized to want. Likewise, the ideal of democracy plays a similar twofold role in respect to what happens in real elections, in which money and control of media play the decisive roles. In every instance, asserting a valued goal becomes the means for misrepresenting and explaining away a reality that has little to do with it, *except* insofar as this reality requires for its continued existence peoples' misuse of this goal. In other words, it is only because most people in the university misunderstand academic repression in terms of an imperfect academic freedom that academic freedom can continue to function so effectively as academic repression. If the practice of academic freedom in capitalism is academic repression, the ideal of academic freedom is the ideology that both permits and provides a cover for its occurrence.

So much follows from privileging the qualities of academic freedom as an ideal, but the contribution that the ideal of academic freedom makes to preserving the status quo also comes from its narrow focus on freedom. Talk of freedom, whether in the marketplace, in politics, or in the academy, assumes equality in the conditions that permit people to use their freedom or the irrelevance of such conditions. For freedom is not just about wanting something, but includes the ability to do or have what one wants. It is a want embodied in a practice, but, unlike the simple want, the practice requires the existence of certain conditions. Unfortunately, in a class divided society, such conditions are never equal and always relevant. Simply put, some people have the money, jobs, education, and so forth to act freely, and others do not. In every case, the privileged few also benefit from a ready-made rationalization of their privileges: they are simply making use of their freedom. Let others, they say, try to do as much.[20]

---

19. For abstraction of vantage point in the critique of ideology, see pp. 70–3.
20. For abstraction of extension in the critique of ideology, see pp. 26, 41, 45–6.

In the academy, the people with power use their freedom to repress radicals in the ways described. If the police mechanisms embodied in the practice of academic freedom give them the means to do this, it is the ideal of academic freedom that gives them an effective way of rationalizing it. Hence the constant patter about exercising their academic freedom as they go about their work of repression. In the university, as throughout capitalist society, a commitment to freedom in the absence of an equally strong commitment to social justice carries with it the seeds of even greater injustice. For the ideal of academic justice to take its place alongside the ideal of academic freedom, however, we shall have to await the coming of a society that no longer needs its universities to help reproduce and rationalize existing inequalities, that is, a socialist society.

So far I have examined the role that the ideal of academic freedom plays in keeping things as they are, but now I am only too pleased to admit that this ideal also plays a part in helping to change them.[21] That is, at the same time that the ideal of academic freedom hides, distorts, and helps to rationalize academic repression by government, university administrations, and departmental faculties, it also opens up a little space and provides some justification for the presentation of critical opinion. Rhetorically and occasionally procedurally, it also serves as a modest defense for radical teachers who avail themselves of this space. While wishing doesn't make it so and error exacts compound interest, what people believe to be true (even it false) and what they consider good (even if impossible) are not without influence. If only through constant repetition, liberal cant occasionally takes hold, particularly on younger members of the academy, producing a subspecies of academic freedom groupies, people too afraid to act upon their ideas but willing to support those who do.[22] With the help of the few real exceptions, liberals who try to incorporate their beliefs into their daily lives (a self-destructive impulse for all but the most established scholars), the ideal of academic freedom sometimes plays a progressive role in the struggle to extend the boundaries of what can be studied in our universities.

The ideal of academic freedom, vague, unclear, contradictory, but repeated often enough, also exercises, in my view, a very general restraining influence on what the perpetrators of academic repression are able and even willing to do. It is not always true that it is better to deal with honest villains than with hypocritical ones. In our understandable disgust with their hypocrisy, many radical critics have neglected to look for its positive side. The complex and occasionally humanizing influence of hypocrisy

---

21. For interpretation of polar opposites, see pp. 14, 48, and 64–5.
22. For quantity/quality change, see pp. 15, 48–9, and 76.

on hypocrites, in the university as indeed throughout capitalist society, requires further, serious examination.

Finally, and most important, the ideal of academic freedom also helps contribute to the development of critical thinking in the university insofar as it contains within itself elements of such thinking. At its best, this means recognizing, as part of the ideal, how the conditions of modern capitalist society have turned the practice of academic freedom into academic repression and used the ideal to cover its tracks. A critically constituted ideal contains within it the conditions of its own misuse as well as the structural changes necessary to reverse this process.[23] Saved from displays of moral outrage, we are freed to work for academic freedom by helping to build the egalitarian conditions that are necessary for it to exist. This includes a demand for academic freedom not just for teachers and students but for workers and others who today are penalized for freely expressing their opinions. In developing this expanded understanding of the ideal of academic freedom, in sharing it in the university and with the public at large, we are beginning the work of putting it into practice. Academic freedom, by this interpretation, lives and grows in the conscious struggle for a socialist society.

Unfortunately, none of these progressive trends are dominant. At present, they are all subordinate to the role played by academic freedom in helping to police the university, and only deserve our attention once this central fact has been made clear. Otherwise, there is a danger of falling victim to all the distortions mentioned above and even contributing to them. But once the capitalist context in which academic freedom appears has been laid out, once its main function in this context is understood, its other role in helping to undermine capitalism requires equal attention.

In summary, academic freedom is about both freedom and repression, how they are linked to each other not only as opposites, but also as preconditions, effects and aspects, each of the other.[24] Their proper order of treatment is first repression and then freedom.[25] In this way, freedom is less distorted and the contribution that freedom (in its ideological form) makes to repression is minimized. The Marxist approach to academic freedom involves analyzing it as a practice, one inextricably tied to capitalist power relations, and as an accompanying ideology.[26] This analysis embodies and helps to develop a new critical practice and an alternative

---

23. For abstraction of extension, see pp. 39–53.
24. For internal relations, see pp. 33–9.
25. For abstraction of vantage point, see pp. 67–78.
26. For abstraction of extension, see pp. 39–53; for level of generality, see pp. 53–67; for vantage point, see pp. 67–78.

vision which can also be subsumed under a now broadened notion of academic freedom.

What then is the situation today? What is the state of these contradictory tendencies in academic freedom in the winter of 1991? [27] The first thing to remark is that there has been a considerable increase in the number of Marxist and other kinds of radical professors in the universities. Together with the growing crisis in capitalism and the inability of most bourgeois scholarship to explain it, this has led to the increased legitimacy of Marxist scholarship in practically every discipline.[28] At the same time, there are also more radical professors not getting hired or tenured.

Probably the most striking development is a gradual breakdown of the three-tiered policing mechanism of academic repression described earlier. With a growth in the number of radical scholars and the increased legitimation of radical scholarship, the bottom tier, professors in the departments, is no longer excluding radicals with the regularity that it once was. I was jolted into recognizing this change by my experience at the University of Maryland, where a search committee made up of ten political scientists chose me, a Marxist, for their chair. I don't think this could have happened ten years earlier. And if this happened in political science, traditionally the most conservative of the social sciences, it is happening (though sometimes very slowly) in all disciplines, and in universities throughout the country (though many exceptions exist). In mine and other cases, this has simply forced university administrations and politicians (the second and third tiers) to take a more direct part in academic repression. But, as I have argued, there are limits to how much they can do without paying what is for them an unacceptable price in terms of legitimacy.

Consequently, on occasion, there have been important victories. Among the more prominent are Fred Block (sociology, University of Pennsylvania) and Dick Walker (geography, University of California-Berkeley), who received tenure, and Edwin Marquit (physics, University of Minnesota) who won promotion—all after protracted struggles. Though the cards are stacked against us, they are not all dealt out, and the way a particular struggle is conducted can count.

---

27. For contradiction, see pp. 15–17, 50–3, 63–5, and 76–7.

28. For the increase of Marxist scholars and the spread of Marxist scholarship in the universities, see Bertell Ollman and Edward Vernoff, eds., *The Left Academy: Marxist Scholarship on American Campuses.* Vol. 1 (New York: McGraw Hill, 1982); Vol. 2 (New York: Praeger, 1984); Vol. 3 (New York, Praeger, 1986). The collapse of the Eastern European regimes that so many have associated (wrongly) with socialism and Marxism has led to a temporary reversal of this trend. I say "temporary", because the worsening problems of capitalism continue to make Marxism necessary as the only adequate means for understanding them and socialism as the only rational and humane means for solving them.

In the coming period, I would expect to see—for reasons already given—a still greater increase in the number of radical teachers, a rise in the amount of academic repression (primarily by university administrators and to a lesser degree by the government), and—as a result of both—a continued weakening of the university's role as a legitimator of capitalist ideology. How these conflicting tendencies will finally work themselves out, of course will depend far more on the social and political struggles of the larger society than on the positions we take within the university. Yet what we do as professors will count for something in the balance, so we must become better scholars, better critics, better teachers. We will also need to be steadfast. Which brings me back to Scott Nearing.

On November 29, 1981, not quite two years before his death at the age of 100, Scott Nearing sent me a letter that he asked me to share with everyone to whom it applies:

"To my comrades in the struggle for a kindlier and juster world, I send fraternal greetings. During the present period of worldwide change and unrest, study and teaching are particularly important. We as scholars have the right and duty to teach and impart what we believe in and what we have learned. The right to do this is the keystone of our profession. The need to do it arises whenever any authority challenges our responsibility to learn and communicate—to study and to teach. The present period offers scholars and students a challenge to meet and a part to play that may have vast consequences for the future of man. My salutations to the brave men and women who are opposing and resisting the forms of reaction, regression, and despotism in North America."

References

Bowles, S., and H. Gintis, 1976. *Schooling in Capitalist America.* New York: Basic Books.
Brown, M. 1979. "The Ollman Case and Academic Freedom," *New Political Science,* Spring.
Fisk, M. 1972. "Academic Freedom in Class Society." In *The Concept of Academic Freedom,* edited by Edmund Pincoffs. Austin: University of Texas Press.
Frumkin, R.M. 1981. "The Eternal Professor: Scott Nearing Is Still Teaching," *ZEDEK* (February).
Metzger, W.P. 1961. *Academic Freedom in the Age of the University.* New York: Columbia University Press.
Ollman, B., and Vernoff, E., eds. 1982. *The Left Academy: Marxist Scholarship on American Campuses.* Vol. 1. New York: McGraw Hill; 1984. Vol. 2. New York: Praeger; 1986. Vol. 3. New York: Praeger.
Schappes, M.U. 1982. "Forty Years Later—But Not Too Late," *Jewish Currents* (April).
Shor, I. 1980. *Critical Teaching and Everyday Life.* Boston: South End Press.
Twain, M. 1899. *Following the Equator: A Journey Around the World.* New York: Harper and Brothers.

8

Studying History Backward: A Neglected Feature of Marx's Materialist Conception of History

History is the story of the past, and like any story, it begins in the past and proceeds forward to the present or however near the present one wants to take it. This is how it happened. This is also the order in which this story is usually told. It doesn't follow, however, that this is the ideal order for studying the meaning of the story, especially as regards its final outcome. Marx, for one, believed that we could best approach how the past developed into the present by adopting the vantage point of the present to view the conditions that gave rise to it—in other words, if we studied history backward.[1] In his words, "the actual movement starts from existing capital—i.e., the actual movement denotes developed capitalist production, which starts from and presupposes its own basis" (1963, 513).

This is not a lesson to be gleaned from most writers on Marx's materialist conception of history, where the most popular debates deal with the nature of the "economic factor" and the effect it is presumed to have on the rest of society, with historical periodization, relative autonomy, and, above all, the paradoxical juxtaposition in Marx's writings of freedom and determinism. Irrespective of their political views, virtually all sides in these debates examine history in the order in which it happened. Thus, whether one takes changes in the forces of production, or in the relations of production, or in economic structures, or in material existence as determining new developments in the social order (and no matter how strong or weak a sense is given to the notion of "determine"), what brings about the change is generally treated first and the change that is brought about second, with the latter being viewed from the vantage point of the former, as its "necessary" result. Basing themselves on the order in which

---

1. For abstraction of vantage point, see pp. 67–78.

Marx often presents his conclusions—"The hand mill gives you society with the feudal lord; the steam mill society with the industrial capitalist"— they have assumed, wrongly, that this is also the order in which Marx conducted his studies and would have us conduct ours (n.d., 122).

Marx's unusual approach to studying history is rooted in his acceptance of the Hegelian philosophy of internal relations, the much-neglected foundation of his entire dialectical method. Based on this philosophy, each of the elements that come into Marx's analysis includes as aspects of what it is all those other elements with which it interacts and without which it could neither appear nor function as it does. In this way, labor and capital, for example, in virtue of their close interaction, are conceived of as aspects of each other. Labor power could not be sold or get embodied in a product over which workers have no control if there were no capitalists to buy it; just as capitalists could not use labor to produce surplus-value if labor power were not available for sale. It is in this sense that Marx calls capital and labor "expressions of the same relation, only seen from the opposite pole" (1971, 491). Likewise, the unfolding of this interaction over time, its real history, is viewed as internally related to is present forms. Things are conceived of, in Marx's words, "as they are and *happen*" (my emphasis), so that the process of their becoming is as much a part of what they are as the qualities associated with how they appear and function at this moment (1964, 57). [2]

With the philosophy of internal relations, a major problem arises whenever one wants to stress a particular aspect or temporal segment of this ongoing interaction without seeming to deny or trivialize its other elements. One of the main ways Marx tried to resolve this problem is with the notion of precondition and result. Like contradiction, metamorphosis, and quantity/quality change—though less well known than any of these— the notion precondition and result enables Marx to pursue his studies more effectively by bringing certain aspects of change and interaction into sharper focus. Specifically, precondition and result is a double movement that processes in mutual interaction undergo in becoming both effects and makers of each other's effect simultaneously. For this, the two must be viewed dynamically (it is a matter of *becoming* a precondition and *becoming* a result), and organically (each process only takes place in and through the other). [3]

According to Marx, capital and wage-labor are "continually pre-supposed" and "continuing products" of capitalist production (Marx, 1971,

---

2. For internal relations, see pp. 33–9.
3. For abstraction of extension, see pp. 39–53; for vantage point, see pp. 67–78.

492). Indeed, "Every precondition of the social production process is at the same time its results, and every one of its results appears simultaneously as its preconditions. All the production relations within which the process moves are therefore just as much its product as they are its conditions. (1971, 507). Besides capital and wage-labor, Marx also treats foreign trade, the world market, money, and the supply of precious metals as both preconditions and results of capitalist production (1971, 253; 1957, 344). Of crucial importance for us is that establishing something as a precondition occurs by abstracting it from a situation that it has not only helped to bring about but of which it is itself, grasped now as a result, a fully integrated part.

Viewing precondition and result as movements, in the process of their becoming, and both of these movements as aspects of a single movement, requires in the first instance an abstraction of their extension (of what all is included) that is large enough to encompass the interaction of the elements referred to over time. Thus, as preconditions and results of one another, capital and wage-labor are each conceived of as including the other throughout the long course of their common evolution. Secondly, integrating the separate movements—in which capital serves as a precondition for wage-labor and simultaneously becomes a result of wage-labor—within a single combined movement without losing the distinctive character of each can only be done by changing vantage points for viewing them in mid-analysis. To treat labor as a precondition for capital, in other words, it is necessary to view labor from the vantage point of capital already grasped as a result, since we only know that one thing is a precondition for another when the latter has emerged in some recognizable form. It is not only that we must have the result in hand in order to examine what served it as a precondition, but it is the very occurrence of the result that transforms its major interlocking processes, its present conditions, into preconditions. Only when capital assumes the form of a result can labor take on the form of its precondition, so that the one becoming a result and the other becoming a precondition can be said to be taking place simultaneously.

However, as we saw, capital always includes wage-labor as one of its aspects. Thus, capital in its form as a result includes wage-labor, now also in the form of a result. And it is by adopting the vantage point of labor in this latter form that we can see that one of its major preconditions is capital. Here, too, and for similar reasons, labor's becoming a result and capital's becoming a precondition occur simultaneously. And this takes place simultaneously with the processes referred to above by which capital becomes a result and labor becomes one of its main preconditions. In both cases, investigating how something that exists came to be proceeds from its present form, the result, backward through its necessary preconditions.

As the interaction between processes in an organic system is ongoing, so too is the acquisition of qualities that makes them into preconditions and results of one another. Wage-labor has been both precondition and result of capital (and vice versa) throughout the long history of their relationship. Nevertheless, at any given moment, whenever either of these processes is singled out as a precondition, it is abstracted in extension as something less developed, possessing fewer of the qualities it eventually acquires in capitalism than the result it is said to give rise to. Such is the case whenever two or more interacting processes are re-abstracted, rearranged, to occur as a sequence. While interacting processes in an organic system are always mutually dependent, viewing their relations diachronically requires that they be abstracted at different phases in what has been a common evolution. This is necessary if Marx is to get at the distinctive influence of particular aspects of that interaction over time, avoiding the opposing pitfalls of a shallow eclecticism, where everything is equally important and hence nothing worth investigating, and causalism, where a major influence erases all others while leaving its own progress unaccounted for. It is Marx's way of establishing dialectical asymmetry, and with it of unraveling without distortion what might be called the double movement, systemic and historical, of the capitalist mode of production.

II. ——————————————————————————

The double movement of precondition and result occupies the central place in most of Marx's historical studies. Searching for the preconditions of our capitalist present is the little appreciated key with which Marx opens up the past. It is what happened in the past that gave rise to this particular present that is of special concern to him, but what exactly this was can only be adequately observed and examined from the vantage point of what it turned into. As Marx says, "The anatomy of the human being is a key to the anatomy of the ape. . . . The bourgeois economy furnishes a key to ancient economy, etc." (1904, 300). Though frequently quoted, the full implications of this remark, especially as regards Marx's method, have seldom been explored. It is essentially a directional signpost intended to guide our research, and the direction in which it points is back. And this applies to unique events and situations as well as to the processes and relations whose level of generality places them in modern capitalism, the capitalist era (the time frame for most of Marx's studies), the period of class history, or the lifetime of our species.[4]

Reading history backward in this way does not mean Marx accepts a cause at the end of history, a "motor force" operating in reverse, a teleology. Instead, it is a matter of asking where the situation under hand comes from and what had to happen for it to acquire just these qualities, i.e., of asking what are its preconditions. In this case, the search for an answer is aided by what we already know about the present, the result. Knowing how the "story" came out, placing such knowledge at the start of our investigation, sets up criteria for relevance as well as research priorities. It also provides a perspective for viewing and evaluating all that is found. Whereas, the alternative of viewing the present from some point in the past requires, first of all, that one justify the choice of just this moment with which to begin. With the result unknown, or only vaguely known and completely unanalyzed, there is no compelling reason to begin at one moment rather than another. Likewise, the choice of what kind of phenomena—social, economic, political, religious, etc.—to emphasize at the start of such a study can only be justified on the basis of a principle drawn from outside history, since the historical investigation that might confirm its value has yet to take place. Also, associated with this approach is the tendency to offer single-track causal explanations of the ties between what has been singled out as the beginning and what is found to come after. By viewing the past from the vantage point of the present, Marx, on the other hand, can focus on what is most relevant in the past without compromising his adherence to a thoroughgoing mutual interaction throughout history.

Marx said his approach used both "observation and deduction" (1973, 460). He starts by examining existing society; he then deduces what it took for such complex phenomena to appear and function as they do; after which, he continues to research in the directions indicated by these deductions. By combining observation and deduction in this way—not once, but again and again—Marx can concentrate on what in the past proved to be most important and show why, while avoiding the parlor game, all too common among historians and the general public alike, of second-guessing what might have been. By ignoring the alternatives that were present at earlier stages, Marx is often misunderstood as denying that people could have chosen differently and that things might have taken another course. But this would only be true if he had begun with a cause located sometime in the past and had treated its subsequent effect as inevitable. Instead, starting with an already existing result, he is concerned

---

4. For abstraction of level of generality, see pp. 53–67.

to uncover what did in fact determine it, what the events themselves have transformed into its necessary preconditions. It is the necessity of the *fait accompli,* and only graspable retrospectively. Necessity read backward into the past is of an altogether different order than the necessity that begins in the past and follows a predetermined path into the future.[5]

In investigating history backward, Marx makes an important distinction between preconditions that are themselves wholly results, albeit earlier forms, of their own results now functioning as preconditions, and preconditions that have at least some features that come from previous social formations. It is the difference between what capitalism requires to develop as compared to what it required to emerge in the first place. In the latter case, one precondition was the appearance in towns of large numbers of people who were willing and able to sell their labor-power and become a proletariat. This condition was met by the massive exodus of serfs from the estates due mainly to the various acts of enclosure that characterized late feudalism. Similarly, the accumulation of wealth that capitalism required in order to get under way could only come from sources other than the exploitation of labor that capital alone makes possible. Once in place, even minimally so, the capitalist mode of production accumulates wealth through its own distinctive means, reproducing in this way one of its major preconditions. In Marx's words, "The conditions and presuppositions of the becoming, of the arising, of capital presuppose precisely that it is not yet in being but merely in becoming; they therefore disappear as real capital arises, capital which itself, on the basis of its own reality, posits the conditions for its realization" (1973, 459).

The developments in feudalism that made the new turn toward capitalism possible were themselves, of course, internally related aspects of that mode of production, but they had no place or role in what came after. Marx refers to these developments as "suspended presuppositions" (*"aufgehobne Voraussetzungen"*) (1973, 461). They were necessary for the creation of capitalism, but there is no need for capitalism, once under way, to reproduce them. Examining currently existing capitalism backward through its preconditions and results leads in due course to the origins of the system. "Our method," Marx says, "indicates the points . . . where bourgeois economy as a merely historical form of the production process points beyond itself to earlier historical modes of production" (1973, 460). At this point, in order to trace the transformation of feudalism into capitalism, distinctively capitalist preconditions and results get replaced as main objects of study by the suspended presuppositions of feudalism.

---

5. For cause and determine, see pp. 36, and 65–7.

The question that guides research still is what capitalism—now viewed in its earliest stage—requires, and the direction in which study proceeds remains as before—backward.

What needs emphasizing is that Marx seldom treats feudalism as just another mode of production alongside of capitalism. Hence, feudalism's most distinctive structures at the high point of their development receive little attention. Also, feudalism is seldom examined as the mode of production that produced capitalism—hence, the relative neglect of the former's internal dynamics. Instead, feudalism almost always comes into Marx's writings as the social formation in which the immediate origins of capitalism are to be found. "The formation of capitalism," Marx says, "*is* the dissolution process of feudalism" (1971, 491). (My emphasis.) It is as an essential part of capitalism that feudalism is studied.[6] Thus, it is the particular ways in which the disintegration of feudalism occurs that is of prime interest to Marx, for it is here that he uncovers the preconditions of capitalism. And the same applies to earlier periods, for the roots of capitalism extend even there. They are all pre-capitalist, and of interest primarily as such. Consequently, moving from capitalism back through its preconditions to feudalism and slavery, there is no pretension of offering these three stages as a model of development through which every country must pass, as too often occurs when they are treated in reverse order. This is another example of the difference between necessity read backward from the present and necessity read forward from some point in the past. What's called the "Marxist periodization of history" is but another unfortunate result of standing Marx's method on its head. In sum, looking back from the vantage point of what capitalism has become to what it presupposes enables Marx to concentrate on specific features in the rubble of the past that he would otherwise miss or underplay, just as it enhances his understanding—essentially transforming the last moments of a dying system into the birthing moments of a new one—of what is found.

To be sure, Marx can also examine the relation of precondition and result from the vantage point of the former, beginning in the past and looking ahead; in which case, it is more accurate to speak of "cause" (or "condition") and "effect," and he occasionally adopts this order (and these terms) in expounding his conclusions, especially in more popular works, such as his Preface to the *Critique of Political Economy* (1904). What makes cause and effect less satisfactory as a way of organizing research is that before we have an effect it is difficult to know what constitutes the cause, or—once we've decided what the cause is—to know where the

---

6. For abstraction of extension, see pp. 39–53.

cause comes from, or—having determined that—to know where in its own evolution as the cause to begin our study. Consequently, the complex interaction by which the cause is itself shaped and made adequate to its task by the effect, now functioning in its turn as a cause, is easily lost or distorted, even where—as in Marx's case—causes and effects are viewed as internally related. If Marx still uses the formulation "cause" and "effect" (or "condition," "determine," and "produce" in the sense of "cause"), this is usually a handy shorthand and first approximation for bringing out for purposes of exposition some special feature in a conclusion whose essential connections have been uncovered by studying them as preconditions and results.[7]

Unable to follow Marx's practice in making abstractions, lacking a conception of internal relations and a workable grasp of the often conflicting demands of inquiry and exposition, most of Marx's readers have forced his words on precondition and result into a causal framework. The components of capitalism get divided into causes (or conditions, generally understood as weak or broad causes) and effects, with the result that the former, separated from their real causes, are made to appear ahistorical, possibly natural, as something that cannot be changed or even seriously questioned. Thus, when Marx presents man as a social product, the multiple ways in which people also create society are distorted if not completely missed. While, conversely, those who emphasize Marx's comments on human beings as creators of society generally miss the full impact of what is meant in his references to people as social products. Whereas, for Marx, man is "the permanent precondition of human history, likewise its permanent product and result" (1971, 491). Unable to sustain this dialectical tension, bourgeois ideology is replete with one-sided distortions that come from causal interpretations of this and other similar remarks in Marx's writings.

III.   —————————————————————————————

The same double movement of precondition and result that dominates Marx's study of the past plays a decisive role in his inquiry into the future. In the philosophy of internal relations, the future is an essential moment in the present. It is not only what the present becomes, but whatever happens in the future exists in the present, within all present forms, as potential. In the same way that Marx's fuller study of the present extends

---

7. For cause/effect, see pp. 36, 65–7.

STUDYING HISTORY BACKWARD *141*

back into its origins, it extends forward into its possible and likely outcomes. For him, anything less would detract from our understanding of
what the present is and our ability to mold it to our purposes. Antonio
Gramsci has said that for a Marxist the question "What is man?" is really
a question about what man can become (Gramsci, 1971, 351). Whether
directed at human beings, a set of institutions, or a whole society, the
unfolding of a potential has a privileged status in Marx's studies.[8] But how
does one go about studying the future as part of the present?

According to Marx, investigating the past as "suspended presuppositions" of the present "likewise leads at the same time to the points at
which the suspension of the present form of production relations gives
signs of its becoming foreshadowings of the future. Just as, on one side,
the pre-bourgeois phases appear as merely historical, i.e., suspend presuppositions, so do the contemporary conditions of production likewise
appear as engaged in suspending themselves and hence in posing the
historical presuppositions for a new state of society" (1973, 461). Whether
studying the past or the future, it is chiefly a matter of looking back,
deriving presuppositions from the forms that contain them. We have seen
Marx apply this to the past grasped as the presuppositions of the present,
but how can he grasp the present as presuppositions of a future that has
yet to occur? Whence the sense of the future that allows him to look back
at the present as its presuppositions?

There would appear to be two answers. First, and especially as regards
the near future (what lies just ahead in capitalism) and the middle future
(represented by the socialist revolution), what is expected is derived by
projecting existing tendencies (laws) and contradictions forward. The
vantage point is the present but a present that has been abstracted in
extension to include the overlapping trajectories and buildup of various
pressures that emerge from the immediate past. As regards the near future,
Marx frequently abstracted the processes he saw in the world as having a
temporal extension big enough to include what they were becoming as
part of what they are, going so far as to use the name associated with
where they are heading but have not yet arrived to refer to the whole
journey there. In this way, all labor that produces or is on the verge of
producing commodities in capitalism is called "wage-labor"; money that
is about to buy means of production is called "capital"; small businessmen
who are going bankrupt and peasants who are losing their land are referred
to as "working class," and so on (1963, 409–10, 396; Marx and Engels,
1945, 16). Marx frequently signals the futuristic bias in his naming practice

8. For abstraction of the future as an aspect of present day processes, see pp. 28–31.

with such phrases as "in itself," "in its intention," "in its destiny," "in essence," and "potentially."[9]

As regards the middle future, the moment of qualitative change not in one or a few processes but in the whole social formation of which they are part, Marx's chief point of departure is the knot of major contradictions that he found in investigating capitalism. "The fact," he says, "that bourgeois production is compelled by its own immanent laws, on the one hand, to develop the productive forces as if production did not take place on a narrow restricted social foundation, while, on the other hand, it can develop these forces only within these narrow limits, is the deepest and most hidden cause of crises, of the crying contradictions within which bourgeois production is carried on and which even at a cursory glance reveal it as only a transitional, historical form" (1971, 84). "Even at a cursory glance," Marx believes, it is clear that capitalism cannot go on much longer. All we have to see is that it builds upon and requires a social foundation—essentially, private appropriation of an expanding social product—that cannot support its growing weight.[10]

Projecting capitalism's major contradictions forward in this manner involves subjective as well as objective conditions—in Marxist terms, class struggle as well as the accumulation of capital—in their distinctive interaction. Marx never doubts that it is people who make history, but, as he is quick to add, "not in circumstances of their own choosing" (Marx and Engels, 1951, 225). Most of Marx's own work is devoted to uncovering these circumstances for the capitalist era, but always in connection with how they affect and are likely to affect the classes (the relevant abstraction for people) operating in them. Responding to pressures from their social and economic situation and to the results of their own internal socialization, these classes are further predisposed to choose and act as they do by the range of alternatives available to them. But all the circumstances pertaining to capitalism and modern capitalism that are mainly responsible for how people behave are changing.[11] Projecting the sum of such changes forward, organizing the narrowing options that they provide as contradictions, Marx can foresee a time when a renewed burst of class struggle will bring the capitalist era to a close. There is nothing, of course, in any of these unfolding and overlapping tendencies and contradictions that allows Marx to predict with absolute certainty what will happen, and especially not when and how it will happen. The future so conceived does

---

9. For abstraction of process, see pp. 28–31; for quantity/quality change, see pp. 15, 48–9, and 76.

10. For contradiction, see pp. 15–17, 50–3, 63–5, and 76–7.

11. For abstraction of level of generality, see pp. 53–67.

not fit together neatly like the pieces of a puzzle, but is itself a set of alternative outcomes, no one of which is more than highly probable. Such is the dialectical form of the future within the present, the sense of "determined" contained in what is meant by "potential."

The second way in which Marx constructs a future from which to look back at the present applies chiefly, though not solely, to the far future or socialist/communist society that he believes will follow the revolution. In studying the presuppositions of the present in the past, Marx's focus is on the capitalist character of the present and its origins in a pre-capitalist past. Unlike the qualities that exist today that partake of the human condition, the qualities that have arisen as part of capitalism can be expected to change drastically or even disappear altogether when capitalism does. Having been posited as a historically specific result, capitalist forms of life can now be posited as the historical premise for what they in turn make possible. We have simply reproduced the relations these present forms were found to have with their real past with their likely future, except that the position and therefore the role of the present has been reversed. The point is that if the forms of life associated with capitalism belong to the order of things that have historical presuppositions—which is to say, if they emerged in real historical time—they are also capable of serving as presuppositions for what follows. And for Marx, as we saw, it is the very analysis that reveals them as the one (as results) that reveals them "at the same time" as the other (as presuppositions), and in the process gives us "foreshadowings of the future."

Marx constructs his vision of the far future by abstracting out the historically specific conditions of capitalism (treating as preconditions what has proved to be historical results) as well as by projecting existing tendencies and contradictions forward, taking full account of changes in criteria and priorities that would occur under a socialist government. We learn, for example, that "The workmen, if they were dominant, if they were allowed to produce for themselves, would very soon, and without great exertion, bring the capital (to use a phrase of the vulgar economists) up to the standard of their needs." Here, the "workers, as subjects, employ the means of production—in the accusative case—in order to produce wealth for themselves. It is of course assumed here that capitalist production has already developed the productive forces of labor in general to a sufficiently high level for this revolution to take place" (1963, 580). Marx begins by removing the historically specific conditions of capitalist production that have made workers into a means for producing surplus-value (itself the result of earlier history) and then projects forward what these workers would be able to do with the instruments of production once left on their own. Having constructed some part of the socialist future from the vantage point of the present, he then reverses himself and looks back at the present from the vantage point of this future to specify one of its major preconditions, which is highly developed productive forces.

In projecting existing tendencies and contradictions into the future (whether near, middle, or far), the eventual outcome is viewed as the further extension of a result that has its central core in the present. With the shift of vantage point to the future, however, the future becomes the result, and what exists now becomes part of its extended preconditions, along with what had formerly been set off as the present's own preconditions. By having its status changed from that of a result to that of a precondition, the way the present instructs us about the future also changes. Taken as a result, present forms are used as a basis for projecting the tendencies and contradictions that constitute its own real history forward. While viewing present forms together with their origins as preconditions of the future allows Marx to use the present to help clarify the future in much the same way that he uses the past to help clarify the present. By examining earlier times from the vantage point of capitalism, as its presuppositions, Marx could learn not only what led to our present but obtain a fuller understanding of capitalism as a later development and transformation of just these presuppositions. Chiefly, it was a way of singling out what had proved to be the most important parts of our history and embedding them, now suitable altered, as essential features in a dialectically arranged present.

Similarly, our image of the future acquires greater definitiveness to the extent that important elements in present day society can be treated as its preconditions. Criteria of relevance and research priorities for studying what is coming into being are also affected. Naturally, there are severe limits that this approach places on the amount of detail Marx can offer about the future. Unlike the free flights of fancy with which utopian socialists constructed their future societies, Marx never severs the internal relations that connect the future to its past, and therefore to the variety of possibilities as well as to the dominant tendencies inherent in that past. Marx gives no detailed blueprints of the future, it appears, because his method does not permit him to have any.[12]

The sequence presented above deserves to be restated: Marx begins by viewing the past from the vantage point of the present (moving from result to precondition). Again, from the vantage point of the present, but

---

12.   This being said, there is a considerable amount of information on what communism will look like scattered throughout Marx's writings. For a reconstruction of the way of life that emerges from these comments, see my "Marx's Vision of Communism," *Social and Sexual Revolution*, pp. 48–98.

including now the ties that have been uncovered with the past, he projects this present forward to some stage of the future (moving from one part of the result to another). Finally, adopting the vantage point of what has been established in the future, he examines the present taken together with its ties to the past (moving from result to preconditions). Marx could not construct any part of the future without treating it as a development out of the present. The present would not exhibit any development unless it was first constituted as a system of interacting processes arising out of its past. And the future would not emerge even to the minimal degree it does in Marx's writings if he had not taken the final step of adopting the vantage point of the future to look back on the present. Paradoxically, it is this last move that also rounds out Marx's analysis of the capitalist present.

The main effect of casting the relation between past, present, and future as part of the interaction of precondition and result is that it enabled Marx to bring into focus for purposes of study the historical movement of the capitalist mode of production without either dismissing or trivializing its organic movement. He can now fix upon the present in a way that throws into the sharpest possible relief the changes (already made) that tie it to its real past and those (in the process of taking place) that connect it to its probable future, pointing to major influences where they exist while holding fast to the mutual interaction that characterizes each stage in the development. Further, viewing the present from the vantage point of its as yet unrealized potential gives to our capitalist present the value of a stepping-stone. From a sense of having arrived, we become newly aware and highly sensitized to the fact of going somewhere, of constructing here and now—from somewhere in the middle of the historical process—the foundations for a totally different future. With this, the project and our intentions as part of it assume a greater place in our consciousness, and in class consciousness, with a corresponding impact on our actions. Marx's future oriented study of the present becomes increasingly relevant, therefore, just as this future, as indicated by this same study, becomes more and more of a realistic possibility.[13]

References

Gramsci, A. 1971. *Selections from Prison Notebooks*. Edited and translated by Q. Hoare and G. N. Smith. New York: International Publishers.

Marx, K. 1904. *A Contribution to the Critique of Political Economy*. Translated by N.I. Stone. Chicago: Charles H. Kerr.

---

13. For a more detailed account of how Marx investigated the future inside the present, see my forthcoming book, *Communism: Ours, Not Theirs*.

———. 1957. *Capital*. Vol. 2. Moscow: Foreign Languages Publishing House.

———. 1963. *Theories of Surplus Value*. Part 1. Translated by E. Burns. Moscow: Progress Publishers.

———. 1971. *Theories of Surplus Value*. Part 3. Translated by J. Cohen and S. W. Ryazan-skaya. Moscow: Progress Publishers.

———. 1973. *Grundrisse*. Translated by M. Nicolaus. Harmondsworth, Eng.: Penguin.

———. n.d. *The Poverty of Philosophy*. Moscow: Foreign Languages Publishing House.

Marx, K., and F. Engels, 1945. *The Communist Manifesto*. Chicago: Charles H. Kerr.

———. 1951. *Selected Works in Two Volumes*, Vol. 1. Moscow: Foreign Languages Publishing House.

———. 1964. *The German Ideology*. Translated by S. W. Ryazanskaya. Moscow: Progress Publishers.

Ollman, B. 1976. *Alienation: Marx's Conception of Man in Capitalist Society*. Cambridge, Eng.: Cambridge University Press.

———. 1978. *Social and Sexual Revolution: Essays on Marx and Reich*. Boston: South End Press.

———. Forthcoming. *Communism: Ours, Not Theirs.*

9

How to Study Class Consciousness . . .
and Why We Should _____

I. _____

According to Marxist theory, a socialist revolution requires a class conscious working class. Consequently, most socialist political activity is directed one way or another to raising worker's consciousness. Yet relatively few Marxists have gone beyond theoretical analysis to studying the class consciousness of real workers. In part, this is due to the belief, widespread among Marxists, that such consciousness is a necessary by-product of capitalist economic crisis, or the belief, equally widespread, that class consciousness can only be observed in political actions (in both cases, studying class consciousness now is impossible or irrelevant). In part, this neglect is due to a post-Lenin overemphasis on developing political strategies and organizations, on the assumption that class consciousness is sufficiently advanced—once effective leadership is provided—for revolutionary activity to occur (in which case, studying it is unnecessary). Proponents of this view often confuse, as Lenin never did, simple anger directed against a boss and trade union consciousness with revolutionary or class consciousness.

Given the complexity of our subject, the paucity of Marxist studies of class consciousness is also due, in part, to lack of a workable method (in which case, such studies are unthinkable). And, finally, if truth will out, this situation is due, in part, to an unhappy tradition in which many renegades from Marxism have begun their descent from grace by noting the non-socialist character of real workers (in which case, investigating class consciousness has appeared to some as politically suspect and even reactionary). The absence, until relatively recently, of Marxist scholars in the universities who might have conducted such studies has only served to exacerbate these tendencies.

There have been, of course, numerous Marxist studies of the working class, particularly by historians and sociologists, that describe important aspects of their class consciousness. E. P. Thompson (1966), Eric Hobsbawm (1984), David Montgomery (1979), Herbert Gutman (1976), Harry

147

Braverman (1974), Andre Gorz (1967), Serge Mallet (1975), Erich Fromm (1984), Michael Mann (1973), John Leggett (1968), Stanley Aronowitz (1973), Eric Wright (1985), Adam Przeworski (1977), John McDermott (1980), and Paul Willis (1981) are some of the chief figures here. But few of these authors have made class consciousness their main focus. And fewer still have made independent studies of the consciousness of today's workers. In the main their evidence comes from non-Marxist research (which they reinterpret), working class actions (which they deconstruct), government statistics, literary texts, personal experiences, anecdotes, and unique events and testimonies. More serious still, there is no consistent method that helps us as readers and potential researchers and political actors to get what we want and to understand what we have once we've gotten it. Usually, we are provided with a highly suggestive collage, generally with many parts missing, of theoretically undigested facts and insights. Until these findings are reformulated in terms of Marx's theory of class consciousness and integrated in turn within Marx's broader analysis of society, their full potential for helping us either understand or change capitalism cannot be realized. Clearly, a better focused, more systematic, and more effectively theorized Marxist study of class consciousness of today's workers remains to be done.

In the meantime, non-Marxist social science has made class consciousness one of its main topics of study, though, of course, the conceptual frameworks that are used have little to do with Marx's own. The preferred approach is the attitude survey, simply asking workers a whole range of questions as to how they feel, think, and act in regard to specified social and political situations. One of the most influential examples of this approach is found in Goldthorpe, Lockwood, Bechhofer, and Platt (1969). Those who conduct such surveys generally assume that the answers they get back are honest, of similar intensity, easy to interpret, and—most suspect of all—relatively stable. But Seymour Martin Lipset, whose many writings on the working class have made extensive use of such materials, admits that no attitude survey has ever foretold any of the great bursts of working class consciousness that have occurred (1983a). Public choice literature offers another, increasingly popular, non-Marxist approach to studying class consciousness. Here, the emphasis is on examining the practical reasoning that leads individuals to make decisions on whether to participate in class actions. Based on a highly individualistic sense of decision making and an extremely egoistic view of human nature, most of the studies that have come out of this school, beginning with the pathbreaking work of Mancur Olsen (1971), have demonstrated conclusively that individual workers have nothing to gain by thinking and acting as members of their class.

A third approach has simply linked class consciousness, or rather the lack of it, to the increasing segmentation of the work force that follows from changes in the structure of the job market. What distinguishes different groups of workers from each other, it is held, has become greater than what they have in common, establishing a variety of occupation or sector consciousnesses in place of class consciousness (Lockwood, 1975). This account is sufficiently materialist and structuralist to attract the support of some radicals (Edwards, 1979), but the class consciousness that is undermined never gets the same attention as what undermines it. Hence, we are in no position to estimate the pull of conflicting forces on workers' consciousness either now or in the future.

But perhaps the most influential non-Marxist approach to studying class consciousness is one that uses cross-cultural data to answer the question, "Why no socialism in the U.S.?" In this case, what workers think is deduced from what they have achieved, especially politically, and what American workers have achieved in this regard is considerably less impressive than the powerful socialist and communist parties and trade unions thrown up by the European working class. By concentrating on what there is in European history and conditions that contributed to these developments (such as a feudal past), and what there is in the U.S. that restricted them (such as greater social mobility), this comparative approach tries to show not only that class consciousness does not exist here, but that it could not have come about and—by implication—will never come about. For the classic statement of this position, see Sombart (1976; first published 1906).[1]

The assumption here, of course, is that there is only one way of becoming class conscious. This is clearly disproved, however, not only by the variety of paths taken by the working class in different European countries but also by the degree of class consciousness that relatively large numbers of American workers achieved in the period just before World War I and again in the 1930s. The point is that capitalism, just like any complex organism, contains many compensating mechanisms, so that the absence of any one of them is not sufficient reason for believing that its function will not find expression through some other form. Conversely, the presence of conditions that exist only in the United States is no guarantee that the sum of capitalism's other conditions will not sooner or later produce a class consciousness equal to, or even greater than, that found in Europe. Be-

---

1. Summarizing much of this work, Seymour Martin Lipset lists close to two dozen differences between the United States and Europe that have been used to explain the relative backwardness of the American working class (1983b,1). Useful surveys of some of the major debates over class consciousness can be found in Wolpe (1970) and Marshall (1983).

sides their conservative implications and the questionable methods adopted by all these non-Marxist studies, they can also be faulted for focusing on only part of class consciousness, which narrowness is also largely responsible for their conservative implications.

II.

Making a Marxist inquiry into the class consciousness of today's workers, on the other hand, requires that we bring the whole of this notion into focus. For this, we must clarify the nature of class and the consciousness of a class in Marxist theory. To begin with the latter, "consciousness" in the expression "class consciousness" does not mean the same thing as it does in the expression "individual consciousness." It is not just a matter of individuals being conscious, or having a certain understanding, of their class. Rather, class is the subject, and, consequently, consciousness is not just a larger version of individual consciousness. What is it then? Before answering we must shift our attention to class.

We find that defining "class"—or indeed any other important notion in Marxism—proceeds from the whole to the part (class, in this case) rather than from still smaller parts (individuals) to class, viewed as some larger composite notion.[2] According to Marx, "the subject, society, must always be envisaged as the precondition of comprehension" (1904, 295). This whole, this society, is capitalism, or more specifically, Marx's analysis of capitalism, which captures both its distinctive character as a social formation and the unique dynamics, or "law of motion," that has transformed it from its beginnings in feudalism to and through the present to whatever future awaits it. Before we can offer more precision on Marx's notion of class, we need to have a better idea of the whole in which it plays such a crucial role.

Capitalism is not a perpetual motion machine destined to last forever and a day. But if it isn't, what is it about the way this system works and develops that will eventually bring on its destruction? Marx believed he found the answer to this question in the process of accumulation and centralization of capital (or wealth producing wealth), especially when viewed in connection with the limited purchasing power of the workers. This relationship is often expressed as the contradiction between social production and private appropriation.[3] Production and consumption follow two different logics. The former is determined by profit maximization;

---

2. For whole/part relation, see p. 12–13, and 33–9.
3. For contradiction, see pp. 15–17, 50–3, 63–5, and 76–7.

the capitalists invest in order to make and maximize profits. While what gets bought and consumed is determined by what people, most of whom are workers, can afford. And, as the capitalist never return as much wealth to workers (in the form of wages) as the workers produce (in the form of commodities), there is a constant pressure on the system to find alternative uses (that is, uses profitable to capitalists) for this surplus.

This contradiction intensifies as the gap between the amount of wealth produced (and producible) and the amount returned to the workers as wages grows, as it invariably does, chiefly through advances in science and technology. Increases in the workers' real wages, which can occur from time to time and from place to place (though, unfortunately, no longer in our time and place), does not seriously impede this process. Every decade or so for the past 150 years this contradiction has resulted in a crisis of overproduction (or, viewed from the perspective of the workers, of underconsumption), with the accompanying destruction and wastage of factories, machines, goods, and workers. Eventually the need to rebuild what has been destroyed or left to wear out together with the appearance of new markets makes investment more profitable. There is a renewed burst of accumulation, and the cycle starts over. The new beginning takes place on a higher level; more is invested, more people, tasks, and area are involved all around the world; more is at stake. Capitalism has been saved, but only at the cost of increasing the scale of risk in the next crisis. In Marx's estimation, capitalism is a little like a drunk who drinks in order to steady his nerves until the time that . . . And that time always comes. Marx's prediction of the downfall of capitalism is not to be read as the prediction of the arrival of a comet on such and such a day, but as the projection of the most likely outcome of a worsening impasse, whose development one can see and study in the past and present.

III. ───

In capitalism, grasped in this way, class is first of all a place in the system, a property of the whole at whose core we find the interrelated functions of capital and wage-labor. The groups of people who realize these functions, i.e., use capital to exploit workers and use labor to produce value, are the capitalists and workers. Marx often refers to capitalists and workers as "embodiments" or "personifications" of capital and wage-labor (1958, 10, 85, 592; 1959, 857f.). Without denying that these classes are composed of real people, this is a way of saying that what makes them classes is not so much the qualities of the individuals but the relation of the group, *qua* group, to a central organizing function of the system. It is clear that workers, in this sense, are no more male than female, white than black, unskilled than skilled. As classes, the capitalists and the workers are viewed as extensions of the functions of capital and wage-labor, which themselves are only meaningful as parts of a system whose functions they are. Marx himself goes so far as to say, "capital is necessarily at the same time the capitalist . . . the capitalist is contained in the process of capital" (1973, 512).

In the labor theory of value and the materialist conception of history, the major theories through which Marx interprets capitalism, capitalists, and workers generally make their appearance as embodiments of capital and wage-labor. When describing the broad lines of capitalist development, the origins of different social pressures and constraints, the opening and closing of options, and especially what happens in the majority of cases over time, Marx did not think it necessary to move much beyond this essentially functional approach to classes. This same approach lies behind his oft-quoted statement that, "The question is not what this or that man or even the whole of the proletariat at the moment considers its aim. The question is what the proletariat is, and what consequent on that being, it will be compelled to do" (Marx and Engels, 1956, 53). What real flesh and blood capitalists and workers did and said and thought and wanted was either deducible from the way the system works and has developed (or else it would not work or have developed like that) or irrelevant (since even without the contribution of these particular individuals the system works and has developed as it has). Both necessary and sufficient conditions are easy to decipher after the fact. For example, that the French Revolution occurred indicates that the conditions for it happening at that time were not only necessary but sufficient. Consequently, where the acts and words of particular individuals are cited in Marx's more general historical and economic writings, it is to illustrate a point or to otherwise facilitate exposition rather than as evidence or as part of an argument for his conclusions.

In dealing with the possibility of socialist revolution in the present, however, whether Marx's present or our own, it is not enough to treat people as embodiments of social-economic functions. As much as this helps us understand their conditions, the pressures they are under, and their options and opportunities, the people involved must still respond to these influences in ways that make what is possible actual. In Marxist terminology, they must become class conscious. To study whether this can actually occur here and now, or at least soon, we must add a subjective, people-oriented, more directly and narrowly human element and focus to the objective, system-oriented view of class that has been presented so far. In short, in analyzing history and political economy, Marx could operate with an essentially functionalist conception of class derived from the place of a function within the system. Class here is something to which real people are attached. In this way, incidentally, it is possible for an individual who serves more than one function (managers and wage-earning professionals, for example) to belong to more than one class.[4] But in analyzing the present state of the class struggle and in developing political strategy, this view has to be supplemented, not replaced, by a conception of class that gives priority to the group of people who occupy this place and perform this function. Sharing a social space and function, they also tend to acquire over time other common characteristics as regards income, life-style, political consciousness, and organization that become, in turn, further evidence for membership in their particular class and subsidiary criteria for determining when to use the class label.[5] Here, class is a quality that is attached to people, who posses other qualities—such as nationality, race or sex, for example—that reduce and may even nullify the influence on thinking and action that comes from membership in the class. Conceived as a complex social relation, in line with Marx's dialectical outlook on the world, class invites analysis as both a function and a group, that is to say, from different sides of this relation.

There is even a third major aspect of class, conceived of as a complex relation, which is the abstracted common element in the social relations of alienated people. Their tendency to interact with each other as instances of a kind rather than as unique individuals, a tendency that is expressed mainly through mutual indifference and competition, takes on independent form in the notion of "class." It is the alienated quality of social life of the individuals who embody the aforesaid economic functions. We will return to class as alienation later in this paper, when we discuss the various difficulties workers experience in becoming class conscious.[6]

All these aspects of class—place/function, group, alienated social relation, and there are others—are mutually dependent, but their relative importance varies with the problem and period under consideration. Each is distinctive for the dimension of reality it brings into focus. Essentially,

---

4. We even learn that it is possible for one person to belong to three classes: peasants, handicraftsmen, and landowners (Marx, 1963, 408). Other examples of the same person belonging to more than one class in virtue of performing different functions can be found on pp. 51, 108, and 409 of this work.

5. For a more detailed discussion of the relation between the development of a group into a class and the evolving criteria that determine Marx's use of the class label, see Ollman (1979, chapter 2).

6. For a discussion of class as an alienated social relation, see Ollman (1976, chapter 29).

they are different ways of cutting up the "pie." Their real content largely overlaps; though the way each organizes its content makes this difficult to recognize.

Returning to the example of the French Revolution, it is clear that the classes involved were not only embodiments of functions, but groups of real people and expressions of social alienation. As people they made decisions, and there was always the possibility that on any given occasion they might have chosen otherwise. However, it does not follow that each of these aspects of class should get equal treatment in an account of this event, or that the aspect of class that is emphasized in an account of an event that has already happened, like the French Revolution, should be emphasized in trying to understand developments that lie ahead. One should be open, in other words, to using "class" in somewhat different ways when analyzing the present and/or future than when analyzing the past.[7]

Corresponding to our two main senses of class—as embodiment of a function and as a group—is a bifurcated conception of class interests. In one case, class interests are attached to class in the sense of function, and in the other to the social group who performs this function.[8] The first can be referred to as "objective interests" and the second as "subjective interests." Thus, in the case of the workers, class interests not only refers to what real workers, viewed as a group, actually believe to be in their interests (these are subjective interests), but it also refers to those practices and changes that serve the workers, being who they are, i.e., in their function as wage-labor (these are their objective interests). The most important of these *objective* interests involve the kind of social structural changes that are required for the mass of workers to realize their *subjective* interests. This is how these apparently independent sets of interests are linked. Capitalist power relations, for example, simply do not permit most workers to get the good, high paying, secure, healthy, interesting jobs they say they want. To understand why this is so and what order of changes would secure these aims, realize these *subjective* interests, requires the kind of analysis of capitalism that Marx made and most workers have not. As a result, most workers are unaware of their *objective* class interests in transforming capitalist power relations.

IV.

Having defined "class" and "class interests" as both objective and subjective, we are now in a position to approach class consciousness. First, as

7.   For the role played by Marx's abstractions of extension, level of generality, and vantage point in constructing his notion of class, see pp. 46–8, 58–60, and 74–5.

8.   For abstraction of vantage point, see pp. 67–78.

regards its content, its main elements include one's identity and interests (subjective and objective) as members of a class, something of the dynamics of capitalism uncovered by Marx (at least enough to grasp objective interests), the broad outlines of the class struggle and where one fits into it, feelings of solidarity toward one's own class and of rational hostility toward opposition classes (in contrast to the feelings of mutual indifference and inner-class competition that accompany alienation), and the vision of a more democratic and egalitarian society that is not only possible but that one can help bring about. These are the main things that a class conscious working class is conscious of. Studying workers' class consciousness, then, is looking for what is not there, not yet present in the thinking of real workers, as well as for what is. How can this be?

It can be, because class consciousness brings together (and is equally a part of) both the function and group aspects of class. To begin with, it is the understanding that is appropriate to the objective character of a class and its objective interests. We can call this the objective aspect of class consciousness. Given this is the place and function of a class and this its objective interests, its class consciousness must be such and such. The one is deducible from the other. It is an imputed class consciousness. George Lukacs (1971) is the Marxist scholar most associated with this view. However, class consciousness is also the consciousness of the group of people in a class in so far as their understanding of who they are and what must be done develops from its economistic beginnings toward the consciousness that is appropriate to their class situation. This is the subjective aspect of class consciousness.

Class consciousness in this subjective sense differs from the actual consciousness of each individual in the group in three ways: (1) it is a group consciousness, a way of thinking and a thought content, that develops through the individuals in the group interacting with each other and with opposing groups in situations that are peculiar to the class; (2) it is a consciousness that has its main point of reference in the situation and objective interests of a class, viewed functionally, and not in the declared subjective interests of class members (the imputed class consciousness referred to above has been given a role here in the thinking of real people); and (3) it is in its essence a process, a movement from wherever a group begins in its consciousness of itself to the consciousness appropriate to its situation. In other words, the process of *becoming* class conscious is not external to what it is but rather at the center of what it is all about.[9]

To claim that class consciousness is a group consciousness is not to deny that individuals also have something that may be called an individual

---

9. For the different kinds of abstraction involved here see discussions of abstraction of extension, level of generality, and vantage point on pp. 39–78.

consciousness, that this may include political and social elements, and that such consciousness both affects and is affected by their group consciousness (or that they may have—really participate in—other kinds of group consciousness, racial, national, religious, and sexual as well as class). Individual consciousness may also be politically in advance of or lagging behind class consciousness. Class consciousness, however, is something other. It is a kind of "group think," a collective, interactive approach to recognizing, labeling, coming to understand, and acting upon the particular world class members have in common. It is a set of mental moves and a store of knowledge and judgments reserved for these common situations and what these situations tap or set into motion, in order to survive and in order to do better than survive, where the individuals's fate is inextricably linked with the fate of the group. It is a manner of thinking that is done in common, most of the time in a common place on common problems, phrased in a common and distinct terminology, pushed forward and held back by common pressures and constraints. It is not only the Australian Aborigines who solve problems in a group (apparently to the point that individual Aborigines have trouble taking Western IQ tests). We all do. It is, at least in part, a professional deformation of intellectuals, of people whose work involves a lot of thinking in isolation, to believe that thinking can only be done by individuals operating on their own, with the result that what I have called "group thinking" is generally either ignored or denied the honorific label of "thinking."

There is nothing mystical here. I am not suggesting that there is a collective "mind" of the same order as individual "minds." On the other hand, neither am I making the commonsensical point that some aspects of individual consciousness are more affected by social interaction than others. Nor am I introducing Jung's collective unconscious by the back door. Instead, some of our thinking is simply being viewed as a cooperative activity, and an activity that is best understood by focusing on the shared conditions in which it occurs, the shared problems it attacks, the common interests that it expresses, and the interactive logic that gives it its structure, rather than on the individual minds (including both conscious and unconscious) in which it continues to take place.

Obviously not all problems are submitted to group thinking, but just those which circumscribe our existence as members of the group, class in this case, though the same thing applies to problem solving as a member of racial, national, religious and sexual groups. Individuals who do not participate in the consciousness of their class in this way, no matter how numerous they are, should be viewed as the exceptions and, no matter how long the wait, as temporary exceptions at that.

Politically, what counts is what an individual understands and does as a member of a class and not his private reflections and intimate behavior. In coming to recognize, as most of us have in this Freudian century, the undeniable influence of the latter on the former (not to mention the reverse), there has been a regrettable conflation of these two forms of consciousness. The study of class consciousness as part of developing a strategy for socialist transformation requires that group and individual consciousnesses, at least initially, be kept quite distinct.[10]

Class consciousness is also different from individual consciousness, as we said, by having its main point of reference in the situation of the class and not in the already recognized interests of individuals. It is this that enables Marx, on occasion, to conceptualize class consciousness as an aspect of class (again, grasped as a complex relation), with the implication that workers are not fully a class until they become class conscious (1934, 19).[11] The main content of class consciousness, therefore, is not to be had by asking members of the class what they think or want, but by analyzing their objective interests as a group of people embodying a particular societal place and function. It is, again, the appropriate consciousness of people in that position, the consciousness that maximizes their chances of realizing class interests, including structural change where such change is required to secure other interests. What these same people, occupying this same place, think before they acquire *this* class consciousness is not really class consciousness, except in so far as it is used to highlight what is not there. In this sense, and to this degree, class consciousness is a consciousness waiting to happen. It exists in potential, not an abstract potential but one rooted in a situation unfolding before our very eyes, long before the understanding of real people catches up with it.[12]

It should be evident now the degree to which "class consciousness" is a theory laden expression, and that what non-Marxists mean by it is not and cannot be the same thing that Marxists mean by it. Therefore, what non-Marxists find in their research into what they call "class consciousness" is not easily transferable into a Marxist analysis. Likewise, what

---

10. The literature on crowds offers many examples of group thinking in connection with less permanent groups. See Brown and Goldin (1973), especially the chapters on disaster. Another fruitful area of investigation into group thinking is the automatic processing of social information. See Bargh (1984).

11. That class consciousness plays the same role in other groups becoming classes is evident from Marx's treatment of the French small-holding peasants (1951, 303). Marx's often quoted distinction between class-in-itself and class-for-itself is another indication of his belief that a class only fully becomes a class when it acquires class consciousness (n.d., 195).

12. For abstraction of extension, see pp. 39–53.

Marxists discover in their investigation of class consciousness will not be readily accepted or even understood by non-Marxists. The questions that Marxists address generally take the form—"Why *haven't* the workers become class conscious?" and "When are they *likely* to do so?" (which inclines us to look for the barriers to such consciousness). While non-Marxists ordinarily ask such questions as "What is the consciousness of workers?" and "Are the workers class conscious?" (which ignores the very analysis, Marxism, that leads us to raise these questions in the first place). The difference is between Marxists—who are looking for something that they believe is already there, in one sense, and not there, in another, something they grasp the broad outlines of from their analysis—and non-Marxists investigating the same subject who appear to be simply looking. But are they? We shall return to this in a moment.

Finally, and possibly what distinguishes it most from individual consciousness as ordinarily understood, class consciousness is elastic and changing, and encompasses all the stages in the process of becoming what it potentially is along with the time it takes for this to occur. As such, class consciousness cannot be captured in any instant, nor can it be expressed in any simple, straightforward description. The time frame is stretched to cover the whole journey, but it is a journey with an end, a goal established by the situation of the class as such and evoked by all the conditions and pressures that constitute that situation, though most members of the class may not recognize this until very late. One of the most puzzling features in Marx's use of "class" is how he could claim that class is "the product of the bourgeoisie" while maintaining that "All history is the history of class struggle," and refer to various pre-capitalist groups as "classes" (Marx and Engels, 1942, 77; 1945, 12). In fact, class (in all of its aspects), class struggle, and class consciousness all develop, mature, become over time, and only in late capitalist society do they realize their full potential. It is in this sense that each may be said to be a product of capitalism. In so far as many of their elements are present earlier, however, class, class struggle, and class consciousness can be said—if this limited sense is kept in mind—to have existed before. Moreover, viewed as historical processes, the mature form of each can be taken as present in its earlier stages and vice versa. Such is the nature of becoming as a dialectical category. As regards class consciousness at the present time, rather than what any single person thinks, class consciousness refers to how, when, from, and toward what a whole class of people are changing their minds.[13]

---

13. For abstraction of process, see pp. 28–31.

Studying class consciousness has something in common with trying to catch a wave at the moment when it breaks. All movement toward this point is treated as development, as preliminary, as the unfolding of a potential. Everything that either contributes to or retards its movement is equally the object of study, but the constant point of repair, the perspective from which the whole process is viewed and interpreted, the event that gives everything that preceded it its distinctive meaning, is the moment at which the wave breaks.[14] Naturally, there is the assumption, derived from a Marxist analysis of capitalism, that the wave will almost certainly break, that sooner or later the worsening problems of the system, together with the reduction and eventual disappearance of system-approved alternatives for dealing with them, will drive most workers to embody the consciousness of their class.

But why do Marxists insist on making Marx's view of the most probable future of class consciousness the key element for understanding its present form? Are we unnecessarily burdening class consciousness with something that just is not there? Why can't we be satisfied with whatever class consciousness emerges from simply questioning workers and leave it at that? Our answer can be summarized in the following points: (1) That class consciousness has *a* future is incontestable. (2) No one can avoid having some idea of what that will be, as evidenced by our expectation, by what surprises us, and by what developments we think need to be explained and accounted for. (3) Marx arrives at his idea of what class consciousness will become through an analysis of the changes going on in the conditions in which people live and work (this seems reasonable). (4) Non-Marxist social scientists also have an idea about the future of class consciousness, though it is generally left implicit (see number two above). Most probably believe that class consciousness will stay more or less the same, while some may believe that every conceivable change is equally possible.

(5) The basis for the first view could only be that it is class consciousness in its present state that determines future class consciousness, or that the other conditions that influence class consciousness, whatever they are, will never change, so that the effect they have now will continue into the future. The basis for the second view could only be that there is nothing we know about our past and present that is relevant to learning about our likely future, or that what we do know suggests that no one outcome, no particular development in class consciousness, is more likely than another. On the surface, none of these arguments seem reason-

---

14. For abstraction of vantage point, see pp. 67–78.

able, so that the beliefs they support—that no change in class consciousness will occur, or that every kind of change is equally possible—are
never openly defended.

(6) Moreover, one's view of future class consciousness, whatever it is,
greatly affects one's understanding of its present state. In Marx's case, it
is what enables him to view much of what today's workers actually think
as false consciousness and ideology. Among non-Marxists viewing future
class consciousness as identical with its present state—what I take to be
the more prevalent alternative view—gives to class consciousness in its
present form an appearance of natural truth. What is becomes reified,
unchanging, and, apparently, unchangeable. The Marxist ideas of false
consciousness and ideology are not only rejected but ridiculed. It is not
just that these non-Marxist beliefs go beyond the evidence; they are held
in the absence of any attempt to get at the evidence. So much for the
notion suggested earlier that non-Marxist social scientists investigating
this subject were simply looking, that they brought no assumptions with
them, and that this might be an advantage. (7) Hence—and finally—it
seems clear that to fully understand what class consciousness is in the
present requires a serious effort to learn about its likely future, using, as
Marx does, all the available evidence.

What if the majority of the workers in capitalist society never become
class conscious? This certainly is a possibility. Our effort to integrate the
probable future into the present is not an exercise in crystal ball gazing. But
imputed class consciousness, the workers' rational understanding of their
situation and of what kind of actions are required to serve their interests,
can be treated as future class consciousness even if it never takes place. It
is after all only the *probable* future as determined by Marx's analysis of the
worker's situation together with its developing patterns and trends. What
needs to be stressed is that the probable future is an internally related part
of the present, and exists there (here) as the point toward which real pressures are directing us. Grasped as "becoming," it is the form assumed by
the future within the present, and as such affects how we understand the
present, how we should study it, and what we can do to help change it.

Does understanding imputed class consciousness as future class consciousness imply that socialism is inevitable? No, because class conscious workers are a necessary but not a sufficient condition for a success-
ful socialist transformation of society. How effectively these class
conscious workers are organized, what political action they take, the
character of the then opposition, and even luck will help determine the
final outcome of the class struggle. Marx himself offered barbarism—what
we would probably call fascism—as one alternative to socialism, but
living one hundred years ago, he did not give it the attention that it would

receive today. The state of the Cold War has led to the recognition that still another all too realistic alternative to socialism is the destruction of the species brought about by nuclear holocaust. Many would even rate this the most likely outcome. While occasionally sympathetic (if this is the right word) to this view, it should be clear that the factors effecting this outcome are, at least to a large degree, of a different order than those that influence the progress of class consciousness. Consequently, the possibility of nuclear holocaust, like the possibility of fascism, does not prevent us from treating imputed class consciousness as future class consciousness within a notion of present class consciousness viewed in the process of becoming.

What emerges from the foregoing is that our object of study, class consciousness, is much larger than the mind or understanding of any individual and much longer than the present moment. It is the class, its interests and self-understanding, in the context of the situation, especially its interaction with opposing classes, that constitute it as a class, and all this as it has developed, is developing, and will continue to develop into the future. At its broadest, the study of class consciousness is a study of an important part of capitalist society, which through its interconnections puts us in touch with the whole. Any investigation of class consciousness, therefore, is simultaneously an investigation into capitalism, into how it works and where it is tending, viewed from the perspective of that moment when the mass of workers have acquired the understanding that is necessary for engaging in revolutionary activity.[15]

Given the spatial and temporal dimensions of class consciousness, it is obvious that examining small pieces of this process, such as the consciousness of individual workers, which is separated from its social context and viewed statically, as it appears in an instant, simply will not do. This is, of course, what happens in most attitude surveys. Even if the questions are fair and the respondents honest (big "ifs"), attitude surveys cannot capture a process, a context, and a potential for change. It is as if one sought to catch the moment a wave breaks by photographing an earlier moment (and small piece) in its movement. But class consciousness is not the kind of thing that shows up in a photo, or even in moving pictures. There are just too many aspects that are not immediately perceptible.

V.

What is the alternative? Until now, I have been constructing a dialectical conception of class consciousness that could be studied directly and not

---

15. For abstraction of large extensions, see pp. 41–2; for vantage point, see pp. 67–78.

only as a dependent aspect of class structure or class struggle. In what follows, I sketch what such a study would look like, its advantages and problems, and its organic ties to political practice. The dialectical alternative to examining class consciousness in the attitudes of individual workers, then, is to study the objective aspects of class consciousness in the situation of the class, and its subjective aspects in the thinking and activity of the group, and both of these over time. On the objective side, what we have called the situation of the class must be studied on two different levels of historical specificity.[16] First, we must clearly establish the place and function of the working class together with its objective interests in capitalism as such, that is in capitalism as it has existed for the past five to six hundred years, in order to derive the class consciousness that is appropriate. Reconstructing this situation not only provides the goal or finished form of class consciousness but puts us in touch with social pressures arising out of the most basic relations of capitalism that move the actual consciousness of living workers in the direction of this goal. Given our concern with class consciousness, the focus is on the workers, and hence the rest of capitalist society comes into view chiefly as part of the necessary conditions and/or results of the workers appearing and functioning as they do.[17] In reconstructing how capitalism looks and works from the vantage point of the working class, there are some tendencies that deserve special attention. Among these are the accumulation and centralization of capital, the falling rate of profit, the increasing rate of exploitation, and the immiseration of the working class (that is relative to the capitalists and viewed on a world scale). Though sometimes referred to as "laws," Marx's tendencies all admit—indeed often require—countertendencies, and should be understood and pursued with this in mind.[18]

The second level on which to study the situation of the working class is the more specific one of world capitalism today. As well as the tendencies mentioned above, which are characteristic of capitalism as such and apply with varying degrees of tenacity to the whole capitalist epoch, there are a number of often contradictory tendencies—each exercising some influence on consciousness—which taken together express what capitalism has become in our day. Among the most important of those helping to expand class consciousness are recent developments in automation and related changes in job structure and employment; the movement of viable industries out of the advanced capitalist countries to the third world

---

16. For abstraction of level of generality, see pp. 53–67.
17. For abstraction of vantage point, see pp. 67–78.
18. For contradiction, see pp. 15–17, 50–3, 63–5, and 76–7.

where labor is cheaper; stagflation, the most distinctive feature of the current economic crisis; the closing off of traditional non-socialist solutions to the problems associated with capitalism's need to expand investment and trade due to the saturation of older markets; the "debt bomb" with, among other things, its implicit threat to the savings workers have in banks that are threatened; the invasion of advanced capitalist countries, especially of the United States, by foreign and international capital, seriously weakening the link between capitalism and nationalism (if most workers could believe "What's good for General Motors is good for America," it is difficult to substitute "Renault" or "Toyota" or "Honda" for "General Motors" and feel the same sentiment); and the increase in workers' "ownership" of industry, whatever its pro-capitalist form and however little it affects who exercises real control (the question of power has been joined and the potential of workers to take and use power for their own ends is that much easier to conceive).

On both of these levels, in capitalism overall as well as in modern capitalism, there are also a number of relations and tendencies that pull in the opposite direction, that make the attainment of class consciousness more difficult. As regards capitalism in general, the most important of these find expression in Marx's theory of alienation: workers are separated from—and hence lack control over—their activity, products, and other people, at work and throughout social life. While the resulting feelings of isolation and powerlessness (both subjective factors) receive most of the attention, the core of alienation lies in the workers' objective situation as workers in capitalism. Oddly enough, Marx never offered the workers' alienation as part of the explanation for the continued inability of the mass of the workers to become fully class conscious, just as he never introduced the progress many workers have made in becoming class conscious as a factor qualifying their alienation. Yet, each condition acts as a major check on the other, and until we succeed in integrating the theories with which Marx grasps these opposed developments—something that must be left for another time—we will not be able to gauge with any accuracy the real potential for change inherent in each one.

As regards modern capitalism, the most important of these restraining relations and tendencies include the increasing segmentation of the labor force (with its accompanying fragmentation of interests), institutional racism, sexism, nationalism and other means of dividing the workers, the enormous expansion of the consciousness industry (some would put capitalist ownership of all mass media at the top of our list), and the spread and then failure of Soviet-style socialism, broadly conceived, as a dystopian model of what happens to all attempts at radical reform. All of this constitutes so many barriers and pressures rooted in the objective situation of workers, in their work, life, and world, against their becoming class conscious.

How the contradictory tendencies (whose main parts I have only been able to list) are related to each other in each modern capitalism and capitalism overall, and how the sum of the tendencies in the former facilitate, give expression to, or inhibit all the tendencies in the latter form the substance of a Marxist study of the objective side of class consciousness. One way of bringing out the objective character of these heterogeneous elements is to subsume them under the notion of class struggle. The class struggle is not, as most commentators left and right would have it, a subjective, consciously chosen form of class behavior. Rather, it is "the form of motion of classes."[19] It is what a class—grasped as a place/ function in the system, as the group of people who embody this function and who as a result tend to develop other common characteristics, and as the common element in their alienated social relations—becomes in and through its complex interaction with other classes, particularly over class interests and the conditions and possibilities for their realization. All that a class does, or what happens to it, that directly or indirectly affects its power vis-à-vis other classes is class struggle. Viewed in this way, class struggle encompasses what Gramsci calls the war of position, the adding and subtracting of advantages and disadvantages, as well as what he calls the war of movement, those occasions when confrontation is open and direct; and it rages throughout all sectors of society (1971, 108–110, 229–235, 238f., 243). The contradictory tendencies referred to above are recast here as internally related causes, expressions, and effects of the interaction of classes.

To be sure, when a class, in the sense of group, is conscious of itself as a class together with its interests, its involvement in class struggle is more purposeful and usually more effective than when it is not. What makes the interaction of classes a "struggle," however, is not the consciousness of the actors, nor even the intensity or undisguised nature of the clash, but the incompatibility of their objective interests and paths of development, both of which are inherent in the structure of capitalism itself. And it is this that makes it possible to organize the key contradictions of capitalism as a class struggle and to treat class struggle as the summary expression of the objective forms of class consciousness.[20]

In most Marxist accounts of this subject the opposite occurs, which is

---

19.   This apt formulation is a gift of the Canadian-American psychologist and philosopher, Bill Livant.

20.   For abstraction of vantage point, see pp. 67–78.

to say class struggle is the main object of study, and class consciousness, to the extent it is addressed at all, is treated as its minor and dependent aspect, as a reflection of class struggle. We have also seen that Marx could conceptualize class consciousness as an aspect of class as such, as something that develops as a class realizes its full potential. While such approaches to class consciousness are adequate for treating the past, where the evidence of what happened is in (so that we know roughly what the level of class consciousness must have been for classes or class struggle to have developed so far), it is my view that a serious Marxist study of how the present is opening onto the future requires as a complementary focus one that makes class struggle a subordinate aspect of class consciousness. (A similar point was made earlier in this essay about the limitations in understanding class simply as the embodiment of an economic function.) This, then, is not an attempt to deny the material basis of Marxism or the priority it gives to activity, political as well as economic, for analyzing capitalism. It is only that the dialectical method allows us to approach capitalist social relations from the vantage point of class consciousness and that for understanding our present moment as well as for affecting it there are certain advantages in doing so.

In investigating the different objective aspects of class consciousness, now conceptualized as class struggle, care must also be taken not to prejudge the particular combination of factors that will carry the wave to its breaking point, or, conversely, will ensure that it not get there, at least not now anyway. As we said earlier, any complex organism, and none is more complex than capitalism, has many compensating mechanisms for what is missing or not working as expected. Consequently, no social feature, either through its presence or absence, exercises an absolute veto on the development of class consciousness. No doubt the way in which consciousness develops has an important influence on the pace and form of the revolution. It does not follow, however, that there is only one road, a royal road, to socialism, and that socialists who are not on it are doomed to failure. Given the changing though still highly structured context provided by the process of capital accumulation, the class struggle allows for enormous flexibility and variety in how workers become class conscious. Yet, it remains the case that some paths of development are more likely—indeed far more likely—to be taken than others, and studying the objective aspects of class consciousness for each time and place is the surest means of uncovering what these are.

While an overly deterministic reading of any of these relations is in error, Marx clearly saw a particularly close connection between worsening economic conditions and improved prospects for socialist revolution. The tie between the two, however, is not automatic and necessary, but probable and mediated through a series of changes that make the development of class consciousness easier and more likely to take place. Such changes include the intensification of capitalist exploitation, which occurs in any crisis, the concentration of capital and the accompanying accentuation of class differences, the closing and narrowing of existing career options (small business, for example), increasing evidence of the irrationality and immorality of capitalism (particularly, conspicuous consumption and waste amid growing poverty), unemployment for many and job insecurity for the rest, the loss of savings, homes, farms, and small businesses, the steady erosion of welfare state benefits acquired in better times, and the evident failure of traditional economic and political strategies (like trade unionism and voting for the Democrats). As various life options that have been available to workers are closed off, as the connections that have to be made appear more obvious, as the material penalties for misunderstanding and not making them grow larger, as the surrounding injustices become more blaring, and as the benefits to be won through a redistribution of economic and political power (what is sometimes called the "revolutionary positive") impose themselves as realistic alternatives, in sum, as the objective forces propelling workers toward full class consciousness become overwhelming, it is difficult for any worker to retain his old outlook. (That many still do is another matter—based chiefly on a different set of considerations—and we will return to this shortly.) Minus many important details and qualifications, this is the most general conclusion to be drawn from studies already done on the objective side of class consciousness.

VI.

Having acquired some understanding of the objective aspects of class consciousness, of the consciousness appropriate to the situation of the class together with everything in the situation that is working toward its full actualization, we are now ready to examine its subjective aspects. Proceeding in the opposite order, dealing with subjective aspects first, there is a serious danger of mistaking a part, usually the psychology of workers, for the whole, and ignoring the objective aspects of class consciousness or treating them as minor conditions and qualifications. Psychology today has become a lot like Pac-Man, gobbling up one discipline after another. The only sure way to avoid psychologizing social problems is by laying out the main objective conditions (pressures, constraints, and options) in which people think and act *first*. Then, and only then, can people's thinking and acting be judged for what they are.

On the subjective side, the study of class consciousness should proceed by dealing with groups of workers as groups, directly, especially in situations where some dramatic change has occurred that triggers off a heightened interaction. Such a change increases their awareness of their place and role in the system as workers and with it the likelihood of thinking, even of personal problems, in class terms. A strike offers one example of this. Visits to the unemployment office is another. Observing what the group does and the interaction and degree of participation of the members, listening to what is said, reading what they write, asking questions aimed at bringing out their understanding and intensity of feeling about whatever is pushing them toward class consciousness and whatever is holding them back, making remarks on similar topics aimed at provoking a response, asking workers what they see in pictures and cartoons that are relevant to their situation, judging their reaction to political jokes, beginning a story taken from their lives and asking them to finish it, taking videos of their discussions—showing it to them—and then asking them to comment on what they have seen, and even acting alongside workers to get a feel for what is going on are all recommended.[21]

It is also extremely important to conduct such inquiries over a period of time to be able to chart both the direction and pace of change. One of the most neglected aspects of class consciousness, largely because the process of becoming is not put at the center of what it is, is the speed at which it can develop (and also, unfortunately, undevelop or come apart). This is still another reason for the priority we have given to the objective side of class consciousness over the psychology of workers. For if class consciousness can develop and spread with the speed of a forest fire, then—sticking with this analogy—it is more important to know the conditions under which this can occur, including the dryness of the grass, the extremes of heat, the duration of the heat wave, what kind of events can start a fire and how likely they are to occur, what techniques of fire prevention are available, etc., than knowing details about the currently nonflammable state of particular blades of grass.

Dialoguing with a group of workers in a stable situation, where nothing dramatic has taken place, is less revealing but still worthwhile. Working class colleges and high schools, hiring halls, trade union meetings, welfare offices, bars and churches in working class neighborhoods, hospital waiting rooms, dances, summer camps, sporting events, funerals, over food, waiting for parades or demonstrations to begin, parks and beaches

---

21. One version of an interventionist research strategy has been developed by the French "action sociologist" Alain Touraine (Touraine, esp. Part 2). Other useful suggestions on where and how to study workers' interactions are found in Blackburn and Mann (1978).

provide some of the occasions for such research. The particular locale chosen, of course, will greatly influence what can and cannot be learned. Still, each of these is an occasion for the group to interact and react to the researcher's questions and provocations as a group, and for studying class consciousness this is crucial. How many people speak, the way in which answers feed into or oppose each other, the intensity with which positions get expressed, the nods of the head as well as the expletives are all raw data for such a study.

It is probably worth stating once again the importance we attach to the group, and therefore to group studies, for understanding class consciousness. Class consciousness is an evolving quality of the class. It progresses in and through the class' developing response to its determinate situation and corresponding interests. The class displays the level of its consciousness, the factors that are currently influencing it most, and the direction and pace of its change whenever workers interact with each other, which occurs in all the different subgroups in which members of this class come together. Approached on their own, individual workers may not even know or feel or be able to put this consciousness into words. For the individual, class consciousness is not so much something they have or do not have as it is something they give expression to or participate in when in a group along with other workers, when acting and thinking in their capacity as group members dealing with the situation and problems that are peculiar to the group. At these times, the people in the group both perceive what is taking place (which includes how they hear the questions of the researcher) and respond to it (intellectually, emotionally, and practically) differently than each individual does or would on his own.

Changes of mind, in particular, are strongly affected by the group. For example, in a group that is moving in one direction, it is easier for the individual, given some degree of identification with the group, to change his mind in the same direction than it would be if he were on his own. While in its more conservative moments, of course, a group may have just the opposite effect. Earlier, I said class consciousness is how, when, and toward what a whole class of people change their minds. It is because most of the changes that make up the content of class consciousness take place in group interaction and can only be observed and correctly estimated in this context that the group must be the focus of our study.[22]

I would also like to insist once again on the need to study class consciousness as a developing rather than a static phenomenon. Examining what is there in light of what is not (imputed consciousness), tracing the changes in the class' objective situation, following a group of workers

---

22. For abstraction of extension as regards people, see pp. 46–8.

over a period of time, stressing sharp transitions in their situations or behavior or thinking, all this is generally not enough. The very concepts we use in which to think about class consciousness, starting with "class consciousness" itself, must be opened up to allow the passage of time, to include where it has come from as well as where it is likely to go as part of its very meaning. Other change-oriented concepts, such as "process," "moment," and "becoming," should be used in preference to "attitude," "factor," and "variable" to convey its relational parts. Only then can everything uncovered at a moment be consistently grasped as arising out of and arching toward something else. Otherwise, temporarily stalled processes are likely to combine with reified social forms and all too frequent intellectual laxness to produce prematurely finished results. Everything in class consciousness is in transition and must be viewed and studied as such.[23]

As for which subsection of the workers should be given priority in choosing people and occasions for study, the answer to this comes from an updated reading of Marx's texts. Besides constituting the largest section of the working class in nineteenth century capitalism, industrial workers worked and lived in conditions that were in the process of becoming generalized. In this as in so much else they led the way. Because of their place and numbers in industry, industrial workers also had the power to bring the entire capitalist system to its knees. Hence, Marx's political as well as economic emphasis on this section of the working class. Today, industrial workers are no longer the majority of the working class, and their proportion as part of the class is becoming smaller, and while they set the pace when material conditions for the whole class were improving, the current drop in real living standards finds them trailing after other less favored, generally less unionized, sections of the class. Granted, they are still the main source of all real (as distinct from paper) wealth in our society, and they still have the force to bring capitalism to a halt by withdrawing their labor-power. From this, it would seem that industrial workers should continue to be a main subgroup in any study of working class consciousness, but—on the basis of current trends in capitalism—they must now share the spotlight with others. As the fastest growing sectors of the working class, highly skilled technical workers, low skilled service workers, and government and office workers should also be heavily represented in studies of working class consciousness.

There are, of course, serious dangers of distortion in conducting the kind of interviews and interventions I have called for, especially those held in less conflictual situations, here I can only sketch the most important of

---

23. For abstraction of process, see pp. 28–31.

these. What does one do, for example, with the people who choose to remain silent, a problem that grows of necessity with the size of the group? In part, and where this is feasible, this can be dealt with by asking everyone for their opinion. Beyond this, one must be attentive to various signs and noises that show how people feel about what is being said and done. Enthusiasm, delight, anger, disgust, disappointment, and resignation are all relatively easy to detect, but the bulk of what constitutes class consciousness remains beyond our perceptual reach. An equally serious problem is that people tend to be more spontaneous and truthful in responding to questions when they are dealing with pressing life problems. Caught at more relaxed moments, their responses are often shaped by demands other than truth. They may not want to appear stupid, or extreme, or to say something that will make them into outsiders in their group. Many respondents also say what they think the researcher wants or expects to hear, and/or will make the researcher like them more. In many cases, it is very difficult to get at the intensity with which people believe and feel something, and therefore to judge what actions may follow or what kind of effort is required to get them to change their views. Avoiding these and similar pitfalls altogether is probably impossible, but their distorting effects can be minimized by giving careful attention to interview tactics, questions asked, language used, and the kind of credentials and prior connections with which one appears on the scene. Unfortunately, these are not matters we can address at this time.

For understanding class consciousness, it is essential—I have argued—to concentrate on groups rather than on individuals; just as earlier I maintained that the objective aspects of class consciousness should precede its subjective aspects in the order of treatment. Given the spatial and temporal dimensions of our subject and, in particular, its character as an evolving quality of the group, this is the best way to avoid one-sidedness and lopsidedness. Having driven home this point, I am now ready to admit that there are some studies of individuals that may also advance us toward our goal. Of these, the least useful are just those attitude surveys that constitute the great bulk of mainstream research on workers' consciousness. Besides suffering from all the problems that beset studies of groups (given above), such studies tend to magnify those aspects of the individual's consciousness that set the individual apart from the group, to reify these aspects, and eventually to substitute them for whatever consciousness the group may have on the same subject. So that in subsequent studies of the group, it is the individual's consciousness that gets expressed and not that of the group or what would have been that of the group. Witness the difference between the attitude toward strikes expressed by most individual workers and that expressed by a group of workers at a union meeting who vote to go on strike. Hence, the preference of most union leaders for mass meetings over secret ballots as a means for deciding whether to strike, and the preference of employers for secret ballots (Mann, 1973, 50). It is also clear that individual consciousness is more likely to reflect the restricted appearances of private life—and to that extent to show less awareness of one's place in the capitalist system—than group consciousness, rooted as it is in the function and interests of the class.

Nevertheless, despite such drawbacks, some aspects of the process of becoming class conscious, even as applied to groups, can be studied on an individual basis.[24] For example, though all social and political ideas are interrelated, the ties that bind any few of them together may be so close as to constitute these ideas as a subsystem, so that a change in any one of them immediately triggers changes in the others. Learning which these ideas are and the nature of their peculiar interaction with each other and with other subsystems of ideas can be accomplished through studies of individuals. Likewise, cognitive dissonance (the coexistence of apparently contradictory views on the same subject), the reliance on authoritarian figures and texts (who they are and how much influence they exert), the complex ties between ideas and emotions, the amount of thinking on social and political matters that is unconscious or automatic (though this is likely to vary a lot depending on whether one is alone or acting as a member of a group), and something of the priorities and weighing given to different parts of the belief system can all be usefully studied on a person by person basis. I also would not neglect in depth interviews of workers who are already class conscious to see how much they can reconstruct of the process that brought them there.

In studying individuals for purposes of understanding class consciousness, it is important to phrase questions as much as possible in ways that presuppose the individual's identity as a member of the group. Here, one does not ask what John Doe, who happens to be a worker, thinks of such and such; but what the worker, John Doe, thinks of it.[25] By directing questions and remarks to individuals as part of their class, one can evoke something of the group's response even with the other members of the group absent, reinforce the individual's identity as a group member, and valorize group consciousness over individual consciousness for the subject under discussion.

---

24. For abstraction of extension as regards people, see pp. 46–8.
25. For abstraction of vantage point, see pp. 67–78.

Concentrating on individuals is probably most valuable, however, in coming to understand the various psychological barriers to becoming class conscious. Some of these barrier like qualities result from the situation of the group and affect to some degree all of its members. Such, as we saw, are the feelings of separation and powerlessness that are the result of the relations of alienation in which the whole class finds itself. Individuals may also posses qualities derived from membership in other groups (racial, national, gender, etc.) or from personal experiences (however socially conditioned) that make it very difficult for them to participate as class members in the thinking of the class. Racism, sexism, patriotism, exaggerated religiosity, and authoritarianism are examples of this. Though social in origin and expressed in a variety of social forms, these qualities currently form a part of individual character, so that person oriented approaches, such as psychology and psychoanalysis, can be used both to analyze and diminish their distorting influence. Wilhelm Reich's conception of character structure, understood as organized habit, as an internalized pattern of early behavioral responses to dangers to the self from both within (anxiety) and without (repression, oppression and indifference), offers a helpful framework in which to investigate such apparently irrational qualities (1961, Part 2).[26]

As Reich said in a related context, what requires explanation is not why a hungry person steals, but why he does not (1972, 294). Why he does or should follows more or less logically from his condition. Why, despite this condition, he does not is the problem for which psychology may supply a large part of the answer. And the same applies to class consciousness, the presence of which is easily explainable in terms of the workers' conditions; whereas its absence requires another order of explanation. By putting us in touch with some of the pressures within each individual that inhibit the development of class consciousness, Freud and his followers have an important contribution to make to our study. But, focusing as they do on the individual, they cannot even begin to see those pressures that promote class consciousness, since all of the latter arise out of the situation of the class. Hence, the one-sided, essentially negative and

---

26. For abstraction of extension, see pp. 39–53. See, too, Ollman (1979, chapter 1), where I approach these barriers to class consciousness from the "other side," treating them as steps in the process of becoming fully class conscious. While still useful as a reconstruction of the contents of class consciousness and as a kind of ideal type map of how its main elements come together, this article suffers from an overly individualistic bias in its treatment of class. At the time, I had an insufficient grasp of the group thinking aspect of class consciousness as well as of the role of imputed consciousness as described by Lukacs.

pessimistic conclusions regarding class consciousness of virtually all psychological studies of our subject.

In summary: asking how can we study class consciousness required that we start by defining "class," "class interests," and "class consciousness." Each was found to have objective and subjective aspects, and in every case it was the relation between the two that was decisive in grasping the notion. In the case of class consciousness, the relation of its main subjective aspect, which is the actual consciousness of the group, to its main objective aspect, which is the consciousness appropriate to the place and function of the class in capitalist society, is a relation of the one developing toward the other. Investigating class consciousness, too, was broken down into inquiring into its objective and subjective aspects, with the latter divided in turn into group and individual consciousness.

Investigating the subjective side of class consciousness was said to involve the following steps: studying groups of workers wherever possible; studying them over time, especially in conflictual situations; tracing sharp transitions in their lives and beliefs; looking for what is not there, a potential gleaned from the analysis of the workers' place in society and the interests that are attached to it; and trying to uncover what inhibits or blocks the actualization of this potential, both in groups and in individual workers. Interacting and provoking responses as well as observing and questioning workers all have a place in this process. As paradoxical as it may sound, from a study of the workers' objective situation we can know in a general way where class consciousness is heading even before we have learned very much about its present state or when, how, and how quickly it will develop in the direction indicated by its potential. Throughout, change and movement are more or less taken for granted, while apparent stability and what causes it are the main problems to be explained. Perhaps most attention in studying the subjective side of class consciousness should be devoted to the various barriers to its development in the group and in individuals. We need to know what they are, how they evolve and work, their intensity, what effects them, etc., and this for each subsection of the class in each stage of its movement toward full class consciousness. It is within this framework and by taking such steps that dialectical inquiry is able to deal with class consciousness in its quality of becoming.

But what class consciousness is becoming involves activity, revolutionary activity, conscious class struggle, as well as a heightened and aroused understanding.[27] Class struggle, as I said earlier, is the law of motion of

---

27. For abstraction of extension, see pp. 39–53.

classes, bringing under one rubric the contradictory forces that underlie class interaction as the summary objective expression of class conscious-ness. Given dialectical relations, class consciousness can also be viewed as the subjective side of class struggle, reflecting both the form and intensity of this struggle at each moment in its development.[28] Though this is—as I have admitted—the standard way of viewing and treating their relationship, in this essay the order has been reversed. Hence, my conclusion: fully class-conscious workers engage in revolutionary activity, of some sort and to some degree. Being the one entails the other, but the steps by which the latter occurs need to be worked out. (It does not follow that workers who are less than fully class conscious cannot under certain circumstances also engage in revolutionary activity, at least for brief peri-ods, but that is another matter and requires detailed study of these circum-stances.) Any thorough study of class consciousness, therefore, has to address such questions as at what point in the development of class consciousness do workers get involved in revolutionary activity? What are the conditions for sustaining class consciousness, and why and how do people lose it? (With so much attention paid to raising consciousness, very few socialist scholars or activists have concerned themselves with the reverse process.) And what is the role of unions and political parties in the movement to attain state power? Does recognizing the role of leadership in the workers' movement imply, as Reich for one believed, a two-tiered conception of class consciousness, one for leaders and another for the mass of workers? (Reich, 1972, 289).

Putting questions that usually lie at the core of most socialist political analyses at the very end of a plan to study class consciousness is not meant to deny the importance of these questions, but rather to indicate another approach to finding answers for them.[29] For example, studying capitalism from this perspective suggests that a class not only gets the party it deserves, but constructs the one it needs, that it is ready for, one that is appropriate to what it is and is becoming. Whereas a party, as hard as it may try—as Brecht informs us and the experience of the American left among others confirms—can never create an appropriate people (1957, 1010).

No effort to induce more Marxist empirical studies is complete without warning against the kind of errors and distortions Marxists are inclined to make because of the systemic character of our subject and our dialectical approach to it. If non-Marxists, for example, often miss the forest for the trees, Marxists just as often play down or ignore the parts in deference to

---

28. For abstraction of vantage point, see pp. 67–78.
29. Ibid.

generalizations about the whole. But the capitalist system can only be grasped through a study of its parts in their interconnectedness.

Marxists also tend to push the germ of any development too quickly to its final form (granted the dialectical relation between the two). This is apparent in many Marxist studies of "Who profits?" and in the reductionism found in most versions of economic determinism. For the problem with which we have been concerned, this takes the form of reducing the long and involved process of becoming class conscious into a simple conditioned reflex, where every sign of progress is viewed as evidence of the finished result. In general, this error comes from not giving enough attention to the complex mediations that make up the joints of any important social problem. The dialectical tension, always difficult to maintain, between identity and difference has collapsed here into simple identity. The alternatives of mistaking what class consciousness can become for what it is (always a sectarian temptation) or what it is as the full measure of what it can become (the dead end of empiricism) can only be avoided by giving both equal attention, as I have tried to do, as moments in class consciousness' process of becoming.

Also, in accounting for the actions of individuals, Marxists often mistake interests for motives; but interest is but one component, however major, in the construction of motives, most other components being of a more personal nature. Aside from these distortions, there is frequently an overestimate of how fast society is changing, with relatively minor cracks on the surface of capitalist stability being mistaken for the start of a revolutionary upsurge. And there is a corresponding underestimation of the barriers to change, especially those located in individual character. The last points could probably be subsumed under wishful thinking—and so they are—but Marxists are also predisposed to make such mistakes because of weaknesses inherent in the very strengths of Marxism. Bringing change into proper focus and emphasizing all the elements that make for change carries with it the danger of undervaluing the forces that support the status quo. Ever present as temptations, these false moves substitute reassuring formulae for the hard work of dialectical inquiry, and have to be very carefully guarded against.

VII.

Finally, it is obvious that studying class consciousness affects it, becomes part of the respondents' social world, and an ingredient in the process by which they come to understand it. Conceiving of class consciousness as a complex relation and as a process, viewing it as something that is always becoming in and through workers' interaction with their environment (including other people), it is clear that every attempt to study class consciousness, which becomes of necessity a part of that environment, will influence its development in some way and to some degree.[30] Where class consciousness is viewed as a given set of beliefs, as something static, it is possible to argue that a careful investigator could leave it as he found it, and studying class consciousness need not change it one way or another. But if class consciousness is constantly changing, chiefly in response to changes in the workers' situation, then introducing a researcher into that situation will either raise class consciousness or lower it. Mainly, this results from the techniques, comparisons, and categories used, the information conveyed or withheld, and the hierarchies legitimized or undermined in the conduct of research, as well as from the publication of what is found, which in conservative studies means the reification of a passing moment in consciousness and its transformation into one more reason for sticking with the present.

For example, one can construct questions that emphasize the individual's identity in the class as the self-definition that is most appropriate for dealing with a particular set of problems.[31] One can supply important facts that most workers do not know. One can introduce comparisons that highlight rather than downplay the injustice of their situation (most judgments involve a comparison with a situation believed to be similar, but there is always a choice of which one to use).[32] One can link up individual opponents into an opposition class, and that class to a set of rules and conditions from which it draws its power.[33] And, perhaps most important, one can make such categories as "class," "exploitation," "capitalism," and especially "class struggle" available to workers to think with, to help them organize more effectively, more politically, what they already know, and to integrate more dialectically what they continue to learn.[34] Care must be taken, of course, not to use these categories until most of what they refer to is already known, albeit in some other form, or else they will strike people as meaningless jargon.

On the other hand, along with most social scientists, one can withhold such categories and encourage workers to think in terms of group identities (race, nation, religion, gender, etc.), "individual attitudes," and "personal choices." The crux is how the subject is introduced (how the stage is set), what gets emphasized, what is assumed, what comparisons are

---

30. For abstraction of extension, see pp. 39–53.
31. Ibid.
32. For abstraction of vantage point, see pp. 67–78.
33. For abstraction of extension, see pp. 39–53.
34. For abstraction of level of generality, see pp. 53–67.

used, how it gets framed, and in what categories all this is formulated. The point is that conducting research in the orthodox mode, remaining tied to traditional disciplinary forms and norms, effectively retards the development of class consciousness, whether one intends that result or not. And, throughout, the more aware a researcher is of the effect he has on his human subjects, whether he wants to or not, the greater the likelihood of his having the effect he wants to.

The question with which we started out—how to study class consciousness—is both about how to investigate something and how we do and can affect it. It is this double sense that I have tried to convey in my title: "How to Study Class Consciousness . . . and Why We Should." The radicalizing potential of doing radical research, particularly on class consciousness, has barely been touched. Yet, how better to combine our interests and skills as scholars and activists? With the greater penetration of bourgeois ideology among workers, conducting a study of classes and class struggle from the perspective of class consciousness is probably more important now than it ever was, both for understanding the possibilities of change and for affecting them. The time has come to move beyond criticizing the ideological biases in mainstream scholarship to undertaking our own research on workers to discover the information we need while helping to produce the results we want. The opportunities for carrying out such studies are also greater than they were in the past. The current crisis in capitalism provides us with conflictual situations aplenty and the growing number of radical scholars in the universities constitute an army of potential researchers. Consciousness studying can become an important part of consciousness raising. The choice is ours.

If there are people who take this interest in influencing what workers think through making a study of their consciousness as a sign of manipulation, I can only answer—again—that every study of class consciousness affects how workers think, one way or another. It is manipulation only where there is dishonesty, or where the researcher does not admit even to himself what he is doing or tries to hide it. The old question, Which side are you on?, cannot be avoided. Openly taking sides at the start, when it is necessary to be on one side or the other, is not only the radical thing to do. It is the honest thing to do. And who, but those whose interests are hurt by the truth, would want us to be dishonest?[35]

---

35. If this essay has the ring of a preliminary proposal, that is because it is. Further systematization of the method, testing it and comparing it to other and, especially, similar approaches remains to be done. It is, in part, the hope of undertaking this work as a collective project that has led me to publish my still incomplete thoughts on this subject at this time. Comrades who see scholarly and political merit in what I have tried to do here should not wait for a personal invitation before joining the fray.

References

Aronowitz, S. 1973. *False Promises*. New York: McGraw Hill.
Bergh, J. 1984. "Automatic and Conscious Processing of Social Information." In *Handbook of Social Cognition*. Vol. 3. Edited by R.S. Wyer and T.K. Srull. Hillside, N.J.: Erlbaum Associates.
Blackburn, R. and M. Mann. 1975. *Ideology in the Non-Skilled Working Class*. In *Working Class Images of Society* Edited by M. Bulmer. London: Routledge and Kegan Paul.
Braverman, H. 1974. *Labor and Monopoly Capital*. New York: Monthly Review Press.
Brecht, B. 1987. *Gesamelte Werke*. Vol. 10 Frankfurt: Suhrkamp Verlag.
Brown, M. and A. Goldin, 1973. *Collective Behavior*. Pacific Palisades, Calif.: Goodyear Publishing Company.
Edwards, R. 1979. *Contested Terrain*. New York: Basic Books.
Fromm, E. 1984. *The Working Class in Weimar Germany*. Cambridge, Mass.: Harvard University Press.
Goldthorpe, J., D. Lockwood, F. Bechhofer, and J. Platt. 1989. *The Affluent Worker*. London: Cambridge University Press.
Gorz, A. 1967. *Strategy for Labor*. Boston: Beacon Press.
Gramsci, A. 1971. *Selections from the Prison Notebooks*. Translated and edited by Q. Hoare and G. N. Smith. New York: International Publishers.
Gutman, H. 1976. *Work, Culture and Society in Industrializing America*. New York: Vintage Books.
Hobsbawm, E. 1984. *Workers: Worlds of Labor*. New York: Pantheon Books.
Leggett, J. 1968. *Class, Race and Labor*. Oxford: Oxford University Press.
Lipset, S.M. 1983a. In a debate with the author on class consciousness sponsored by the Caucus for a New Political Science at the September 1983 meetings of the American Political Science Association.
———. 1983b. "Radicalism or Reformism: The Sources of Working Class Politics," *American Political Science Review*, 77.
Lockwood, D. 1975. "Sources of Variation in Working Class Images of Society." In *Working Class Images of Society*. Edited by M. Bulmer. London: Routledge and Kegan Paul.
Lukacs, G. 1971. *History and Class Consciousness*. Translated by Rodney Livingston. Cambridge, Mass.: M.I.T. Press
Mallet, S. 1975. *Essays on the New Working Class*. St. Louis: Telos Press.
Mann, M. 1973. *Consciousness and Action Among the Western Working Class*. Atlantic Highlands, N.J.: Humanities Press.
Marshall, G. 1983. "Some Remarks on the Study of Working Class Consciousness." *Politics and Society*, 12.
Marx, K. 1904. Introduction. *Critique of Political Economy*. Translated by N.I. Stone. Chicago: Charles H. Kerr.
———. 1934. *Letters to Dr. Kugelmann*. London: International Publishers.
———. 1958. *Capital*. Vol. 1. Translated by S. Moore and E. Aveling. Moscow: Foreign Language Publishing House.
———. 1963. *Theories of Surplus Value*. Vol. 1. Translated by E. Burns and edited by S. Ryazanakaya. Moscow: Foreign Languages Publishing House.
———. 1973. *Grundrisse*. Translated by M. Nichlaus. London: Allen Lane.
———. n.d. *Poverty of Philosophy*. Moscow: Foreign Languages Publishing House.
Marx, K. and F. Engels, 1942. *German Ideology*. Translated by R. Pasqual. London: Lawrence and Wisehart.

———. 1945. *Communist Manifesto*. Translated by S. Moore. Chicago: Charles H. Kerr.

———. 1951. *Marx/Engels Selected Writings*. Volume 1. Moscow: Foreign Languages Publishing House.

———. 1956. *The Holy Family*. Translated by R. Dixon. Moscow: Foreign Languages Publishing House.

McDermott, J. 1980. *The Crisis in the Working Class*. Boston: South End Press.

Montgomery, D. 1979. *Workers Control in America*. Cambridge, Eng.: Cambridge University Press.

Ollman, B. 1976. *Alienation: Marx's Conception of Man in Capitalist Society*, 2nd ed. Cambridge, Eng.: Cambridge University Press.

———. 1979. *Social and Sexual Revolution: Essays on Marx and Reich*. Boston: South End Press.

Olson, M. 1971. *The Logic of Collective Action*. Cambridge, Mass.: Harvard University Press.

Przeworski, A. 1977. "From Proletariat to Class." *Politics and Society*, 7:4.

Reich, W. 1961. *Character Analysis*. Translated by T.P. Wolfe. New York: Noonday Press.

———. 1972. *Sex-Pol: Essays 1929–1934*. Edited by L. Baxendall. New York: Vintage Books.

Sombart, W. 1976. *Why Is There No Socialism in the U.S.?* New York: International Arts and Science Press.

Thompson, E.P. 1966. *The Making of the English Working Class*. New York: Vintage Books.

Touraine, A. 1981. *The Voice and the Eye*. Cambridge, Eng.: Cambridge University Press.

Willis, P. 1981. *Learning to Labor*. New York: Columbia University Press.

Wolpe, H. 1970. "Some Problems Concerning Revolutionary Consciousness." In *The Socialist Register, 1970*. Edited by R. Miliband and J. Saville. London: Merlin Press.

Wright, E.O. 1985. *Classes*. London: Verso.

Select Bibliography on Marx's Dialectical Method

Adorno, T.W. 1973. *Negative Dialectics*. Translated by E.B. Ashton. New York: Seabury Press.

Alker, H. R., Jr., ed. 1982. *Dialectical Logics for the Political Sciences*. Amsterdam: Editions Rodopi.

Allen, J. 1983. "In Search of Method: Hegel, Marx and Realism." *Radical Philosophy* (Autumn).

Althusser, L. 1969. "On the Materialist Dialectic." *For Marx*. Translated by B. Brewster. New York: Vintage Books.

Beamish, R. 1992. *A Study of Marx's Intellectual Labor Process*. Chicago: University of Illinois Press.

Bhaskar, R. 1992. *Dialectics*. London: Verso.

Bologh, R.W. 1979. *Dialectical Phenomenology: Marx's Method*. London: Routledge and Kegan Paul.

Carver, T. 1975. Prefaces. *Karl Marx: Texts on Method*. Edited and Translated by T. Carver. Oxford: Blackwell.

Colletti, L. 1975. "Marxism and the Dialectic." *New Left Review* (September–October).

Cornforth, M. 1960. *Materialism and Dialectical Method*. New York: International Publishers.

Dietzgen, J. 1906. *The Positive Outcome of Philosophy*. Translated by W. W. Craik. Chicago: Charles H. Kerr.

Dunayevskaya, Raya. 1982. *Philosophy and Revolution: From Hegel to Sartre and from Marx to Mao*. Atlantic Highlands, NJ: Harvester.

Engels, F. 1962. *Anti-Dühring*. Moscow: Foreign Languages Publishing House.

———. 1950. "Ludwig Feuerbach and the End of Classical German Philosophy." In Marx, K., and F. Engels. *Selected Works in Two Volumes*. Vol. 2. Moscow: Foreign Languages Publishing House.

———. 1957. Preface, in Marx, K. *Capital*. Vol. 2. Moscow: Foreign Languages Publishing House.

———. 1964. *Dialectics of Nature*. Translated by C. Dutt. Moscow: Progress Publishers.

———. 1976. "Review of Karl Marx, *A Contribution to the Critique of Political Economy*," in K. Marx, *Preface and Introduction, A Contribution to the Critique of Political Economy*. Peking: Foreign Languages Press.

Fisk, M. 1973. *Nature and Necessity*. Bloomington: University of Indiana Press.

Freiberg, J. W. "Dialectical Method." Distributed by Red Feather Institute for Advanced Studies in Sociology: Boulder, Colorado.

Godolier, M. 1972. "Structure and Contradiction in *Capital*." *Ideology in Social Science*. Edited by R. Blackburn. London: Fontana/Collins.

Goldmann, L. 1969. *The Human Sciences and Philosophy*. Translated by H. White and R. Anchor. London: Jonathan Cape.

Gollobin, I. 1986. *Dialectical Materialism: Its Laws, Categories, and Practises*. New York: Petras Press.

Gould, C. 1978. *Marx's Social Ontology*. Cambridge, MA: M.I.T. Press.

Gramsci, A. 1971. *Selections from the Prison Notebooks*. Part III. Edited and Translated by Q. Hoare and G N. Smith. New York: International Publishers.

Guest, D. 1939. *A Textbook of Dialectical Materialism*. New York: International Publishers.

Hahn, A. 1879. *The Rabbincal Dialectics: A History of the Dialecticians and Dialectics of the Mishnah and Talmud*. Cincinnati: Bloch and Co. Publishers.

Hartsock, N. 1993. "Objectivity and Revolution: the Unity of Observation and Outrage." *From a Feminist Standpoint: Essays on Politics, Power, and Epistemology*. Boulder: Westview.

Hegel, G.W.F. 1892. *The Logic of Hegel* (Part 1 of *The Encyclopedia of the Philosophical Sciences*). Translated by W. Wallace. Oxford: Oxford University Press.

Heilbroner, R. 1980. "The Dialectical Vision." *New Republic* (March 1).

Hook, S. 1966. *Reason, Social Myths and Democracy*, Part II. New York: Harper and Row.

Horton, J. 1972. "Combatting Empiricism: Towards a Practical Understanding of Marxist Methodology." *Insurgent Sociologist* (Fall).

Horwath, R. J., and K.D. Gibson. 1984. "Abstraction in Marx's Method." *Antipode* (April).

Ilyenkov, E.V. 1977. *Dialectical Logic*. Translated by H.C. Creighton. Moscow: Progress Publishers.

————. 1982. *The Dialectic of the Abstract and the Concrete in Marx's* Capital. Translated by S. Svrovathin. Moscow: Progress Publishers.

Israel, J. 1979. *The Language of Dialectics and the Dialectics of Language*. London: Harvester.

Jackson, T. A. 1936. *Dialectics*. London: Lawrence and Wishart.

James, C. L. R. 1980. *Notes on Dialectics*. Westport, CT: Lawrence Hill.

Jameson, F. 1971. *Marxism and Form*. Princeton, NJ: Princeton University Press.

Jay, M. 1982. *Marxism and Totality*. Berkeley: University of California Press.

Kain, P.J. 1986. *Marx's Method, Epistemology, and Humanism*. Dordrecht, Holland: D. Reidel Publishers.

Kolakowski, L. 1971. "Karl Marx and the Classical Definition of Truth." *Marxism and Beyond*. Translated by J.Z. Peel. London: Paladin.

Korsch, K. 1970. *Marxism and Philosophy*. Translated by F. Holliday. London: New Left Books.

Kosik, K. 1976. *Dialectics of the Concrete*. Boston: D. Reidel Publishers.

Lefebvre, H. 1968. "The Dialectical Contradiction." *Historical Materialism*. Translated by J. Sturrock. London: Jonathan Cape.

————. 1969. *Logique formelle, logique dialectique*. Paris: Anthropos.

Lenin, V.I. 1980. *On the Question of Dialectics: A Collection*. Moscow: Progress Publishers.

Levins, R., and R. Lewontin. 1985. *The Dialectical Biologist*. Cambridge, MA: Harvard University Press.

Levy, H. 1938. *A Philosophy for Modern Man*. London: Victor Gollanz.

Little, D. 1986. *The Scientific Marx* (chapters 4–6). Minneapolis: University of Minnesota Press.

Low, D. B. 1987. *The Existential Dialectic of Marx and Merleau-Ponty*. New York: Peter Lang.

Lukacs, G. 1971. *History and Class Consciousness: Studies in Marxist Dialectics*. Translated by R. Livingston. Cambridge, MA: M.I.T. Press.

————. 1978. *The Ontology of Social Being: Vol. II, Marx*. Translated by D. Fernbach. London: Merlin.

Mandel, E. 1972. "The Laws of Motion and the History of Capital." In *Late Capitalism*. Translated by J. De Bres. London: New Left Books.

Mao Tse-Tung. 1968. *Four Essays on Philosophy*. Peking: Foreign Languages Press.

Marcuse, H. 1964. *Reason and Revolution: Hegel and the Rise of Social Theory*. Boston: Beacon Press.

————. 1961. "Dialectic and Its Vicissitudes." *Soviet Marxism*. New York: Random House.

Markovic, M. 1974. "Hegelian and Marxist Dialectics." In *The Contemporary Marx*. Bristol: Spokesman Books.

Marquit, E., P. Moran, and W. H. Truitt, eds. 1982. *Dialectical Contradictions: Contemporary Marxist Discussions*. Minneapolis: Marxist Educational Press.

Marx, K. 1961. Afterword to 2d German edition. *Capital*. Vol. 1. Moscow: Foreign Languages Publishing House.

————. 1966. *Poverty of Philosophy*. Chapter 2. Moscow: Progress Publishers.

————. 1975. "Notes on Wagner." In *Karl Marx: Texts on Method*. Edited and translated by T. Carver. Oxford: Blackwell.

————. 1976. Preface and Introduction. In *A Contribution to the Critique of Political Economy*. Peking: Foreign Languages Press.

[Unfortunately, many of Marx's most insightful comments on dialectics do not appear in these works but are spread throughout his writings, early and late, as evidenced by most of the citations to Marx in this book.]

McBride, W. 1977. *The Philosophy of Marx*. New York: St. Martin's Press.

McCarthy, G. 1988. *Marx's Criticism of Science and Positivism*. Dordrecht, Holland: Kluwer Academic Publishers.

Meikle, S. 1985. *Essentialism in the Thought of Karl Marx*. London: Gerald Duckworth.

Mepham, J., and D.-H. Ruben, eds. 1979. *Issues to Marxist Philosophy*. Vol. 1, Dialectical Method. Atlantic Highlands, NJ: Humanities Press.

Murray, P. *Marx's Theory of Scientific Knowledge*. Atlantic Highlands, NJ: Humanities Press.

Nicolaus, M. 1973. Foreword. In Marx, K. *Grundrisse*. London: Penguin.

Norman, R., and S. Sayers. 1980. *Hegel, Marx and Dialectics*. Brighton, Sussex: Harvester Press.

Novack, G. 1963. *Introduction to the Logic of Marxism*. New York: Pioneer Press.

Novak, L. 1980. *The Structure of Idealization: Toward a Systematic Interpretation of the Marxiam Idea of Science*. Dordrecht, Holland: Reidel Publishing Company.

O'Brien, K. 1987. *Reason and the Art of Freedom*. Chapter 2. Philadelphia: Temple University Press.

Ollman, B. 1971. *Alienation: Marx's Conception of Man in Capitalist Society*. Cambridge, England: Cambridge University Press.

————. 1976. "Response to My Critics: More on Internal Relations." In Appendix 2, *Alienation*. 2d edition. Cambridge, England: Cambridge University Press.

————. 1978. "Marxism and Political Science: Prolegomenon to a Debate on Marx's Method." In *Social and Sexual Revolution: Essays on Marx and Reich*. Boston: South End Press.

O'Malley, J. 1970. "Method in Karl Marx." *Review and Politics* (April).

Petrovic, G. 1967. *Marxism in the Mid–20th Century*. Part 3. Garden City, NY: Anchor Books.

Popper, K. 1962. *The Open Society and Its Enemies*, Vol. 2. Princeton: Princeton University Press.

Prokopczyk, C.Z. *Truth and Reality in Hegel and Marx*. Amherst: University of Massachusetts Press.

Rader, M. 1979. *Marx's Interpretation of History*. New York: Oxford University Press.

Resnick, S.A., and R.D. Wolff. 1987. *Knowledge and Class: A Marxist Critique of Political Economy*. Chapter 2. Chicago: University of Chicago Press.

Roosevelt, F. 1984. "Cambridge Economics as Commodity Fetishism." In *Growth, Profits and Property*. Edited by E. Nell. Cambridge, England: Cambridge University Press.

Rosdolsky, R. 1977. *The Making of Capital*. Part 1. Translated by P. Burgess. London: Pluto Press.

Rubel, M. 1981. "The Plan and Method of the 'Economics.' " In *Rubel on Marx*. Edited by J. O'Malley and K. Algozin. Cambridge, England: Cambridge University Press.

Ruben, D.-H. *Marxism and Materialism*. Atlantic Highlands, NJ: Humanities.

Rosental, M. M. 1960. *Dialectical Logic*. Moscow: Progress Publishers.

Sartre, J.-P. 1967. *Search for a Method*. Translated by H. Barnes. New York: Alfred A. Knopf.

———. 1976. *Critique of Dialectical Reason*. Edited by J. Rée, translated by A. Sheridan. London: New Left Books.

Sayer, D. 1979. *Marx's Method*. London: Harvester Press.

———. 1987. *The Violence of Abstractions: The Analytic Foundations of Historical Materialism*. Oxford: Blackwell.

Sayers, A. 1981. "Abstraction: a Realist Interpretation." *Radical Philosophy* (Summer).

Sayers, S. 1984. "Marxism and the Dialectical Method: A Critique of G.A. Cohen." *Radical Philosophy* (Spring).

———. 1985. *Reality and Reason: Dialectics and the Theory of Knowledge*. Oxford: Blackwell.

Schaff, A. 1960. "Marxist Dialectics and the Principle of Contradiction." *Journal of Philosophy*. 58 (March).

Sherman, H. 1976. "Dialectics as a Method." *Insurgent Sociologist* (Fall).

Smith, T. 1990. *The Logic of Marx's Capital: Reply to Hegelian Critics*. Albany: S.U.N.Y. Press.

Sohn-Rethel, A. 1978. *Intellectual and Manual Labor*. Translated by M. Sohn-Rethel. London: MacMillan.

Stojanovic, C.Z. 1980. *Between Ideals and Reality*. Translated by G.S. Sher. New York: Oxford University Press.

Suchting, W. A. 1986. *Marxism and Philosophy*. New York: New York University Press.

Sweezy, P. 1964. "Marx's Method." *The Theory of Capitalist Development*. New York: Monthly Review Press.

Taylor, C. 1966. "Marxism and Empiricism." In *British Analytic Philosophy*. Edited by B. Williams and A. Montefiore. London: Routledge and Kegan Paul.

Thomas, P. 1976. "Marxism and Science." *Political Studies*. 24 (March).

Trotsky, L. 1986. *Trotsky's Note Books, 1933–35*. Edited and translated by P. Pomper. New York: Columbia University Press.

———. 1971. "ABC of Dialectics." In *In Defence of Marxism*. London: New Park Publications.

Vaillancourt, P. M. 1986. *When Marxists Do Research*. New York: Greenwood.

Warren, S. 1984. *The Emergence of Dialectical Theory*. Chicago: University of Chicago Press.

Wilde, L. 1989. *Marxism and Contradictions*. Brookfield, England: Gower Press.

Wood, A. 1981. *Karl Marx*, Part V. London: Routledge and Kegan Paul.

Zeitlin, I. 1967. "Theory as Guide to Study of Society." In *Marxism: A Re-examination*. New York: Van Nostrand Reinhold.

Zeleny, J. 1980. *The Logic of Marx*. Translated by T. Carver. Oxford: Blackwell.

Index of Names and Ideas*

---

*In line with my argument for internal relations, I have made a special effort to bring out the connections between the ideas treated in this book by a heavy use of synonyms and cross-references and by my ordering of subsections under key concepts. The specialized vocabulary associated with dialectical method has also been emphasized throughout. Finally, footnote references only appear in the index if they involve a substantive point.

labor, 12, 29, 30, 34, 35, 38, 43, 46, 49, 51,
53, 57, 62, 68, 69, 70, 75, 78, 122, 134,
141, 143 (*see also* production)
division of, 36, 56, 57, 60, 61, 63, 66, 79,
97, 103, 122
power, 15, 34, 47, 49, 113, 134, 138, 169
theory of value, 49, 61, 62, 152
wage, 30, 55, 76, 77, 134, 135, 136, 141,
151, 152
landlords (land owners), 47, 58, 75, 153
language, 36, 37, 125 (*see also* concept)
law, 45, 94, 104, 105, 106, 126
in Marxism, 17, 64, 65, 77, 78, 80, 141, 142,
150, 162, 173 (*see also* tendency and
countertendency)
*Left Academy: Marxist Scholarship on Ameri-
can Campuses*, volumes I, II and III, 131
Legget, J., 148
legitimation, 98, 106, 112, 115, 123, 124, 125,
127, 131, 132, 176 (*see also* ideology
and false consciousness)
Leibniz, G.W., 35
Lenin, V.I., v, 89, 147
liberal, 103, 115, 116, 129
Lipset, S.M., 148, 149
Livant, B., 164
logic: formal, Aristotelian, 13, 16, 29, 34 (*see
also* external relations and non-dialectical method)
Lukacs, G., v, 23, 26, 172
Lycurgus, 102

Madison, J., 102
Mallet, S., 148
Mann, M., 148
Mannheim, K., 68
Mao Tse-Tung, v, 26
Marcuse, H., 79
market, 30, 49, 51, 61, 63, 70, 72, 112, 113,
115, 116, 117, 128, 135, 151, 163 (*see
also* exchange)
Marquit, E., 131
Marshall, G., 149
Marxism: general descriptions only, v, 1, 2–
3, 9–10, 26, 27, 35, 43, 44, 45, 59, 73, 75,
78, 131
"Marxism and Political Science: Prolegome-
non to a Debate on Marx's Method," 4
material world (foundations), 25, 27, 165
force, 45

scarcity, 60
materialism, 44, 117
materialist conception of history, 44, 62–3,
80, 133–45, 152 (*see also* production)
Mattick, P., 79
McDermott, J., 148
mediation, 17, 48, 166, 175
Meikle, S., 27
memory, 81
Mepham, J., 79
metamorphosis, 48, 49–50, 52, 53, 63, 64,
76, 134 (*see also* interaction, form, and
system)
of value, 43, 49–50, 63, 64, 76
Milibaud, R., 78–9, 89
Military-Industrial Complex, 99
Mitchell, T., 94–101
moment, 15, 18, 31, 32, 33, 68, 76, 81, 140,
161, 169, 175, 176 (*see also* process and
abstraction of extension)
money, 15, 26, 29, 30, 31, 32, 34, 35, 41, 43,
49, 50, 51, 52, 69, 75, 104, 135, 141 (*see
also* value)
Montgomery, D., 147
Moore, B., 3
Moore, G.E., 34
Moore, S., 120
morality, 45, 106, 130
Moses, 102
motive, 175
mystery (mystification), 62, 96, 98, 102, 103,
112, 114, 122 (*see also* fetishism and
ideology)

naming, 28, 31, 141 (*see also* conception)
Napoleon III, 59
nation, 60, 75, 176
nationalism, 60, 163 (*see also* illusory community and ideology)
nationality, 153, 155, 172
nature (natural world), 11, 14, 29, 35, 42, 44,
45, 53, 54, 56, 64, 65, 70, 74, 114 (*see
also* society)
necessity, 19, 89, 92, 93, 133, 137–9, 152, 160,
165 (*see also* determine and freedom)
negation, 2
negation of the negation, 27, 48, 64
need, 53, 59, 63, 104, 143, 174
Nearing, S., 119, 120, 132
New Deal, 100